P9-DWE-632

DATE DUE

MR 25 '94		
MY 27 '94		
JE 30 '94		
DE 22 '95		
DE 14 '98		
JE 7 '06		

Humanitarianism
Across Borders

Emerging Global Issues
Thomas G. Weiss, Series Editor

Published in association with the
Thomas J. Watson Jr. Institute for International Studies,
Brown University

Humanitarianism Across Borders
Sustaining Civilians
in Times of War

■

edited by
Thomas G. Weiss
Larry Minear

Lynne Rienner Publishers   ■   Boulder & London

Published in the United States of America in 1993 by
Lynne Rienner Publishers, Inc.
1800 30th Street, Boulder, Colorado 80301

and in the United Kingdom by
Lynne Rienner Publishers, Inc.
3 Henrietta Street, Covent Garden, London WC2E 8LU

Library of Congress Cataloging-in-Publication Data
Humanitarianism across borders : sustaining civilians in times of war
/ edited by Thomas G. Weiss and Larry Minear.
    p.   cm. — (Emerging global issues)
    Includes bibliographical references and index.
    ISBN 1-55587-428-2 (alk. paper)
    1. War relief. 2. International relief. 3. International
relations. 4. Humanitarianism. I. Weiss, Thomas George.
II. Minear, Larry, 1936– . III. Series.
HV639.H88   1993
363.3'4988—dc20
                                               93-14130
                                                   CIP

British Cataloguing in Publication Data
A Cataloguing in Publication record for this book
is available from the British Library.

Printed and bound in the United States of America

 The paper used in this publication meets the requirements
of the American National Standard for Permanence of
Paper for Printed Library Materials Z39.48-1984.

Contents

Preface

THOMAS G. WEISS & LARRY MINEAR

Widespread and endemic conflicts have presented humanitarians with formidable challenges in recent years. The initial euphoria surrounding the waning of the Cold War now has given way to a more realistic appraisal of the likelihood of continuing—perhaps even increasing—violence. The prospects for the lives of civilians caught in the throes of war are chilling.[1]

In areas such as Afghanistan, Mozambique, and Somalia, conflicts kindled largely by superpower rivalry have taken on lives of their own.[2] Other conflicts dampened for decades by the existence of the Cold War are being rekindled in the Balkans and various republics of the former Soviet Union. In conflicts with no direct links to East-West rivalry—such as those in the Sudan, Liberia, and Sri Lanka—seething ethnic tensions are fueling a new micronationalism. Violence and chaos have reached such levels that the term "failed states"[3] has been coined to describe political entities that no longer can be characterized as functioning in any normal sense.

Whether between or within nations, strife has increased the need for humanitarian assistance and protection—and increased the difficulty of providing international relief effectively. In many of the areas of seemingly endless violence and warfare, humanitarians themselves—like the persons in need of assistance—have been harassed and held hostage, injured, and killed. Aid convoys have been hijacked and blocked, relief activities commandeered and shut down. Withholding food and medicine is often a ready weapon in the arsenals of governments and insurgents.

Confronted with burgeoning need and yet faltering institutional responses, the world is poised between the Cold War and an embryonic new humanitarian order. Emerging from an era that made humanitarian values subservient to geopolitical considerations, the world is groping toward arrangements in which life-threatening suffering and human rights abuses become legitimate international concerns irrespective of where they take place. Moving from a controlling paradigm in which state sovereignty has served as an all-purpose rationalization for the abuse of civilians within a state's borders, the world is now infusing sovereignty with a greater sense of humanitarian obligation. Humanitarianism across borders seems to be the direction of the future, even though the geographical state remains the cornerstone of world politics.

To help the humanitarian community and the institutions—civilian and military, public and private—with which it interacts forge an analytical and practical understanding of this transitional moment, we launched the Humanitarianism and War Project in 1991. Based on the analysis of interviews with practitioners and other data gathered in conflict areas, the project seeks to identify lessons from recent humanitarian experience within conflict and to recommend institutional strategies for the future. A list of project publications appears at the end of this book.

This book is the second of three, each with a different audience in mind. The first volume was designed for agencies and individuals whose task involves the actual provision of assistance and protection. *Humanitarian Action in Times of War: A Handbook for Practitioners*,[4] identifies eight principles of humanitarian action and presents practical strategies for improving the operational effectiveness and accountability of the international humanitarian network.

Scheduled for publication next year, the final volume, *Humanitarianism and War: Reducing the Human Cost of Armed Conflict*,[5] is written with the concerned international public in mind. Sustained and effective humanitarian action requires the active support of an increasingly well-informed constituency. Consequently, we seek to convey to concerned but nontechnical readers the challenges of expressing international solidarity in today's complex, interconnected world. We plan to analyze the organizations involved, review the tough choices they face, and highlight some of the creative ways that have succeeded in reaching civilians trapped in situations of conflict.

Positioned between these two volumes, this book spans those two audiences. It is designed for practitioners concerned with the broader context of their day-to-day tasks, and also addresses persons not directly associated with humanitarian organizations—be they policy- or opinionmakers, media professionals, scholars, analysts, or ordinary citizens—who wish to explore some of the critical humanitarian issues facing the world today.

This is a collection of thoughtful essays by nine authors who have been involved in one way or another in efforts to alleviate civilian suffering in times of war. We sought them out because of the constructive roles they have played in recent years and the respect they have earned among their colleagues. They reflect the diverse makeup of the humanitarian family: practitioners, academics, journalists, military people, UN and private organization officials, and persons from nonprofit and commercial sectors.

The work is organized into three interrelated parts that represent crucial aspects of the global effort to improve the international humanitarian system:

values, the use of military force, and the future shape of humanitarian institutions. Preceding each of the three sections, our commentary places the contributions of the authors within current debates about how best to sustain civilians in times of war. We identify how each author adds to an understanding of the most critical issues regarding the norms (Part 1), processes (Part 2), and institutional structures (Part 3) of humanitarian action. We also frame questions arising from each chapter that merit additional analysis, reflection, and action.

The authors write in their personal capacities rather than speaking on behalf of organizations with which they are or have been affiliated. Their essays have benefited from a conference in Providence, Rhode Island, in December 1992, at which the authors presented their chapters to one another and to a carefully selected group of humanitarian professionals. Following the conference, which was funded by the French government and hosted by Brown University, the authors revised their chapters to take into account the critiques of colleagues.

Three assumptions have influenced the topics addressed by the authors and our commentary. First, the focus is on widespread civilian suffering resulting from international or internal armed conflict rather than on the havoc wreaked by so-called natural disasters.[6] While the intent is not to ignore humanitarians in other operational landscapes—such as those responding to droughts and floods—the difficulties in helping civilians in such disasters are exacerbated during conflict. A recent document from an international group of experts correctly argues that coping with armed conflict is *the* principal remaining obstacle to eliminating famine in our time.[7]

Second, our use of the concept of humanitarianism is positive rather than pejorative. We employ it, even though in some quarters the term conveys high praise, while in others it rings of do-goodism and naiveté. The ambiguity is complicated by the fact that over the years the term has not been defined clearly in international law or codified in national legislation with the same precision accorded concepts such as human rights or refugees. Our book encourages self-criticism rather than self-congratulation and endorses humanitarian action, but of a variety that matches warmhearted compassion with toughmindedness.

Third, the expression "across borders" in the title is not intended to imply that all action geared toward sustaining civilians in times of war comes from outside a given country or region in conflict. Our case study of the Gulf crisis concluded that the most immediately available humanitarian assistance to third-country nationals fleeing Kuwait and Iraq came not from the international community and its established institutions but from the Jordanian and Iranian people themselves.[8] In many circumstances and at many points in the relief and reconstruction process, however, humanitarianism across borders is indispensable. In Somalia, for example, the breakdown of political and civil institutions rendered massive outside involvement essential. Yet even there, local resources existed that were not used. In Somalia and elsewhere, the challenge is to find ways of supporting and supplementing indigenous capacity with action across borders.

This book reflects the contributions of many persons and organizations. The two institutions cosponsoring the Humanitarianism and War Project deserve special thanks: Brown University's Thomas J. Watson Jr. Institute for International Studies in Providence, Rhode Island, and the Refugee Policy Group of Washington, D.C., have provided us with an institutional home for our research and writing. We would like in particular to acknowledge the encouragement and assistance of RPG's executive director, Dennis Gallagher.

Financial contributions from many quarters lend both breadth and credibility to our work. Current sponsors include ten nongovernmental organizations (Catholic Relief Services, Danish Refugee Council, Lutheran World Federation, Lutheran World Relief, Mennonite Central Committee, Norwegian Refugee Council, Oxfam-UK, Save the Children–UK, International Federation of Red Cross and Red Crescent Societies, and Canada's International Centre for Human Rights and Democratic Development); six UN organizations (UNICEF, UN High Commissioner for Refugees, UN Special Emergency Programme on the Horn of Africa, UN Development Programme, Department of Humanitarian Affairs–UNDRO, and World Food Programme); four governments (France, the Netherlands, the United Kingdom, and the United States); and three foundations (the Pew Charitable Trusts and the Rockefeller and Arias Foundations).

The text of this volume has profited immensely from reflections and comments by numerous colleagues and friends throughout the humanitarian community, too numerous to name here. We would like to single out Mary Anderson, however, who not only contributed a chapter but also helped identify the issues addressed in our commentary. We are also indebted to Fred Fullerton, Mary Lhowe, Susan Costa, and Amy Langlais of the Watson Institute for editorial assistance; and Judy Ombura at the Refugee Policy Group for her administrative help.

We note in conclusion that the task of analysis and commentary is far less daunting than the daily challenges faced by humanitarians on the front line in conflicts around the world. Their perilous efforts and excruciating experiences, frequently involving great personal hardship and risk, inform this volume. We share their commitment to forging a humanitarian regime that more effectively assists and protects all those in need.

T.G.W. and L.M.

Notes

1. For a discussion of these developments, see Thomas G. Weiss and Meryl A. Kessler (eds.), *Third World Security in the Post–Cold War Era* (Boulder: Lynne

Rienner, 1991); Thomas G. Weiss and James G. Blight (eds.), *The Suffering Grass: Superpowers and Regional Conflict in Southern Africa and the Caribbean* (Boulder: Lynne Rienner, 1992); and Brian Job (ed.), *The Insecurity Dilemma: National Security of Third World States* (Boulder: Lynne Rienner, 1992).

2. For a discussion of reconstruction costs from Cold War conflicts, see Anthony Lake (ed.), *After the Wars: Reconstruction in Afghanistan, Indochina, Central America, Southern Africa, and the Horn of Africa* (Washington, D.C.: Overseas Development Council, 1990).

3. Gerald B. Helman and Steven R. Ratner, "Saving Failed States," *Foreign Policy* 89 (Winter 1992–93): 3–20.

4. Boulder: Lynne Rienner, 1993.

5. Boulder: Lynne Rienner, forthcoming 1994.

6. See Randolph Kent, *Anatomy of Disaster Relief* (London: Pinter, 1987).

7. "The Bellagio Declaration: Overcoming Hunger in the 1990s," reprinted in *Food Policy* 15 (August 1990): 352–358.

8. See Larry Minear and Thomas G. Weiss, "Groping and Coping in the Gulf Crisis: Discerning the Shape of a New Humanitarian Order," *World Policy Journal* 9, no. 4 (Fall/Winter 1992–1993): 755–788.

List of Acronyms
and Abbreviations

ABC	American Broadcasting Corporation
ACUNS	Academic Council on the United Nations System
BBC	British Broadcasting Corporation
CBC	Canadian Broadcasting Corporation
CBS	Columbia Broadcasting System
CGIAR	Consultative Group for International Agricultural Research
CIREFCA	Conferencia Internacional para los Refugiados en Centro-América
CNN	Cable News Network
CPAF	Cambodian People's Armed Forces
CRS	Catholic Relief Services
DAC	Development Assistance Committee
DHA	Department of Humanitarian Affairs [UN]
EC	European Community
ECOMOG	Economic Community Monitoring Group
ECOSOC	Economic and Social Council
ECOWAS	Economic Community of West African States
EPLF	Eritrean People's Liberation Front
FAO	Food and Agriculture Organization of the UN
FMLN	Frente Farabundo Martí para la Liberación Nacional
GNP	Gross National Product
ICRC	International Committee of the Red Cross
ICVA	International Council of Voluntary Agencies
IDF	Israeli Defense Forces
IFRC	International Federation of Red Cross and Red Crescent Societies
ILO	International Labour Organisation
IMF	International Monetary Fund
IOM	International Organization for Migration

ITN	Independent Television News
ITV	Instructional Television
JUSMAT	Joint United States Military Advisory Team
LWF	Lutheran World Federation
MIA	Missing in Action
MSF	Médecins Sans Frontières
MTV	Music Television
NATO	North Atlantic Treaty Organization
NBC	National Broadcasting Company
NGO	Nongovernmental Organization
OAU	Organization of African Unity
OECD	Organization of Economic Co-operation and Development
OLS	Operation Lifeline Sudan
ONUMOZ	United Nations Observer Mission in Mozambique
ONUSAL	United Nations Observer Mission in El Salvador
PBS	Public Broadcasting System
PVO	Private and Voluntary Organization
RENAMO	Mozambique National Resistance
RPG	Refugee Policy Group
SPLA	Sudanese People's Liberation Army
TPLF	Tigray People's Liberation Front
UK	United Kingdom
UN	United Nations
UNDP	United Nations Development Programme
UNDRO	United Nations Disaster Relief Organization [DHA]
UNFPA	United Nations Population Fund
UNHCR	United Nations High Commissioner for Refugees
UNICEF	United Nations International Children's Emergency Fund
UNIFEM	United Nations Development Fund for Women
UNITAF	Unified Task Force [Somalia]
UNITAR	United Nations Institute for Training and Research
UNOSOM	United Nations Operation in Somalia
UNPROFOR	United Nations Protection Force in the Former Yugoslavia
UNSEPHA	United Nations Special Emergency Programme for the Horn of Africa
UNTAC	United Nations Transitional Authority in Cambodia
UNCTAD	United Nations Conference on Trade and Development
USAID	United States Agency for International Development
WFP	World Food Programme
WGBH	PBS television and radio station in Boston, Massachusetts
WHO	World Health Organization
WWF	World Wide Fund for Nature
ZDF	Das Zweite Deutsche Fernsehen

■ Part 1 ■
Humanitarian Values

Commentary

THOMAS G. WEISS & LARRY MINEAR

The most logical place to begin a discussion of humanitarianism across borders is with a review of the values that inform and motivate humanitarian activity. These values are being scrutinized intensively at today's pivotal moment in modern history. The Cold War has ended and its era is passing; the post–Cold War order is just beginning to take shape. Yet to emerge are the values around which a new order will be constructed and the institutions that will put them into practice.

During the Cold War, geopolitical considerations infiltrated fundamental values such as the sanctity of human life. In the frenzied competition between communism and anticommunism, promoting political ideology became more important than protecting human life. The right to food and freedom from persecution were not treated as absolute or universal. Rather, the key factor was whether the use of food as a political weapon or the violation of fundamental civil and political rights were perpetrated by "friendly" or "unfriendly" regimes.

Depending upon which superpower made the judgment, a Nicaraguan life was more or less important than a Salvadoran, a Cambodian refugee more or less valuable than a Filipino. Responses to human rights violations in East Timor were calibrated according to the perceived importance of the Indonesian government. Entire regions of the world, and the people who lived in them, were valued according to their strategic significance.

The Horn of Africa, for example, was caught in the crossfire between Washington and Moscow. Initially, the principal U.S. client was the Ethiopian government of Emperor Haile Selassie, the Soviet Union's the Somali regime of Siad Barre. Shortly after Selassie was ousted in a Communist takeover in 1974, the superpowers exchanged clients and adjusted

1

flows of military and economic aid accordingly. The Reagan administration delayed the U.S. response to the famine of 1983–1985 because Ethiopia was viewed as the Soviet Union's responsibility. After a late start, however, the United States eventually became the major outside provider of humanitarian relief, joining the Soviet Union and Eastern European countries.[1]

While East-West tensions did not divide the world neatly into two camps, the division was surprisingly clearcut. Whose side a government was seen to be on in the global struggle affected the international attention given to an emergency and the longer-term human needs of its people. Even the work of the United Nations and other intergovernmental organizations was politicized. As the near-total isolation of Vietnam throughout the 1980s suggests, the country allocations of many specialized UN agencies and the World Bank took their cues from the United States. The UN Security Council, the international community's most influential political body, rarely addressed humanitarian issues during the Cold War.

In the post–Cold War era, humanitarian crises no more serious than those earlier ignored by the Security Council are viewed as "threats to international peace and security." In fact, "humanitarian intervention" has become a household word. In April 1991, following the defeat of Iraq and the subsequent flight of Kurds from their homes, UN Resolution 688 determined that the mass upheaval constituted precisely such a threat. The Security Council insisted that humanitarian organizations receive access to the dislocated civilian population within Iraq and authorized military force to guarantee that access.

In the wake of the Security Council's unprecedented invocation of life-threatening suffering among Iraq's Kurds as the rationale for military intervention in northern Iraq, humanitarian considerations have figured in the authorization of subsequent commitments of UN-related military forces to such places as Somalia and Bosnia. Yet the same groups that lamented the marginalization of human needs during the Cold War are now seeing in their post–Cold War elevation another danger. The new attention to threats to humanity is, of course, welcome. However, in the absence of mechanisms to ensure that all suffering exercises equal claim on Security Council attention, the necessary equity in the protection of human life remains elusive. The serious needs in the world's Somalias will continue to upstage the even more catastrophic plights of the Sudan and Liberia.

This swing of the humanitarian pendulum confronts the international community with the fundamental issues that it chose to ignore during the Cold War. What is the nature of humanitarianism and its relation to sovereignty? When national borders are becoming more porous, do human values exercise transnational claims on political authorities, be they seated government or insurgent challengers? Under what kind of accountability does the international community respond to violations of humanitarian norms? What are the mechanisms for assuring such accountability?

The three chapters in Part 1 of the book deal with the values that are at the core of humanitarian action. Are humanitarian values universal or culturally specific? Do they impel emergency lifesaving action only, or do they also encompass a more inclusive and wide-ranging set of concerns and initiatives? Do they comprise a reliable force that supports and demands strong international responses, or are they uneven and unreliable as the basis for consistent and systematic humanitarian action?

Where does one turn for an informed and thorough discussion of humanitarian values? Ironically, organizations that provide daily assistance and protection to vulnerable populations may not be the best sources to articulate and elaborate them. Practitioners tend to be action oriented; their strength is saving lives. Caught up in the turbulence of sustaining civilians in one emergency after another, humanitarian organizations and their staffs typically consider discussions of values to be luxuries for a sunny day when demands for their services ebb. Such a day, unfortunately, seems a long way from dawning.

Philosophers, theologians, political theorists, and ethicists sometimes better explain humanitarian values. Based upon their views of human nature and institutions, human interaction and behavior, they can identify the determining forces behind economic, social, and political organization and action, be they respect for life and responsibility to other human beings or security and self-aggrandizement. Surveying the universe of humanitarian organizations, they also identify shared values and principles. But these do not always work in the rough-and-tumble circumstances of wars, in which norms are challenged by powerful self-interests and humanitarian acts are more opportunistic than principled.

A middle course is charted by the Humanitarianism and War Project, which seeks to examine the values affirmed by humanitarian organizations in the difficult terrain of armed conflicts. Growing out of our field research and discussions to date, we have identified eight principles that should guide humanitarian action. These principles are presented not as moral absolutes but as norms toward which humanitarians should strive; their formulation and implications require further debate and refinement, since a variety of viewpoints and trade-offs exist. However, principles are benchmarks against which performance can be measured; they help to prevent pragmatism from degenerating into unprincipled opportunism.

We offer these Providence Principles[2] as a backdrop for the chapters in Part 1, which seek to identify and explore humanitarian values. These principles also provide the context for discussions in Part 2 about the use of military force, which some see as a violation of humane values and others as a protection of them. Such principles are also central to the discussion in Part 3 about the shape of future institutions needed to protect and advance humanitarian values.

1. *Relieving Life-Threatening Suffering:* Humanitarian action should be directed toward the relief of immediate, life-threatening suffering.

2. *Proportionality to Need:* Humanitarian action should correspond to the degree of suffering, wherever it occurs. It should affirm the view that life is as precious in one part of the globe as another.

3. *Non-Partisanship:* Humanitarian action responds to human suffering because people are in need, not to advance political, sectarian, or other extraneous agendas. It should not take sides in conflicts.

4. *Independence:* In order to fulfill their mission, humanitarian organizations should be free of interference from home or host political authorities. "Humanitarian space" is essential for effective action.

5. *Accountability:* Humanitarian organizations should report fully on their activities to sponsors and beneficiaries. Humanitarianism should be transparent.

6. *Appropriateness:* Humanitarian action should be tailored to local circumstances and aim to enhance, not supplant, locally available resources.

7. *Contextualization:* Effective humanitarian action should encompass a comprehensive view of overall needs and of the impact of interventions. Encouraging respect for human rights and addressing the underlying causes of conflicts are essential elements.

8. *Subsidiarity of Sovereignty:* Where humanitarianism and sovereignty clash, sovereignty should defer to the relief of life-threatening suffering.

Domestic and international humanitarian agents generally subscribe to these principles, although different organizations and practitioners may interpret them differently or assign them different relative priority. This becomes particularly evident during wars when sustaining civilians presents tough trade-offs between various principles. Although the Providence Principles are less moral absolutes than norms toward which practitioners should strive, they represent fixed points on a shared compass that also stimulate dialogue and focus discussion.

Are the values that motivate humanitarian action universal, or are they culturally specific? Are concrete expressions of solidarity a feature unique to so-called advanced societies, or are they perhaps more essential to peoples whose existence is harsher and may require greater mutual support? Is compassion an instinct basic to humankind, or is it more often an expression of caring by those who are reasonably well-off? Does humanitarianism have religious and cultural roots? What is its relation to religious fundamentalism, which often seems to politicize human obligation and action? Does the recent upsurge in brutality in the former Yugoslavia and elsewhere confirm the Hobbesian suspicion that people are inherently selfish and nasty, or is it the result of the willingness of politicians to play on ethnic fears to serve their own narrow objectives?

Our exploration of these matters begins with the chapter by Ephraim Isaac, "Humanitarianism Across Religions and Cultures." A scholar of ancient religions and a linguist with a working knowledge of some fifteen languages, Isaac brings a rich background to his assignment. An Ethiopian by nationality, he has played a role in efforts to build peace in his country and to use the opportunity provided by the change in governments to work at reconciliation within his country. An orthodox Jew with catholic interests, he is ideally situated to explore the extent to which humanitarian impulses and institutions are universal, as well as culturally specific. He examines humanitarian obligations and practices in the major religions and traditional practices in Africa.

The issue of universality is important in theory and praxis alike. It is generally believed that the concept of humanitarianism is most fully developed in the jurisprudence and culture of Judaeo-Christian nations. Popular stereotypes suggest that only these nations place a high value on human life and care enough to assist their own or other distressed populations. Wealthy industrialized nations have not only the resources but also the established traditions that have given humanitarianism a peculiarly Western flavor.

The most actively involved governments and the most well-established and best-known humanitarian organizations are indeed Western in origin and constituency, in personnel and approach. However, recent research and writing has noted with increasing frequency that the concept and practice of humanitarianism is rather more widespread. Fundamental tenets of humanitarianism are more understood to resonate with central elements in non-Western traditions of religion, law, and ethics.[3]

A major catastrophe in today's global village generally activates a bewildering array of organizations. Working side by side will be Christian, Muslim, and secular groups; persons from nearby communities and countries and from around the world; governmental, intergovernmental, and nongovernmental workers; and civilian and military personnel. How these organizations and their employees express their values and relate to others has a direct bearing on the success of their endeavors and of the larger effort.

Inadequate understanding of other traditions of assistance, local values, and institutions can negatively affect the success of humanitarian activities. Outside responses based purely on Western legal and cultural traditions often obscure the reality that the most effective relief is probably that which corresponds to local mores and energizes the affected individuals and institutions. Consonance with local values also widens the ownership and accountability for humanitarian action, frequently making the difference between successful and failed undertakings.

When help comes from outside a society whose capacities are

temporarily overwhelmed, an appreciation of local values encourages humanitarian practitioners to build upon and strengthen indigenous resources. Fostering empowerment and institution building will help the affected community move toward self-reliance rather than remaining disaster prone and dependent upon outside assistance. Cultural sensitivity, however, is more than simply a means toward more effective programming. It also reflects a fundamental commitment to the importance of human life, whatever its cultural context.

An appreciation of the humanity of those affected by life-threatening crises is an essential element in the emerging international humanitarian order. Even a cursory examination of history suggests that an appeal to the universality of human rights and humanitarian law is a distinctly modern phenomenon. History is filled with examples of supposedly superior cultures and values around which states and empires were organized. Distinctions between the sacred and the profane, the citizen and the barbarian, the metropole and the hinterland reflected the conviction that certain human lives were more valuable than others. While altruism may be more widespread in non-Western cultures than many in the West realize, universal human-itarianism is nonetheless a distinctly radical value; it is a notion that has received widespread support only in the modern period.

The second chapter in Part 1, "Development and the Prevention of Humanitarian Emergencies," explores some universal and specific operational implications of humanitarian values. The relief of life-threatening suffering, for example, does not automatically ensure that response to emergencies will occur in ways that strengthen local institutions. In some circumstances, working through local organizations may delay international responses. However, faced with a choice between saving lives and respecting local mores, practitioners may opt for the former. In the northern Sudan in the mid-1980s, international nongovernmental organizations and donor governments brushed aside the Khartoum authorities in their rush to save lives threatened by the widening famine. In Somalia in 1992, some aid officials placed a premium on averting famine deaths, relegating until later any discussion of how relief aid would affect prospects for reconstruction and development.

The author of Chapter 2, Mary B. Anderson, and a colleague, Peter J. Woodrow, carried out an extensive field review several years ago of the strategies and results of some forty relief projects by nongovernmental groups. *Rising from the Ashes: Development Strategies in Times of Disaster*[4] has become a cornerstone of efforts to reconceptualize humanitarian interventions. A private consultant based in Boston, Anderson frequently has been enlisted by United Nations organizations, the U.S. government, and private agencies to improve the effectiveness of their activities in economic and social development, particularly on matters of sensitivity to gender and culture.

As a relief specialist, Anderson believes that humanitarian action must be cost-effective in terms of the immediate delivery of relief and the mitigation of suffering. As a development economist, however, she suggests that emergency relief must also address other objectives. Since urgent human need is rooted in underlying problems of poverty and powerlessness, humanitarian action should improve the medium- and long-term prospects for equitable economic development and peace, or at a minimum should not undermine or delay those projects. In other words, emergency aid should be provided in ways that will help a society care for itself.

Her examination suggests the artificiality of the traditional dichotomy between rapid responses to urgent needs and advancing the cause of development and peace. Drawing on illustrations from her field research in several regions, Anderson argues that it is possible to relieve immediate suffering through well-conceived programs that augment the capacities of beneficiaries to meet their own long-term needs. Analysts traditionally have identified discrete points on a spectrum, moving from short-term emergency relief through reconstruction of essential infrastructure to medium- and long-term development. Her approach explores interactions along the spectrum between emergency interventions and efforts to reduce poverty and enhance local capacities, a subject with which development organizations themselves increasingly are struggling.

In this regard, there may be a negative lesson to be learned from the most conspicuous and preoccupying international crises of 1992 and 1993, those involving Somalia and the former Yugoslavia. In each, the failure to resolve long-standing tribal and ethnic tensions erupted into bloody warfare, dramatizing the costs of ignoring the interactions along the emergency-to-development continuum. Anderson herself examines the specific operational and institutional difficulties, even for agencies that make the connections between emergencies and their underlying causes, in implementing programs that adequately take them into account. In fact, as the linkages become understood more fully, the difficulties become more operational than conceptual.

One of the most dramatic problems for development agencies is that the public and their parliaments frequently respond far more readily to appeals for assistance in complex emergencies rather than attack long-term problems. A recent UNICEF report distinguishes between "loud" emergencies in war zones that make headlines and the "silent" emergencies of existence for poor families who suffer daily from malnutrition and preventable diseases. The report points out that the world community was horrified enough to act because about half a million children under the age of five had died in 1992 in war-ravaged Somalia, but did little to prevent the deaths of the thirteen million other children, or about thirty-five thousand per day, who died during the same period from poverty.[5] This aberration is particularly unsettling because every dollar expended in such silent emergencies is an estimated ten to twenty times more effective than in loud ones.

The concerns with differential reactions to and support for various types of emergencies lead naturally to the final chapter in Part 1, Edward Girardet's "Public Opinion, the Media and Humanitarianism." A journalist with experience in print media, radio, and television, Girardet's reporting during the 1980s for the *Christian Science Monitor* provided for many Americans the major source of information on the war in Afghanistan and its humanitarian toll. More recently, his special reports on Somalia have been widely viewed on U.S. and British television. Concerned about increasing the responsibility and accountability of the media in its coverage of humanitarian issues, he helped found and now edits a new periodical, *Crosslines*, a forum for media professionals to reflect on such issues.

Girardet presents the findings of survey work in which he has been involved that suggest coverage of global humanitarian problems is more limited and selective than in the past. Calling for more continuous and accurate coverage of complex emergencies, he examines the collection and dissemination of information by the media and its impact upon public opinion in the West. Taking a hard look at the harsh economics of covering humanitarian crises and the media's penchant for depicting only the graphic violence of war, he urges his colleagues in the media, and in particular network television, to address more consistently the subtleties of poverty and the underlying sources of ethnic conflict.

Without doubt, the media can and has become a partner with the humanitarian community in fostering support for international assistance and respect for human rights, and in sensitizing the international public to the underlying causes of emergencies. That impact is suggested by the fact that during 1992, the Cable News Network aired some 434 items on Somalia as contrasted with six on the Sudan, where human suffering was equally or more widespread. Additional research would probably show that by its reporting on the deteriorating situation in Somalia, CNN reinforced international efforts to respond. The converse is probably also true: that the absence of media attention to the Sudan crisis contributed to the lower priority it received from media-sensitive decisionmakers.

The important role played by the media in humanitarian affairs has led aid organizations to invest significant resources in facilitating media coverage of major crises. Yet the current economic and institutional constraints that Girardet describes make it difficult for the media to move beyond reporting international ambulance chasing and spectacular atrocities to the insidious long-term effects of war and deprivation on the victims. To the extent that it depicts the relief of suffering in war rather than the less graphic but equally essential efforts to overcome the poverty and injustice beneath the conflicts, the media contributes to a vicious cycle. Because there is so little public and political attention to the underlying causes of emergencies, those emergencies recur with greater frequency. Moreover, such coverage exacerbates the difficulties of aid organizations, noted in Chapter 2, in mobilizing resources for indispensable reconstruction and development activities.

At the Providence conference described in the Preface, the Girardet chapter sparked intense debate. Particularly contested was its assertion of a direct and necessary connection between a responsible media, informed public opinion, and enlightened public policies. Girardet was asked what evidence demonstrates actual impacts of the media and public opinion on pragmatic initiatives and policy changes in the humanitarian field? Research about public opinion and policy formation has focused mainly on issues of arms control and the former Soviet Union. Different dynamics there may be at work as humanitarian action, when conventional wisdom suggests that public opinion also drives the policies of Western governments. Girardet's basic hypothesis about the media's influence on public opinion and the resulting changes in humanitarian policy needs more research and analysis. Public outrage generated by the BBC documentary on the Ethiopian famine in October 1984 and rock concerts for the benefit of the victims widely are believed to have forced the U.S. and British governments to focus on the tragedy and step up relief efforts. Public outcry about the plight of Kurds in northern Iraq in April 1991 seems to have forced the reluctant allied coalition to seek the passage of Security Council Resolution 688 as the basis to establish safe havens.

True in some circumstances, the pressure of public opinion hardly explains action in others. Decisions by George Bush just before the Republican convention in August 1992 to mount a U.S. airlift from Mombasa to Somalia, and in December of the same year—in the final months of his lame-duck presidency—to send soldiers to protect humanitarian operations there, seem to have reflected less pressure from public opinion than the interests of the president and other elite decisionmakers. His desire to be associated with humane instincts during the election campaign and, when not reelected, to be remembered as a kinder, gentler chief executive surely figured in his decisions. After months of media coverage of the horrors of internecine violence, the public was predisposed to go along with the President's decisions but public opinion did not cause them.

The first three chapters suggest a number of issues requiring further reflection regarding the nature of humanitarian values and their implementation by the international community in its efforts to sustain civilians in times of war.

1. Humanitarian values resonate with a basic human instinct of compassion and with obligations common to the world's great religious traditions. However, certain fundamentalist approaches to religion now are associated with intolerance, parochialism, and a lack of solidarity and sympathy with some who suffer. To what extent does religious extremism constitute a threat to a more effective global humanitarian system?

2. Even if humanitarian values are indeed more universal than generally realized, many of the world's principal humanitarian organizations still employ a predominantly Western approach and constituency. What are the operational implications of a more universal approach to humanitarian action for the culture of today's aid institutions? How can existing institutions become more attuned to the cultures in which major humanitarian crises are set? How can institutions that are more indigenous to crisis areas increase their comparative advantages?

3. Humanitarian action and hopefulness go hand in hand. Efforts to assist, protect, and sustain the vulnerable reflect the conviction that however deep-seated current racial, ethnic, tribal, political, and other antagonisms, and however barbaric current behavior, they should not be allowed to triumph. If the opposite of humanitarianism is not inaction but cynicism, what are some of the ways, ranging well beyond the sphere of humanitarian action itself, by which the international community can nurture and sustain the forces of hopefulness in the post–Cold War world?

4. At a time when differences between majority and minority populations are increasingly erupting into civil strife, the principle of tolerance for ethnic diversity is no longer axiomatic. In this perspective, the issue in Bosnia is not territorial aggrandizement but rather the viability of multiethnic living. An alternative viewpoint would suggest that ethnic cleavages are such that a separation of ethnic groups as in Cyprus may be necessary temporarily and perhaps even permanently. To what extent do basic humanitarian values necessitate multiethnic societies?

5. The media are both a valuable asset to a more effective system of global humanitarian action and a dangerous liability. Recent experience suggests that through publicizing assaults against humanity, the media can energize international action. However, media coverage is uneven, sporadic, and short-lived as new crises push still-unresolved crises off the screen. What can be done to utilize the media more routinely in impelling and sustaining humanitarian action? How can the media contribute to a more serviceable humanitarian system that includes a more fail-safe system of early warning devices and longer-term follow-through?

6. In a number of recent civil wars, the abuse of humanitarian activities has been so egregious that organizations have considered suspending—and in some cases have actually suspended—activities to protect their integrity. For agencies whose purpose is to save lives, the idea of voluntarily refusing to carry out their mandates is contradictory. Yet it is undeniable that circumstances may exist, such as rampant violations of international law and morality, in which humanitarian values may require calling a halt to activities that would continue to be manipulated by powers with no serious commitment to their success. How might decisions to withhold or temporarily suspend assistance and protection efforts represent not a denial of humanitarian values but actually an affirmation of them?

7. With the passing of the Cold War, humanitarian values have an opportunity to become a new cornerstone of international relations. No longer subservient to an East-West agenda, human needs may exercise a claim on international action because of their intrinsic importance. Yet countervailing factors may prevent humanitarian values from coming into their own. These include realpolitik, resource constraints, compassion fatigue, and a reluctance among outsiders to engage in highly fractious conflicts. What strategies should be adopted to assure that in the post–Cold War era humanitarian values become preeminent?

Notes

1. For a more extended discussion of the politicization of humanitarian activity, see Larry Minear, "The Forgotten Humanitarian Agenda," *Foreign Policy* 73 (Winter 1988–89): 76–93.

2. These are elaborated in Larry Minear and Thomas G. Weiss, *Humanitarian Action in Times of War: A Handbook for Practitioners* (Boulder: Lynne Rienner, 1993): chap. 1.

3. See, for example, *International Dimensions of Humanitarian Law* (Dordrecht: Martinus Nijhoff, 1988); Marcel A. Boisard, *L'Humanism de l'Islam* (Paris: Michel, 1979); Jack Donnelly, *Universal Human Rights in Theory and Practice* (Ithaca: Cornell University Press, 1989); David P. Forsythe, *The Internationalization of Human Rights* (Lexington: Lexington Books, 1991); Emmanuel Bello, *African Customary Humanitarian Law* (Geneva: ICRC, 1980); and T. O. Elias, *New Horizons in International Humanitarian Law* (Dobbs Ferry: Alphen aan den Rijn, 1979).

4. Boulder: Westview, 1989.

5. See *UNICEF Emergency Operations*, document E/ICEF/1993/11, February 19, 1993, para. 5–8.

▪ 1 ▪
Humanitarianism Across Religions and Cultures

EPHRAIM ISAAC

There is a tendency to associate humanitarianism with the twentieth-century West, which has become known for many and varying philanthropic activities. Even in comparative studies of philanthropy, there is an emphasis on the Western roots of humanitarian thought and its primacy in Western practices: D.J. Constantelos tells us that "Charity, . . . man's reciprocal love for God expressed in acts of love for fellow men, a conception so central to the Western tradition, is not explicitly stated in Buddhism, Hinduism, and Islam." The same author also claims that "in the practical application of charity [Christianity] went beyond Jews, Greeks, and Romans."[1] This statement is untrue as far as Judaism is concerned, which influenced early Christianity and ultimately the concept and practice of charity.

"Humanitarianism" is a feeling of concern for and benevolence toward fellow human beings. It is a universal phenomenon manifested globally and throughout the ages. Humanitarianism as practical generosity or philanthropic activities to promote the well-being of others is also a universal phenomenon. All peoples respect and appreciate humanitarian activities that form part of a common human vocabulary. While the international legal aspects of humanitarianism across borders have begun to be documented,[2] the same cannot be said for religions and cultures, which is our task here.

The twentieth century formalized philanthropy; it did not invent it. Private or collective generosity and giving for public purposes—especially to vulnerable groups (orphans, widows, strangers)—has been a laudable human undertaking for a long time. Whether we call it "humanitarianism," "charity," "almsgiving," "philanthropy," or "civic spirit," the phenomenon occurs in all places and times. The pragmatic side of humanitarianism is relative; it varies from culture to culture and from individual to individual within the same culture.

This essay begins with a survey of the sources of humanitarianism in a sample of writings from a variety of the world's most important religions. It then examines the impact of traditional beliefs in African societies on the development of humanitarian practices and of similar beliefs in other "preliterate" societies. The purpose is to suggest the extent to which humanitarian actions and impulses are part of the common heritage of humankind. There are clearly operational implications of this wider ownership of humanitarianism.

Humanitarianism and Its Religious Roots

In the West, concern for the well-being of others has deep historical roots going back to the Hebrew biblical teachings of love and sharing. In the New Testament, Saint Paul called "charity" the highest good (although there may be disagreements among scholars as to what exactly he meant by this term). Early Christianity championed the founding of institutions for the poor, sick, aged, and orphans. The beliefs and activities of pre-twentieth-century Diggers, Quakers, other radical religious thinkers (William Penn's colony, John Bellars [1654–1725], and Thomas Chalmers [1780–1847]) and early missionary societies (Society for the Promotion of Christian Knowledge [1698] and Society for the Propagation of the Gospel [1707]) included the practice of charity, despite critics who argued that public charity is dehumanizing and demoralizing.[3]

In the ancient world, and even today, humanitarianism has been related to religious beliefs and ethical teachings. Among the qualities of a good person, the Egyptian Book of the Dead lists giving food and water to the hungry and thirsty, clothing the naked, and helping travelers.[4] The ancient Egyptians regarded benevolent acts as very important in the eyes of the gods, who would reward them. In ancient Mesopotamia, acts of benevolence were believed to be decreed by divine powers as part of social justice. Concern for the destitute and the less fortunate is found in texts throughout the ancient Near East from Ugaritic inscriptions to the Babylonian Code of Hammurabi.[5] The god Shamash (Sumerian Utu) and the goddess Nanshe cared for orphans, sheltered refugees, and defended the poor.[6] We inherit from the Greeks and Romans words such as philanthropy (*philanthropia*, "love of mankind"), charity (*caritas*, "gift," "favor," "grace"), and alms (*eleemosyne,* "pity," "mercifulness"). In pre-Classical Greece, Homer and Hesiod held *philoxenia*—hospitality (literally "love of strangers")—as ethical virtues.[7]

But nowhere else in the ancient world do we find so many institutions and as much emphasis upon giving and concern for the needy as in ancient Judaism. The Hebrew Bible (Old Testament) is replete with references to the subject. Whereas private or collective giving in most societies is generally a voluntary act, in ancient Israel it was a religious obligation. "You should open your hand wide to your brother, to your poor, to the need in your land" (Deuteronomy 15: 11) is a command. Biblical law requires one to leave the corners of the field, the gleanings of the harvest, and the crop of the seventh year for the poor (Leviticus 19: 9–10). Love in the biblical sense also means concern for one's fellow human being (Deuteronomy 10: 17–18, 15: 7–10; Psalms 145: 15–16). From a historical perspective, the story of Joseph (Genesis 37ff.) is one of the earliest known references to international food distribution in time of famine.

In later Judaism, helping the needy was regarded as not only a matter of compassion but also justice (*sdqh*). The references to giving, such as the quality of charity and its obligatory nature, charitable work, charity boxes (*kuppah*) and public institutions, free lodges for strangers,[8] and related subjects in intertestamental, Rabbinic, and medieval Jewish literature, would fill volumes. For example, in the Talmud there is the reference to "act(s) of loving kindness," meaning humanitarianism is thought to be one of the three foundations upon which the world was erected (Aboth 1: 2). Wealth is divine grant, and the poor are entitled to share it. The primary focus of giving is, therefore, the needy themselves. However, donors also get certain benefits, including health, escape from death, forgiveness of sin, and even eternal life (Ecclus 3: 30, 29: 12; Tobit 1: 3 and 16, 4: 7ff., 12: 8–9; Aboth R. Nathan 4, 7, and 8; Shab. 151b; Kid. 28a; Yeb. 79a). A reference from the Jewish historian Josephus has been described as the first historical mention of systematic relief work (Ant. 20: 2–5).

The two daughters of Judaism, Christianity and Islam, have inherited these values in different degrees. In Christianity, helping the poor is catalogued with prayer and fasting (Matthew 6: 1–18), and the parable of the Good Samaritan illustrates its significance. Paul's letter to the Corinthians puts charity above two important Christian values—faith and hope. By charity, Paul meant pure love or *agapé*, the love of God and the spiritual love of human beings. To what degree *agapé* involves practical charity is a matter of debate.

Unlike Judaism, which put great emphasis on good deeds as central to righteousness and heavenly reward, Christianity emphasized the primacy of faith as the means to salvation and divine acceptance (Romans 2: 12–5: 21). A minority of the founders elevated good deeds to the level of faith and taught the importance of good deeds for eternal reward (James 1–2). They taught charity as not only a social but also a spiritual obligation—and even as a means of propitiation for sins. In Eastern Orthodox churches, as in medieval Europe, they established institutions for orphans and widows and hospices for the sick and others in need of assistance.[9]

According to Islam, humans serve God through good works, which include almsgiving and generosity towards orphans and the elderly. This is the general principle of statement in the Koran (Surat 23–39). There are basically two degrees or types of charity: legally prescribed (*zakāt*) and voluntary (*sadaqāt*). *Zakah*, almsgiving (from *zakah* "to be worthy," "pure"), is one of the five pillars of Islam.[10] It is a form of self-taxation to help the needy. Giving a portion of one's wealth above and beyond what one needs for sustenance legitimizes one's wealth. Zakah is giving alms directly, or indirectly through the state. Its purpose is to assist destitute travelers, soldiers, and freed slaves and to contribute to other benevolent deeds. All Muslims are assessed for zakah. While homes and personal possessions are exempt, zakah is determined as tithes on land production, livestock, or varying proportions on goods and merchandise and other properties.

Humanitarian deeds in Islam are not limited to such obligatory minimums. There is also *sadaqah* (deeds of kindness and generosity), which designates what is voluntarily given above and beyond the obligatory. A form of sadaqah is the distribution of about two quarts of grain or its monetary equivalent for every member of a household to the poor at the end of the fast of Ramadan ('Id al-Fitr). Property also may be donated for charitable purposes to the state in perpetuity. Such donations, referred to as *waqf* ("standing," "stopping," or "perpetuity," called *habs* in North Africa), are managed by the government for charitable distribution or the maintenance of religious institutions.

More controversial is Islamic thought pertaining to war and prisoners of war. In this respect, Western Orientalists tend to be critical of Islam as harsh and inhumane. In particular, they refer to such passages as Surat 8: 67–68 and 47: 4 of the Koran and argue that Islam teaches victory over infidels at any cost. They hold that Islamic law treats non-Muslims and slaves unjustly and undemocratically. But Muslim scholars and writers defend Islam as just and democratic. They argue, quoting the same or similar passages from the Koran and other texts from the tradition, that according to Islam "all men are equal," that Islam "enjoins justice to enemies" and prisoners of war, and that it is even in harmony with the spirit of the Geneva Conventions and Additional Protocols.[11]

The other major religions of the world also uphold humanitarian activities as important religious values. In Hinduism and Buddhism, giving to the poor is an important spiritual act, albeit primarily for the benefit of the giver. Hinduism is said to be a religion that emphasizes personal ethics. Although *karman* means hospitality, courtesy, and good deeds, a realization of *dharma* results from an inner predilection. According to the Upanishads, each individual has personal, social, and economic self-responsibility. If done properly, society will be perfect and there will be no need for charity.[12]

Jainism carries this idea even further, more explicitly emphasizing the notion of self-edification over social involvement as a means of bettering the world and overcoming poverty. This also implies that people who care for themselves also care for others.[13]

In the Eightfold Path, the Five Precepts of Buddhism, there is no mention of *dana*, giving to the needy, but it is an important religious quality (Sutta Nipata 263), even if not equivalent to giving dharma (Dhammapada, 354). Love and compassion toward the less fortunate are integral components of the Four Noble Truths (*catvāri-ārya-satyāni*). The social and public expression of the spiritual qualities of *miatri* (kindness), *karunā* (compassion), and *mudită* (respect) for good deeds, are believed to alleviate suffering. One king, Sivi, gave his eyes; another gave not only his kingdom but also all his possessions, including his family.

In China, philanthropy has a long and established history and much has been written about it.[14] Confucius and Mencius taught that giving is virtuous. The extended family and the state itself were viewed as a philanthropic institution. The Taoist Chuang Tzu seems to have considered philanthropy a perversion.

Traditional Beliefs and Humanitarian Practices in Africa

There are many stories about famine in Africa. From ancient Egypt to modern Ethiopia, there are records and stories of suffering during famine. Many of these point to gathering food during times of plenty and sharing it with affected communities in times of want. "Feed the hungry, give water to the thirsty" is not only a saying found in ancient Egypt, but also throughout traditional Africa. The Yoruba proverb, "a yam remains warm to the touch even after twenty years," means that feeding a stranger has its own reward years later.

Even in good times, hospitality and feeding strangers are seen as important customs in Africa. From Herodotus to David Livingston, travelers in Africa have been impressed by African hospitality. The famous episode from the life of Mungo Park is a classic example. One author described the story of his rescue by a gentle motherly African woman as follows:

> She took him to her home, revived him with a refreshing meal, and then as he slept the women folk resumed their spinning, singing the while far into the night how
>
> > "The winds roared, and the rains fell;
> > The poor white man sat under our tree;
> > He has no mother to bring him milk,
> > No wife to grind his corn
> > [refrain]
> > Let us pity the white man,
> > No mother has he."
>
> Surely no more touching picture of unselfish compassion has been recorded in history; . . . it was not an exceptional case."[15]

Many similar incidents have been reported by early Europeans in Africa. For example, one traveler wrote about the Wolof in Senegal: "The unfortunate, the helpless, and the infirm are objects of commiseration; they are received in every household with the greatest alacrity, and are instantly provided with food, and even with clothing if their condition requires it." The same author reported from the opposite side of Africa: "The visitor is greeted with the usual salutation of yambo [sic]; a stool is offered to the guest while the master of the house is seated on the ground. A meal is instantly prepared, and the stranger is regaled with the best the larder affords."[16] Going farther south, another observer noted: "The Hottentots [Khosa] . . . display extreme kindness towards strangers; and so natural with them is the exercise of hospitality that they look with contempt on the selfish members of the community who eat, drink, or smoke alone. All the aged and infirm are generally cared for."[17] This type of gesture remains a characteristic in today's Africa as well.[18]

Today, Africa receives so much humanitarian aid that the world does not view Africans as philanthropists. Much of Africa seemingly has become so impoverished that African humanitarianism is invisible. Nonetheless, Africans are still very active, if not in financial aid, then in human energy and mutual assistance. To this day, an important institution of the Oromo in Ethiopia is called *dabo*, a communal assistance system of farmers at the time of ploughing, sowing, weeding, and harvesting. It is a social and moral obligation for every adult in a village or surrounding regions to participate in dabo. Likewise, the *sanbate* among Christian Ethiopians is an old mutual economic assistance system. Similar customs exist elsewhere in Africa.

In African folklore, the rescue motif is very common: A woman risks her life to save her husband; she carries him on her back, brings him home from a distant forest, and saves him from the brink of death; a son rescues his father; a man rescues his brother. Although many stories are about the heroic rescuing of relatives, the emphasis is upon the value of rescuing human life itself. Concern only for oneself is valueless. Greed is not only ridiculed, but is also regarded as a sure path to spiritual and perhaps physical death. The story of the tragic end of three greedy men, who fear even a single fly from sharing their food and plot against each other for total possession of the remnants, is found throughout Africa.[19] In folklore and in many African proverbs, helping others and sharing are highly regarded common themes. "Eat alone, die alone," says a popular Ethiopian proverb. Another proverb says, "threads united can tie even a lion," meaning that the way for people to be empowered is by banding together for common social causes. Those who do not give do not or cannot appreciate receiving. Africans appreciate modern Western philanthropy because they have known giving.

Contrary to conventional wisdom, most African peoples who are followers of traditional (i.e., non-Christian, non-Moslem) religions share a great deal of religious and cultural beliefs and values. Their worldview is essentially sociocentric, not individualistic. Emphasis is not on the private but on the common good. Anthropologists have been impressed by the emphasis on the value of human life among many African peoples. "A high value is placed on human life. An aspect of western civilization that puzzles the Louvedu is that we tolerate the loss of human life involved in the use of motor traffic. Are people not more important than speed?"[20] The need for even a chief to respect his subjects, upon whom he depends for a following, is summed up in the saying *"Uuhosi gi vathos,* chieftainship is people."[21]

Underlying the principles of African moral ideas is the very essence of the African worldview: the belief that there is harmony and mutual interdependency between the spiritual and physical, and between the individual and social realms. The activities of nature, such as plants, animals, rain, sunshine, rivers, and forests, were believed to be spiritually effective and meaningful. All forms of individual and collective human activity—including individual and social and experiences like birth, puberty, marriage, and death, as well as rites like circumcision or sacrifice—are associated with daily or seasonal human experience, and are believed to have full spiritual value because they benefit the community, not just the individual.

From this comprehensive point of view, rituals are important to African communal life. A rite is by definition a function and not an individual performance. As many scholars of African religions and other cultures agree, there are several examples of security and protection of the individual by a dominant tribal or state cult, which also sanctions proper conduct in all social relations and subactivities. The Abaluiya and the Lele, for example, may confine their rituals to households, kin groups, or the local community, even though they commonly believe in supernatural forces or beings. Moreover, they believe that ancestral beings protect the living and authorize their conduct. These beings are not necessarily tribal ancestors or from a royal line, but rather from kin groups that define their own power and authority.

Beliefs and rituals are often a reflection of social integration. Economic self-sufficiency and political freedom is in direct proportion to the partition of rituals from the objects of worship. In contrast, closer integration of economic activity and social control indicates that basic concepts and rituals are socially broader and better linked. One could say that humanitarianism is itself a form of ritual in Africa.

Humanitarianism Among Other "Non-White" Peoples

Non-African peoples have similar traditions that should be mentioned briefly. For example, American Indians, who were viewed as "preliterate," have long-standing traditions of humanitarian gestures. According to one author:

> No friendly stranger ever left an Amerind village hungry if that village had a supply of food. The hungry Indian had but to ask to receive, and this no matter how small the supply or how dark the future prospect. The Amerind distribution of food was based on long custom, on tribal laws; food was regarded . . . as a necessity that should in distress be [given] without money and without price. Hospitality was a law . . . a hungry man of any color is cheerfully fed . . . the Europeans would have starved to death in some instances had it not been for the timely aid.[22]

In the nineteenth century much was written about the altruism of other "primitive" or "savage" peoples. Altruism, a term coined by Auguste Comte and meaning devotion for the well-being of other,[23] is opposed to the evolutionary theory of self-preservation as taught by Charles Darwin, Aldous Huxley, and their followers, who viewed life as a successful struggle against the weak.[24] Thomas Hobbes wrote *"homo homini lupus."* "Man is a wolf toward man."

In contrast, some ethnologists called altruism "mutual helpfulness" and thought that it was tribalistic and ruled by customary habits that were based on underdeveloped moral consciousness. This view is based on Darwin's theory about animal sociability and solidarity[25] that postulates there is a natural animal instinct of mutual helpfulness and sympathy. The two opposing views reflect a condescending attitude toward altruism.[26]

However, according to some observers, altruism was "an indispensable factor in the evolution and survival of the human race and the development of civilization." Consequently, mutual helpfulness had to be a high virtue. As altruism then came to be regarded as good, it was attributed to the "higher" forms of religion, and not thought to be characteristic of early or "primitive man." When it was thought to exist among even the so-called primitive peoples, it was argued that "the feeling . . . is not limited to cultured peoples, but is an attribute of humanity, itself, one which goes back to the rudest societies, which share it in common with many animals—many groups of birds and mammals, and even insects (bees, ants)."[27] At any rate, altruism ultimately has been recognized as good and as very important among all peoples, including the so-called preliterate peoples.

Aristotle rightly said that an individual who is "sufficient for himself" must be "either a beast or a god."[28] No individual can find personal fulfillment outside the life of others. Aristotle therefore expresses admiration for the foreign practice of benevolence, which virtue is lacking among the Athenians.[29] In the West, the objective of the moral life is often seen by philosophers, including Aristotle, as self-realization or perfecting an individual life. In the African tradition, the end of moral life is altruism or sacrifice to perfect society (the tribe). Many Western philosophers argue that true self-realization cannot be separate from realizing social ends. The Stoics taught that "a good man is a citizen of the world, *homo sacra res homini*."[30] Christianity, which teaches that a person must work out his/her own salvation, also teaches sacrifice for others.[31]

Conclusion

At the end of the twentieth century, our planet is regarded as a village, in which humanitarianism takes on a new and growing significance. The village is crowded and the needy are multiplying daily. There is no doubt that humanitarian activities are going to increase in importance. It is a common heritage of humankind and will continue to be so.

In both ancient and modern thought, there is a view that humanitarianism should not be an end in itself. Humanitarianism should not be a mere stopgap, but a new beginning for the needy. Alongside the growing activities of philanthropy, strong educational and development initiatives must be conceptualized and executed to enable the needy to continue helping themselves. The operational implications of this holistic conception of humanitarianism are treated elsewhere in this volume. The most important impact, however, is that external assistance would not be perceived as an alien intrusion but rather as a reinforcement of local values and structures.

Notes

1. D. J. Constantelos, "Charity," in M. Eliade, (ed.), *The Encyclopedia of Religion* (New York: Macmillan Publishing Co., 1987): 224. See also E. Grubb "Philanthropy," in *Encyclopedia of Religion*, 837; and A. D. Ross, "Philanthropy," in *International Encyclopedia of the Social Sciences* (New York: Macmillan & Free Press, 1968): 73.

2. See *International Dimensions of Humanitarian Law* (Dordrecht: Martinus Nijhoff, 1988); Jack Donnelly, *Universal Human Rights in Theory and Practice* (Ithaca: Cornell University Press, 1989); and David P. Forsythe, *The Internationalization of Human Rights* (Lexington: Lexington Books, 1991).

3. K.L.M. Pray, "Charity," in *Encyclopedia of the Social Sciences* (New York: The Macmillan Co., 1937): 340–344.

4. E. A. Wallis Budge (ed. and trans.), *Book of the Dead* (London: Kegan Paul, 1910): 273.

5. T. J. Meek (trans.), "The Code of Hammurabi," in J. B. Pritchard (ed.), *The Ancient Near East: An Anthology of Texts* (Princeton: Princeton University Press, 1958): 138–172; and J.C.L. Gibson, *Canaanite Myths and Legends* (Edinburgh: T. & T. Clark Ltd., 1977): 102 (originally edited by G. R. Driver [Edinburgh: T. & T. Clark Ltd., 1956]).

6. S. N. Kramer (trans.), "A Sumerian Myth," in Pritchard, *Ancient*, 29–30; E. A. Speiser (trans.), "The Epic of Gilgamesh," in Pritchard, *Ancient*, 54–58; Robert H. Pfeiffer, "A Pessimistic Dialogue Between Master and Servant," in Pritchard, *Ancient*, 247, 250.

7. Constantelos, "Charity," 223.

8. According to some rabbis, a guest house has to be built with four entrances, each facing in one of the four directions, so that tired strangers coming to them would not be inconvenienced.

9. See C. Constantelos, *Byzantine Philanthropy and Social Welfare* (New Brunswick: Rutgers University Press, 1968).

10. Fazlur Rahman, *Islam* (Chicago: University of Chicago Press, 1979): 15, 37, 208.

11. See M. K. Ereksoussi, "The Koran and the Humanitarian Conventions," *International Review of the Red Cross* B, no. 43 (May 1962); Y. B. Ashoor, "Islam and International Humanitarian Law," *International Review of the Red Cross* (March–April, 1980): 1–11; and Marcel A. Boisard, *L'Humanisme de l"Islam* (Paris: Michel, 1985).

12. See *The Upanishads* (London: George Allen & Unwin, 1963; New York:

Harper and Row, 1963); T. Organ, *The Hindu Quest for the Perfection of Man* (Athens: Ohio University Press, 1970); and N. C. Chaudhuri, *Hinduism* (London: Chatto & Winds, 1979).

13. H. Zimmer and J. Campbell (ed.), *Philosophies of India* (Cleveland: The World Publishing Co. [Meridian Books], 1951): 279 and 196n.

14. See Yu-Yue Tsu, *The Spirit of Chinese Philanthropy* (New York and London: Friendship Press, 1912); J. Legge (ed. and trans.), *The Chinese Classics* (Oxford: Oxford University Press; Hong Kong: Hong Kong University Press, 1893–1895); and H. H. Dubs, *Hsuntze: The Moulder of Confucianism* (London: Probsthain, 1928; New York: Paragon Book Gallery, 1966).

15. A. H. Keane, "Charity, Almsgiving," in J. Hastings (ed.), *Encyclopedia of Religion and Ethics* (Edinburgh: T. & T. Clark, 1908–1926; New York: Scribners, 1979–81): vol. 2, p. 378.

16. A. Featherman, *Social History of the Races of Mankind: The Nigritians* (London: Trübner & Co., 1885): 349 and 96.

17. Keane, "Charity, Almsgiving," 378.

18. The author knows the meaning of African hospitality and care not from stories but from experience, traveling on muleback in remote regions of Ethiopia in the late 1950s. Although generally food was carried, it was enough to be announced as tired strangers in order to get ready assistance, including free lodging.

19. R. M. Dorson, *African Folklore* (New York: Doubleday, Anchor Books, 1972): 498n, 402, and *passim*. See also Y. Diallo, *Humanitarian Law and Traditional African Law* (Geneva: ICRC, Feb.–Jan. 1976).

20. J. D. and E. J. King, "The Louvedu of Transvaal," in D. Forde (ed.), *African Worlds* (London: Oxford University Press, 1954): 77.

21. P. Tempels, *Bantu Philosophy* (Paris: Présence Africaine, 1959).

22. F. S. Dellenbaugh, *The North Americans of Yesterday* (New York and London: G. P. Putnam's Sons, 1901): 354n, 447.

23. *Webster's New Twentieth Century Dictionary*, 2d ed., s.v. " altruism."

24. See, for example, Charles Darwin, *On the Origin of Species* (London: John Murray, 1859); and J. S. and T. S. Huxley, *Evolution and Ethics* (London: Pilot Press, 1947).

25. See Charles Darwin, *The Descent of Man and Selection in Relation to Sex* (London: John Murray, 1871).

26. For a discussion, see J. Iverach, "Charity, Almsgiving," in *Hasting's Encyclopedia of Religion and Ethics* (Edinburgh: T. & T. Clark, 1908–1926): vol. 1, 354n; Merle Curti, "Philanthropy," in *Dictionary of the History of Ideas* (New York: Scribners, 1973–74): vol. 3, 486; and H. Spencer, *Data of Ethics* (New York: D. Appleton and Company, 1879).

27. Keane, "Charity, Almsgiving," 376.

28. Aristotle, *Politics* (London: W. Heineman; Cambridge: Harvard University Press, Loeb Classical Series, 1950): I, 2: 14.

29. Ibid., I, 6: 5.

30. Seneca, *Ad Lucilium Epistulae Morales* (London: W. Heineman; Cambridge: Harvard University Press, Loeb Classical Library, no. 75–77, 1961): Ep. 15: 3.

31. See also Plato, *The Republic* (London: W. Heineman; Cambridge: Harvard University Press, Loeb Classical Series, 1930–35, 1935–37, reprint, 1956); and Aristotle, *Politics*, I, 2: 9.

■ 2 ■
Development and the Prevention of Humanitarian Emergencies

MARY B. ANDERSON

If humanitarian assistance today contributes to a famine tomorrow, can it truly be considered humanitarian?

If humanitarian assistance buttresses the regime of a repressive government that spends its own funds on weapons to turn against its citizens, can it truly be considered humanitarian?

If humanitarian assistance is amply distributed to a needy population but later studies show that female-headed households never received any aid, can it truly be considered humanitarian?

Indeed, if humanitarian assistance does nothing to prevent future humanitarian emergencies, can it truly be said to be humanitarian?

The Dilemma

Questions such as these increasingly plague the providers of humanitarian assistance. The simple act of putting "a cup of cold water in the hand of a thirsty man"[1] proves to be complex and politicized, and genuine generosity too often leads to embedded inequality and degrading dependency. In some cases, aid has kept people alive only to face ongoing or increased difficulties. People whose lives have been saved through short-term food and medical assistance frequently survive in conditions of worsening impoverishment and, in areas of conflict, expanding violence. Humanitarian relief too often has done nothing to address the causes of suffering of those whom it is intended to help.

This chapter confronts this critical dilemma. Is it possible for humanitarian assistance to do more than just meet the urgent and immediate needs of those who suffer in emergencies? Can such assistance also address the root causes of the suffering so that the likelihood of recurrence of such emergencies is reduced?

Many people think not. They believe that humanitarians face an either/or choice. *Either* they can work directly to relieve immediate human suffering and save lives, *or* they can work with people to help build their capacities for meeting their own long-term needs, or for negotiation and political action aimed toward achieving peace. There is an inevitable contradiction between these activities because the former requires speed and efficiency, while the latter requires time and patience for interaction and consultation. Some humanitarians believe that people who are suffering have no capacity, either physical or psychological, to give their attention to long-term issues. They believe that the urgency required for emergency assistance and the slower pace required for development and peacemaking force an inevitable trade-off between relief work and development or peace work.

This chapter contends that the urgency versus development and peace trade-off is fallacious. To pose the alternatives in either/or terms is both damaging and unnecessary. Any valid definition of "humanitarian assistance" must include consideration of the long-term developmental or political impacts of this assistance and means; those who would help save lives should assume responsibility for the long-term impacts of their help.

The argument rests on an understanding of the causes of humanitarian emergencies and the relationships between these causes, humanitarian assistance, and the long-term conditions in which people live. To consider how humanitarian assistance can promote solutions to the problems that cause emergencies, it is necessary to understand the two ends of the emergency spectrum—root causes and long-term outcomes—and their relationships.

These relationships are examined in the pages that follow, keeping in mind the model in Figure 2.1. Poverty and conflict are the basis for human suffering in emergencies: The desired future is one in which everyone enjoys the economic security of development and the physical security of peace. In the middle, humanitarian assistance is offered in response to emergencies. The question is: To what extent, and how, can such assistance actually contribute to future sustainable development and peace?

The following section examines the root causes of humanitarian emergencies, namely, poverty and conflict.[2] Next is an exploration of the

Figure 2.1 Humanitarian Assistance Model

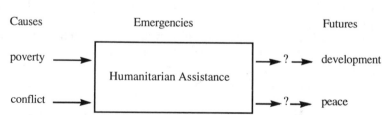

conditions of development and peace as the desired futures in which people do not face repeated emergencies. The next section presents two important lessons for humanitarian assistance providers that emerge from an understanding of causes and futures. The last section considers how the provision of humanitarian assistance simultaneously can alleviate immediate human suffering and contribute to the processes that ultimately bring development and peace.

Poverty and Conflict as Causes of Emergencies

Humanitarian emergencies are situations in which people cannot sustain life by their own efforts. The causes of these situations can be grouped into two essential categories: economic and political. Impoverishment and conflict are the basic economic and political forces that underlie the suffering to which humanitarian assistance responds. While some emergencies are entirely poverty related, today's humanitarian emergencies are often complex. They are the result of both poverty and conflict. In some cases, drought and famine precede fighting (in Somalia, for example), and in others the impoverishment of many people has been a result of war (as in Bosnia).

While poverty and conflict reinforce each other, there are other causes for both. An understanding of what lies behind poverty and conflict is necessary in order to link humanitarian assistance to their solution.

Poverty

Poverty results from a lack of access to adequate or appropriate resources from which to gain a livelihood. In some cases, there simply are not enough resources to support the number of people in a given area. In places where populations have increased and land is limited, the land's carrying capacity is insufficient so that formerly secure people may slip into poverty. More often, resources are sufficient to sustain the population, but they are unequally or unjustly distributed so that some people—or groups of people—are consigned to live in poverty while others enjoy plenty. In other situations, resources are degraded (as when land or forests are depleted by unwise use) or destroyed (as when factories are bombed in war). Degradation and destruction cause people who once lived economically viable lives to decline into poverty.

There are two additional facts about poverty-based emergencies that are important to understanding the relationship between humanitarian assistance and long-term outcomes. The first of these is that humans play a central role in causing all disasters. Poverty-based emergencies never arise entirely from natural causes. Drought, winds, rains, and earth movements are natural events that destroy resources on which people depend, but are not emergencies. They become emergencies only when they overwhelm people's abilities to sustain themselves. Poor people who live on the margin in the best of times are more vulnerable to being overwhelmed by such events than wealthy people. A drought becomes a famine emergency when people are unable to maintain sufficient food surpluses to outlast a failed crop, or when they do not have access to systems that redistribute food from surplus areas if their crops fail. Earthquakes, winds, and floods result in injury, death, and property loss for people (often the poor) who live in vulnerable locations, or when insufficient measures have been taken that could prevent or lessen the impacts of these natural forces (often the case in poorer societies).

Human agency, human choices, human actions, and human decisions create the circumstances in which natural events become emergencies. If humans are involved in causing emergencies, then humans can also take actions to prevent them. Humanitarian emergencies that arise from poverty do not have to happen.

The second crucial fact about poverty-related emergencies is that people need more than physical resources to survive.[3] Survival depends also on social and psychological capacities. The interaction between physical and nonphysical resources and capacities determines people's vulnerability to emergencies. Education, skills, and general know-how are capacities that, when applied to the physical resources of land, tools, seeds, and equipment, affect people's productivity. Family and community structures through which people gain both physical and psychological support often make the difference as to who suffers most—and least—in emergencies. People's experiences in decisionmaking and management affect their sense of efficacy and control and also have an important effect on productivity in normal times and on survival during emergencies.

The interactions between physical resources and nonphysical capacities can trap people in a cycle of poverty or can help them break out of poverty. In poor families that depend on the work of all their members for survival, children are unable to take advantage of schooling. They miss out on education, which could help them improve their options and productive capacities. Technologies require capital for purchases and knowledge for implementation, so the poor who have neither capital nor education lack access to them and consequently a chance to increase productivity and break the cycle of poverty. Time (that is, unallocated time during which one can rest, attend a meeting or class, clear a new field, or do something to improve one's economic base) is also a resource that is more limited for people who live marginally and must scramble constantly to survive than for those who are better off.

In contrast, social, organizational, or psychological capacities also can help people break out of physical poverty. When people who are materially poor live in close-knit and mutually supportive communities, they may be able to organize their work and savings in ways that lead to economic progress for the whole group. This has been one model pursued by poor immigrant families as they successfully enter new societies. Community development and organization sometimes promote economic growth among people who, without effective alliances, had lived economically marginal lives for many years. The gains from such community-based activity derive from the organization of group action that increases the efficient use of labor and resources, and from the psychological boost that people experience when they take control of their lives and work together effectively.

The third fact to be recognized about poverty-related emergencies is that although poor people often are caught in a cycle of poverty that makes them vulnerable to such emergencies, they also have capacities that, if built upon, can comprise the basis for breaking this cycle. Most people who live in poverty work hard to eke out sustenance for themselves and the people for whom they care. They are seldom either idle or passive in their normal (preemergency) lives. Their problem is not inactivity, but a lack of access to adequate or appropriate physical and nonphysical resources with which to sustain their lives.

Conflict

The causes of conflict are even more complicated than those of poverty. In fact, one cause of conflict is poverty. The unjust distribution of resources has been at the root of many wars throughout history. Disputes over limited resources have also fueled conflict. However, conflicts over scarce resources (such as land or water) frequently arise from ideological or political motivations rather than from an actual need for the resource. Thus, poverty is only one, and seldom the overriding, cause of conflict. (History no doubt would show that greed, more than poverty, has been the economic motivation for wars.) Poor people seldom start wars, although they often become the footsoldiers and front-line fighters in wars begun by those who are richer and more powerful.

Other causes of conflict are historical and political. Many of the wars of the 1990s are based in historical animosities coupled with some recent political shift. In the former Yugoslavia, parts of the former Soviet Union, and Somalia, deep-seated intergroup rivalries reemerged as power relationships changed. According to analysts,[4] a sudden power vacuum caused by rapid political realignments invited political opportunism on the part of some leaders who excited old passions and rekindled former animosities. While the motivations of the leaders may be sinister, not all combatants can be accused of selfish motives. Some engage in war from a sense of loyalty, others for justice, and others out of fear of another group's excessive and potentially repressive power.

Many of today's conflicts originated in the context of the Cold War. When the two superpowers armed different sides of local or regional political struggles, these often became surrogate fighters for causes that lay beyond their own borders and interests. However, promoting struggles proved easier than ending them, as circumstances in Angola, Sudan, Iraq, Iran, and

Afghanistan attest. Sales from European and North American arms industries accompanied setting up warring surrogates. Many wars now appear to continue because guns are available rather than because those who use them believe that fighting will achieve their goals more effectively than negotiation. Once arms are in the hands of many people (as in Somalia, Sri Lanka, Lebanon, Cambodia, and Liberia), it has proved so far virtually impossible to retract them.

Several additional points about conflict-related emergencies are important in understanding how these may be affected through emergency assistance. As for poverty-related emergencies, conflict emergencies also arise from human actions and decisions. There is nothing natural about war, although many scholars cite the fact that throughout history societies have resorted to conflict to solve their problems as proof that it is in human nature to do so. As was the case in poverty-caused emergencies, humans can solve the problems humans cause. Conflict emergencies are not inevitable.

Conflicts involve reinforcing processes and are self-perpetuating and spiraling. In many cases, what begins as a war of purpose and meaning becomes more a war of habit and revenge. People perceive few alternatives for settling differences or establishing justice other than the one that has been used, reused, and misused often—namely, guerrilla action or battlefield attack. When one onslaught is "successful," it generates a desire for retribution or revenge. In the name of "equalizing" the price that has been paid by warring sides, each adds to the rationale for future attacks.

Most wars today are fought among civilians, and the percentage of deaths and casualties suffered by them has risen steadily in proportion to deaths of combatants.[5] Those who fight are seldom those who decide when, where, and whether to continue a conflict. These decisions are usually made in council rooms far from the battlefront.

The Relationship Between Poverty and Conflict

Poverty and conflict often occur together, and humanitarian assistance is often required in circumstances where both are causes of an emergency. As previously stated, poverty is one but not necessarily the overriding cause of conflict. However, conflicts are a major cause of increasing impoverishment. As people are forced to move from their homes and jobs; as factories, offices, and infrastructure are destroyed; as communities are split both physically and psychically; as more resources are channeled toward weapons and the support of armies rather than toward meeting civilian needs; in general, as people confront shortages of the goods required both to sustain life and to carry out production, wars produce dire immediate and long-term needs. Wars at least temporarily impoverish many people, some of whom were previously well-off.

The impoverishing power of conflict does not always differentiate between the poor and wealthy. However, in many wars, the degree of poverty prior to a conflict determines how much people will suffer. Frequently, people with some wealth have options or opportunities for escape, while those who are poor are trapped in war zones.

Poverty can also play a role in prolonging conflicts. For example, when young men (and sometimes women) who have no viable economic base are recruited as warriors, their service in combat provides some economic security. With this community of allies and a purpose in life, they may be reluctant to give up their involvement in war. Under these circumstances, strategies for ending conflict may have to include the introduction of productive opportunities and the likelihood of at least as much economic security for stopping fighting as for perpetuating it.

Development and Peace

Development and peace represent futures in which people do not experience humanitarian emergencies. There is sufficient economic security with development and sufficient social and political security with peace so that people can sustain their own lives by their own efforts. Neither impoverishment nor conflict threaten people to the extent that they require external assistance.

Development is best understood as a process rather than as a fixed state. Though it has been described most often in economic or material terms (GNP, income per capita, and meeting basic needs), these are no longer considered satisfactory as the sole measures of development. Since the first publication of the *Human Development Report* by the United Nations Development Programme in 1990, more comprehensive indicators of development have been introduced and legitimized. The *human development index* includes measures of educational and health access and status, political involvement, and even distributional issues such as the relative access to resources and status of women and men.[6] Development is now widely understood as a social and political as well as an economic process.

Peace also is a comprehensive idea. It can mean anything from the absence of overt conflict to a condition where such perfect and universal justice prevails that even the potential for conflict is eliminated. Development is not a necessary precondition for the absence of war. It is important, however, in the realization of justice, which is the foundation for a sustainable peace. On the other hand, development cannot occur without minimal peace—the absence of overt conflict; such peace is a necessary but insufficient condition for development. An expanding and inclusive process of development can promote and nurture a widening peace, which can inspire and promote the processes of development. As poverty and conflict are interrelated, so also are development and peace. These relationships are crucial to understanding how to provide humanitarian assistance that promotes viable futures.

Lessons from Understanding Causes and Futures

The discussion of the causes of poverty- and conflict-related emergencies and of development and peace as futures leads to two critical lessons for humanitarians.

Lesson 1: Human Causes—Human Solutions

The first lesson derives from the central role played by human decisions and actions in creating emergencies: Effective humanitarian assistance must be based in recognition of the human role in causing—and solving—emergencies, and must incorporate elements that focus on affecting human behavior as much as on the delivery of supplies and services. Emergencies are not technical problems. They are human problems that involve physical, social, political, and psychological realities. Purely technical approaches that focus on tonnage, transport, caloric content, and financial accountability to donors will never effectively reduce human vulnerability to future emergencies.

Lesson 2: Human Suffering—Humane Assistance

The second lesson stems from the awareness that people need more than physical resources to survive and that those who suffer in emergencies possess useful resources and capacities that are the basis for their ability to manage their own survival. The lesson is that effective humanitarian assistance must be based on recognizing that the delivery of aid directly interacts with the recipients' own physical, social, and psychological capacities and must be designed to support and build on these. When assistance providers ignore these capacities, they negate and undermine them, leaving those whom they intended to help even less able to survive in the future. Why does this happen?

Extreme poverty and conflict put people into situations where they cannot physically sustain life. Therefore, humanitarian assistance naturally focuses on the physical needs of the sufferers. Because these are dire and visible, assistance must be quick and efficient. But the best of motivations—providing help as quickly as possible—often translates into an unnecessary and harmful process. In the interest of efficiency, distribution systems for providing food and medical care are established, managed, and controlled entirely by external providers. Aid providers lose sight of the capacities of those who are in physical need. People who receive aid that is given in this manner become physically inactive and mentally dependent. They internalize the perception (conveyed by the procedures through which assistance is provided) that they are incapable of handling their own survival and that others are better equipped to do this. Aid recipients become passive dependents on the competence of outsiders.

What can humanitarian agencies do to avoid this syndrome? The answer involves both intangible and tangible elements. The most important factor that determines the long-term impacts of aid is the attitude conveyed by providers and their procedures toward the recipients. When providers trust and respect recipients, they approach their job as workers alongside those needing help. They rely on the recipients, whose knowledge of the situation they trust and respect. When the capacities of recipients are recognized and form the basis of the procedures that are adapted for providing aid, this can create greater efficiency for distributing goods, setting priorities among competing needs, improving managerial know-how, and establishing calm in a stressful situation.

When providers are primarily concerned with control and accountability to donor organizations and funders, they set up systems for distributing and rationing aid that guard against theft. With their food and medicine, aid recipients receive a clear message that they are not trusted or trustworthy. They are transformed into beggars whose survival task becomes asserting more need, finding ways to persuade or trick the donor into providing more, and competing with other recipients for extra favors. The assistance enterprise becomes one in which donor and recipient are pitted against each other; one protects the aid against abuse from those whose need prompted the initial generous act of giving, while the other asserts the remaining vestiges of self-confidence and control through attempts to manipulate the donors and donations. It also pits recipients against one another, creating or reinforcing mistrust and competition among them as they vie for limited aid controlled by outsiders rather than collaborating to decide jointly how to set priorities among their various needs.

Humanitarian assistance provided to Europeans by U.S. and Canadian agencies during and after the two world wars exhibited many characteristics of trust, respect, and sympathy that enable sufferers to rebuild their lives quickly and competently. Assistance provided by many of these same agencies to Asians and Africans since the 1970s too often has exhibited the characteristics of mistrust and the need to control that undermine the confidence and capacities of the recipients.

Suffering Europeans looked familiar to aid providers, who identified with the recipients and knew them to be educated, moral, and intelligent. War clearly caused their suffering. In Asia and Africa, the people who required aid appeared poor, uneducated, and unfamiliar.[7] Their suffering seemed at least partially their fault. Too often, assistance reflects racism and classism. This obstructs the providers' identification with sufferers and, correspondingly, undermines trust and respect.

At the heart of humanitarian assistance is the basic message that the procedures of assistance communicate. Though intangible, the trust and respect—or lack thereof—communicated through assistance are real. Rather than setting up systems to control the flow of goods, donors should engage the recipient community in setting up systems to distribute the goods; rather than guarding they should focus on giving.

When people who are accustomed to hard work suddenly find their daily tasks taken from them, they are physically drained and mentally depressed. When donors trust and respect recipients, and rely on them to carry out many of the tasks associated with aid, the recipients work rather than wait, are active rather than passive, and decide rather than have decisions made for them. They retain their physical energy and reinforce their sense of efficacy and dignity. The minimal requirement to ensure that humanitarian assistance promotes the future potential of the recipients is that it treats people to whom it is given as human.

Humanitarian assistance providers also should seek and utilize all opportunities for strengthening the resources and capacities of recipients. An opportunity for training exists when someone is willing to work but lacks the experience or skills for the task. When daily survival tasks during emergencies do not fully employ the needy (because food is provided rather than cultivated and harvested, and because water is fetched from a tank provided to the users rather than from a well miles away), this is an opportunity to initiate training and education that will enhance the people's future resource base. People who never before had "free" time find that in an emergency setting they can attend a class or participate in an organizing meeting for the first time in their lives.

Givers of assistance always have opportunities to demonstrate trust and respect within the first hours of an emergency, both in their own attitudes and in the systems and procedures they establish for providing assistance. Within a very short time after the beginning of an emergency, givers of assistance can always find opportunities for improving the nonphysical resource base of the recipients. These actions can directly affect the abilities of those who have suffered in an emergency to recover and move forward in their own lives.

Providing Short-Term Humanitarian
Assistance for Long-Term Results

Humanitarian assistance alone cannot bring either development or peace. Development is not something that can be done by outsiders and outside assistance for poor people. Genuine and sustainable development must be achieved by peoples and societies that rely on their own resources and capacities. Similarly, no one can make someone else's peace. Outsiders may impose a cease-fire on warring people and stop overt conflict, but the conditions for a sustainable, justice-based peace must be created by people for themselves.

Although humanitarian assistance cannot bring either development or peace, it cannot avoid becoming interlinked with the poverty and conflict in which emergencies are rooted. If those who provide assistance do not recognize and address the causes and contexts of emergencies, they often reinforce and compound them. At a minimum, humanitarian assistance must be offered in ways that avoid reinforcing the problems that underlie emergencies. Better still, true humanitarian assistance would maximize every opportunity for addressing and correcting these problems. However, as noted, many external factors underline emergencies that are beyond the control of those who suffer directly and of those who provide aid. What kind of role can humanitarian assistance play to address these factors?

Recent studies have demonstrated that relief assistance in poverty emergencies can help promote and support the processes of systemic development.[8] It can be provided in ways that meet urgent needs and simultaneously support activities by recipients to break the resource constraints that perpetuate their poverty. In India during the drought of the mid-1980s, distribution of food to peasants in Gujarat and Rajasthan was linked to communal terracing and reforestation projects designed to lessen the impact of future water shortages. Relief was also provided directly to families who used their enforced idleness (because they could not engage in normal agricultural activities) to improve their own houses, ponds, food storage facilities, and irrigation systems, thus improving their economic base and potential for future survival. In 1984, during the worsening famine in Ethiopia, people in a northeastern province were able to use support from an international aid agency to build many kilometers of roads so that food could be distributed near their homes rather than their having to gather in a centralized feeding camp beside the highway.

In these two examples, food aid was accompanied by technical assistance (how to terrace fields, build roads). Aid met urgent needs quickly and efficiently, and also addressed some of the contextual factors (land degradation, lack of infrastructure) that contributed to the emergencies. Meeting a short-term need was linked to altering fundamental constraints on economic productivity that before the assistance appeared to lie outside the control of the aid recipients. Furthermore, relief was given in a manner that supported the recipients' abilities to achieve their own development. The recipients were in charge of the activities that changed their environmental context.

Are there parallel or comparable activities that assistance agencies can undertake in conflict-related emergencies that will promote peace and reconciliation and also meet urgent needs? Everyone involved in international humanitarian assistance in times of war has engaged in discussions about ways that aid providers affect and are affected by the political contexts of wartime emergencies. How can givers of aid avoid complicity with repressive regimes and still respond to the urgent human needs of the people who live under them? Is there a role for aid providers in reconciliation and negotiation to help bring conflict emergencies to an end? How can humanitarian assistance agencies do anything about the maldistribution of resources underlying the exploitation and injustice that fuel conflict?

These are central issues for emergency aid providers. Many answers and insights are provided by other authors, including the contributors to this volume, and especially the editors.[9] These deal with the relationships between humanitarian assistance agencies and governments, and with the juxtaposition of moral responsibility to those who suffer and political realism. Rather than review these issues and arguments, the rest of the chapter focuses specifically on the opportunities that exist for humanitarian assistance agencies to encourage and empower the recipients of their relief aid so that they—the recipients—can begin to address the factors that force them into crisis. Several examples from recent experience suggest possibilities that deserve further exploration.

In Lebanon during the worst years of factional warfare, a humanitarian assistance agency established health clinics well behind the lines of fighting so that those in need could reach them without direct exposure to danger. The staff of this agency worked with people from all sides of the conflict. During the sixteen years of open warfare, people had virtually no opportunity to cross borders and interact with those who lived on the other sides. When the first tenuous cease-fire finally took hold in 1990, suspicion and mistrust among groups were strong. The humanitarian assistance agency therefore considered shifting the locations of its clinics to border areas to draw people from former warring factions into the same care facility. As they sat next to each other in waiting rooms, as they saw each other's sick children receive treatment, and as they received the same health care as their former enemies, perhaps their suspicions could begin to subside and neighbors could be reacquainted across factional lines.

Also in Lebanon during the worst fighting, another humanitarian assistance agency started a children's magazine called *Sawa*, which means "Together." Each edition included stories about Lebanon's history or cultural treasures so that children, who could not visit or know of them across fighting lines, could learn of a common Lebanese heritage. Each issue included sections on protecting health so that those children whose lives were at risk could learn the importance of taking care of themselves for a future. Each also included empty pages on which children were invited to write their own stories or poems, or draw pictures to send back to the magazine for publication in later editions. Consequently, children who spent many hours and even days in bomb shelters would have some positive activities (and the paper with which to do them), and possibly develop a sense of a shared culture that, if peace began, could become a basis on which to build. A reader wrote a "peace pledge" and submitted it to the magazine; soon children and their parents signed this pledge and returned it to the magazine, where all of their names were published in later editions. Because the mail services were not reliable, the humanitarian agency clinics became the mail drop-off and magazine distribution points. The pages of *Sawa* became recognizable as aerograms and were carried across borders by the people who delivered medical and food supplies.

In Cambodia, as the refugees who fled to Thailand began to return under the auspices of the United Nations High Commissioner for Refugees (UNHCR) repatriation program, suspicions persisted between those who stayed and those who left. Several humanitarian agencies in the Thai border camps initiated a series of meetings between women from the camps who belonged to the well-established Khmer Women's Associations and women who remained in Cambodia and were members of the far-reaching Cambodian Association of Women. It was suggested that repatriation funds be earmarked for projects initiated jointly by these women. In addition to the usual criteria related to economic viability, another criterion would be that women from the two groups must work together on a project's conception, planning, implementation, and benefits. Postwar, short-term assistance could assist the transitional needs of the returnees and provide an impetus to joint projects that had potential for promoting reconciliation and reintegration.

In Somalia, even as the fighting persists, a growing number of villages reportedly have established themselves as small areas of civil order or peace.[10] Refusing to be caught up in the clan-based conflict and to be manipulated by the warring factions, these villages created their own protection systems. When representatives of the warring clans tried to enter these villages to recruit fighters or to steal food, residents banded together to stop them. In some cases, groups of raiders were killed. In others, they were arrested and held. In some, they were tried, found guilty, and executed. These villages have refused to engage in the larger war; they have established independent systems for local civil governance over which they maintain control. Although no humanitarian assistance agency was involved in establishing these nonconflict areas, their existence challenges the assumption that small groups of people can do nothing to protect themselves from surrounding wars. Could external agencies not adapt these experiences and develop humanitarian support for groups to help them withdraw from conflict and establish pockets of peace?

In discussing the relationships between development and peace, it was clear that the continuation of war actually serves the economic needs of certain groups, even among those who were poor prior to a conflict. A challenge facing agencies is how to remove profits from war. How can the young men and women who find both economic security and life purpose by serving in militias be employed in distributing aid, establishing and policing pockets of civil order and peace, and building a basic infrastructure for future development? If initiatives could be devised for major alternative employment opportunities, poor people might be enabled to walk off the battlefield.

Each of these examples represents a fragile idea or attempt to enable people to step away from conflict and toward peace. Some may be effective in situations of overt war, while others are only possible in circumstances of relative calm. The examples are important because they suggest the potential for humanitarian assistance to link aid in conflict-related emergencies to approaches that help people affect the causes of their suffering.

If the lessons concerning the relationship between relief and development have been clearly demonstrated, and if these small but promising examples of the relationship between relief and peace pose a realistic challenge, why is it that most relief assistance has not incorporated these lessons and promises? There are at least three reasons: institutional, psychological, and practical.

Humanitarian assistance agencies sharply separate their emergency response work from their development and peace work. Most are structured so that emergency work, development work, and advocacy or education (often related to analysis or political organizing around the causes of conflict) are administered by different departments and staff. This is partly an accident of history; more often, it reflects an institutional belief that the three are truly unrelated. Agencies separate peace work from relief or development work because overt political action can (and often does) jeopardize the activities undertaken for short- or long-term humanitarian assistance. Agencies find that often they can raise funds more easily for short-term emergency assistance than for long-term development. They separate the programming to facilitate both fund raising to initiate programs and financial accounting for programs that are under way.

There is also a psychological resistance on the part of humanitarian assistance agencies and staffs to incorporating the lessons about the long-term impacts of short-term humanitarian assistance. Most agencies and individuals who work in emergencies have been called to do so out of a deep reaction against the suffering they witness and a strong moral urge to act in the face of the suffering. The motivation to do good in the face of evil and horror must be strong and selfless. It is not surprising that motivated individuals and agencies that undertake extremely difficult work under dangerous and harsh conditions resist any intimation that the long-term impact of their work may damage the people they long to help. In a world fraught with complications, the straightforwardness of emergency assistance has offered one area of clarity. It is exceedingly difficult to give this up.

There are also myriad practical problems that intrude on efforts to promote development and peace through emergency assistance. Many complex factors affect the circumstances of emergencies, and one agency or one staff member can never control all processes and outcomes. Even when an agency recognizes the capacities of the people to whom it provides assistance and relies on these and promotes them in the way it delivers aid, and even when the design of its program addresses some fundamental cause of the problem that led to the emergency, so many other factors are at work that the outcome is never clear. The people whom one sets out to respect and empower may be scared, selfish, or lazy rather than brave, generous, and active. While it is clearly good to feed a hungry woman, save an ill child, or to put a cup of cold water in the hand of a thirsty man, it is never clear where the end of the development or peace road may lie. It is particularly unclear if we accept the premise stated earlier in the chapter that development and peace are not done or given by aid providers; people must achieve them themselves.

In short, the reasons why humanitarians do not always pursue development and peace while they provide aid arise primarily from the frustration that follows the acknowledgment that there is no clarity and no purity in assistance. Nonetheless, many humanitarian assistance agencies are attempting to adopt and adapt the lessons learned about how to relate relief assistance to long-term development in their own programming. Recognizing their role in shaping the long-term futures of the people they assist, humanitarians are accepting the importance of trying new approaches, and they are learning the lessons—both positive and negative—that have been garnered through the extensive experience of many agencies in diverse emergencies.

What is now required is an additional openness to experiment with the modest lessons learned about relating relief assistance and peace. If the peoples of Somalia, Bosnia, Iraq, Afghanistan, Liberia, and all the other areas of the world where conflicts rage must wait passively until a new world order is agreed upon by the states that negotiate such arrangements, then much suffering will inevitably occur. If they can be supported in ways that help them assert their own will for peace, perhaps this can add momentum toward the resolution of conflicts. The point is not that humanitarian assistance should bring development and peace. Rather, the point is that if such assistance is not based on the lessons learned through past experience, it will, at worst, continue to perpetuate the suffering that it is intended to relieve by perpetuating the dependence of aid recipients on outside support. It will certainly miss opportunities to provide aid in ways that are more developmental and more supportive of long-term peace.

The challenge to humanitarian agencies and their staffs is to assist people in ways that enable them to create safer and more secure futures for themselves, and thus to contribute not only to the relief of immediate dire suffering but also to the ultimate prevention of the emergencies that cause this suffering.

Notes

1. Clarence Pickett quoted in Milton Mayer, "The Idea of the American Friends Service Committee," *What Can a Man Do?* (Chicago: University of Chicago Press, 1964): 122.

2. The concern here is with proximate causes: the roots of poverty and conflict that are relevant in *real time* to the planner of humanitarian assistance. Their historical roots are also important and interesting, but would require more pages than available here and have been dealt with by many other economists, historians, political scientists, and psychologists.

3. See Mary B. Anderson and Peter J. Woodrow, *Rising from the Ashes:*

Development Strategies at Times of Disaster (Boulder and Paris: Westview and UNESCO Presses, 1989). The authors describe three categories of capacities that people have that are critical for survival and the lack of which increases disaster vulnerability: the physical/material realm, the social/organizational realm, and the attitudinal/motivational realm.

4. Off-the-record private conversation with a former Soviet political leader; not for attribution.

5. Larry Minear, *Helping People in an Age of Conflict: Toward a New Professionalism in U.S. Voluntary Humanitarian Assistance* (New York: InterAction, American Council for Voluntary International Action, 1988): 8.

6. *Human Development Report 1992* (New York: United Nations Development Programme, 1992): 21.

7. An exception to this general experience was found in the camps in Malaysia that received Vietnamese refugees in 1979. Many of these refugees were highly educated, formerly well-to-do individuals with professions in city planning, water management, health and medical care, and the like. Among the refugees were eighty-four medical doctors and over three hundred nurses to serve about thirty-six thousand refugees at the peak. In these camps, the refugees themselves carried out most of the management and caretaking tasks. (Reported in private conversation by Peter J. Woodrow, December 1992.)

8. See, for example, the case studies in Anderson and Woodrow, *Rising from the Ashes*.

9. See especially, Minear, *Helping People in an Age of Conflict*; and Larry Minear and Thomas G. Weiss, *Humanitarian Action in Times of War: A Handbook for Practitioners* (Boulder: Lynne Rienner, 1993). Also, an important article on this topic is by Hiskias Assefa, Nairobi Peace Group, entitled "Humanitarian Activity and Peacemaking in Protracted Armed Conflicts: Challenge for NGOs," May 15, 1991, Nairobi, Kenya.

10. Private conversations with John Rogge, December 1992.

■ 3 ■

Public Opinion, the Media, and Humanitarianism

EDWARD GIRARDET

The withdrawal of the last Red Army troops from Afghanistan in February 1989, the fall of the Berlin Wall, and the collapse of the Soviet empire are landmarks of the end of four decades of cold war between East and West. They were also images reported and packaged by the Western media, governments, and politicians in a manner readily understood by the general public: the victory of democracy over communism; the overthrow of one-party dictatorship; and a new era of freedom, with democratic self-determination for everyone. It all looked and sounded so neat and simple.

Although the conclusion of the Cold War may have ended ideological rivalry between the Western democracies and the former Soviet-led Eastern Bloc, it has opened a Pandora's box of disruption. Since the end of the 1980s, this new world order has tolerated, if not provoked, tribal and ethnic conflicts—Liberia, Somalia, Armenia, and the former Yugoslavia to name a few—more horrific than most people could have imagined when the Western media still considered the Lebanon war its barometer for civil atrocities. Given current trends, it seems more probable than possible that such conflicts will become the norm for the next few years, not only in Africa and Asia, but also in parts of Europe and the former Soviet republics.

The question today is to what extent the media, public opinion, and policymakers are prepared to direct their attention toward issues of civil atrocities. Another question is whether this attention will prompt the international community to intervene more decisively in *le droit d'ingérence*, or the right of intervention, be it diplomatic, military, humanitarian, or a combination of these.[1] While some analysts may disagree, the media and public opinion are key factors in helping to determine whether society will stand on the sidelines or intervene. Considerable responsibility for conveying the challenges of humanitarian predicaments also lies with policymakers and international governmental and nongovernmental organizations. But even the most astute policymakers must rely on the media for information and to communicate their views. Public criticism can often pressure, even shame,

39

governments into deciding whether they can condone by their inaction the brutalization of civilian populations by repressive regimes or warring factions. Public criticism also demands decisions on whether it has become morally reprehensible to argue that the Liberias and Yugoslavias are simply "too far away" or "none of our concern" to merit international attention.

As media coverage of the Vietnam War, Ethiopia in 1984–1985, and famine and war in Somalia have demonstrated, governments, policymakers, and international organizations are often prompted, if not forced, into action by public exposure of the gruesome realities of war. The media can impose accountability in a manner not always assured by other institutions, while public reaction (e.g., recent demonstrations in Europe against racism) can send demands to governments for clearer action. It is unlikely that the United States would have risked military intervention for purely humanitarian reasons in the Horn of Africa had there not been broad public sympathy for the Somalis' plight, much of it prompted by saturation media coverage. The media also showed that both the U.S. government and the United Nations could derive considerable public kudos through action.

In this chapter, the focus will be on the Western media because of its overwhelming control of world information sources. Through the international shortwave radio networks, the cable and satellite broadcasters, and the wire services, the Western press commands an extraordinary outlet for influencing world audiences and governments. Indeed, organizations like the BBC World Service provide some of the most informative, and sometimes the only consistent coverage of humanitarian crises.

To gauge Western media coverage of humanitarian issues and its influence on the public, the author conducted a series of interviews with newspaper and magazine editors, journalists, foreign correspondents, television producers, and radio broadcasters in North America and Europe.[2] What emerged is a disturbing decline in the reporting of international humanitarian issues over the past decade, especially since the end of the Cold War. Not only is there less coverage, but according to editors and journalists, the quality of the reporting is deteriorating, particularly on television.

Television, the most powerful medium in many Western countries, is confusing professional broadcast reporting with a superficial form of entertainment news, critics say. This disconcerting confusion is often promoted by live reporting via mobile satellite units from the field. This form of reporting is supposed to inform, but in reality it does not necessarily enhance the quality or reliability of news. To some critics, including veteran foreign correspondents, this was clearly apparent during much of the network reporting of the 1991 Gulf War.

Mainline U.S. audiences have never been well informed about foreign matters. Yet today, the general public on both sides of the Atlantic may be far less informed about international issues than it was a decade or two ago, even though technology is better. A poorly informed public places less pressure on policymakers to resolve conflicts, shows less interest in assuming a more activist role in international affairs, and offers less support to the aid organizations to carry out their work.

A Changing Situation

One principal drawback of communicating humanitarian predicaments is the unwillingness of the media to provide quality or consistency in reporting foreign news. It is not so much journalists who are at fault (there has never been a shortage of reporters willing to cover overseas issues), but the refusal by editors to commission such coverage. Editors and journalists lamenting this apparent deterioration say that many newspapers and broadcasters are simply unwilling to provide the space or time needed to explain complex issues. They often are less interested in providing in-depth coverage to inform and educate than in obtaining good ratings through on-the-spot reports. Sufficient background reporting often is replaced by quick, costly visits by high profile anchormen and anchorwomen for trendy situations such as the Gulf War or Somalia.

There also is a tendency to move away from discerning background reporting that is vital to understanding historical causes of conflicts. During the 1950s, 1960s, and 1970s, major newspapers and broadcasters maintained their own teams of foreign correspondents. This allowed them to thoroughly research specific stories while using the news services to cover day-to-day events. Today, partially because of economic cutbacks but also because of lack of vision, editors are reluctant to probe issues before they explode into major news stories. Few bother to follow up on issues that tumble into oblivion. Based on this writer's experience reporting wars, refugee situations, and other humanitarian predicaments, balanced coverage is as dependent on a perspicacious and risk-taking editor as it is on the reporter's ability.

"Many editors, particularly in television, prefer to wait until a story has appeared in the *New York Times* or on the BBC before sending out a reporter, and then the reporter does not really bring back any new insights," said Tala Skari, an editor for *LIFE* magazine in Paris. "With editors reluctant to risk investigating the unknown, journalists are no longer encouraged to come up with original coverage." Matt Miller, Pacific Rim correspondent for the *San Diego Union-Herald,* said, "This is increasingly representative of a major malaise in American journalism. Newspapers are running scared. What is needed is commitment by high-thinking editors."

This trend toward "safe" coverage means that there is less chance of the public being alerted to the horrors of a Sudan or a Liberia before they become crises. Either the stories are not covered, or they are not picked up by network television and other leading media. Another problem is that too many newspapers, magazines, and networks indulge in the use of conventional timeworn images of war or famine that fail to describe current realities. As some editors maintain, this eventually produces a public reaction that is no longer as much compassion fatigue as outrage fatigue.

The media should explain events rather than merely present them. Without this information, the public cannot begin to understand what is happening in the conflict or disaster zones of today and tomorrow. High-quality reporting is equally important for policymakers. When assessing Iran, Afghanistan, and Central America, policymakers in U.S. government circles or think tanks relied too much on official sources that produced inaccurate assessments, and this led to disastrous policies. Reports from independent journalists sometimes provided the only forms of reliable information from the field to help correct, if not expose, such inaccuracies.

Instant Aid, Instant Solutions?

Most conflicts are not short-term events; they can continue for months, years, even decades. Many are colored by tribal or ethnic animosities, which cannot be reported like a simple fire or robbery. When few editors are willing to provide consistent coverage over extended periods, the public often is left with the impression that massive bursts of humanitarian aid are sufficient to resolve a problem. The media is prepared to grant high-profile coverage to a particularly dramatic story for two or three months, and even longer if public compassion or outrage can be sustained. But it can turn with equal fervor to another issue and leave behind the previous one. The story has been covered, and the food and medicines have been airlifted, but little progress has been made to end the hunger and strife.

Randal Ashley, foreign editor of the *Atlanta Constitution*, a regional paper that covers Africa as a priority, admits that such fickleness is a major problem. Yet he argues that focus can be maintained by reporting on the efforts of relief agencies such as "the French doctors;"[3] by responding to local interest through reader columns, or by interviews with individuals passing through the Martin Luther King Center or the Disease Control Centers in Atlanta. "We try not to be extreme about it, but there are different ways of assuring public awareness," he said. "I just don't see donor fatigue happening. The public interest is definitely there."

It is unclear whether the apparent decline in high-quality international reporting causes or responds to a fall in public interest. If there is a drop in public concern, as some editors maintain, is it because the inhabitants of Edmonton, Cleveland, or Saint-Étienne have lost their curiosity for world affairs? Or is it because they simply are not receiving appropriate information?

All Quiet on the Humanitarian Front

Some analysts also question the nature of the reporting needed to rouse the interest of the public and policymakers in the world's less visible problem areas. One current example is the prospect of Yugoslavia-style conflicts in the former Soviet Union. While some journalists and aid specialists have been trying to alert Western governments, few appear to be paying serious attention.

For a long time, many people did not really care (and many still do not) about Somalia, Sudan, or Liberia because these were black or brown Africans killing each other in tribal and clan warfare, and for years, many did not care much about the Kurds either. They were being bombed, gassed, and executed by the Iraqis, Iranians, Syrians, Turks, or whichever government decided its Kurds were in need of repression. To many Westerners, the Kurds were either a lemon dessert or a strange, turbaned people who lived in some far-off mountainous region. When Europe, which had not known such a conflict since World War II, was caught with savage tribal war in its own backyard, impotence and indecision also prevailed. Excuses previously used for Africa and Kurdistan were then directed toward the Yugoslavs: "They have always fought amongst themselves. It's historic. You can't do anything about it." Ordinary civilians in Africa, Europe, and other parts of the world continue dying, sometimes in the full, albeit momentary, glare of the media, but more often than not they are ignored.

These conflicts affect the West politically, economically, and ethically. They produce refugees and economic migrants, threaten regional stability, ignite other conflicts, and help undermine world economies. They also raise the question of whether society has learned anything from the holocausts that descended on Nazi Europe, Idi Amin's Uganda, or Pol Pot's Cambodia. In all these outrages, people and governments stood by as fellow human beings were massacred, tortured, starved, or worked to death because of their race, tribe, religion, political persuasion, or education.

The media still finds it easier to dwell on the genocides of the past than on those of the present. What can be said about a society that self-righteously condemns the persecution of Jews, Gypsies, socialists, and Christians by the Nazis, but neglects to act against those who rape, pillage, and murder their victims sometimes less than two hours away by train or plane? For the generations of today and tomorrow, the horrors of World War II are of no consequence unless people recognize their similarities to current humanitarian emergencies. One German television producer said people should imagine that "whenever Liberians are murdered because they are of the wrong tribe or Bosnians have their throats slit because they are Muslim, that these are in fact Jews. Or Germans. Or Americans. Maybe we might react differently."

The New World Order

Undoubtedly, the end of superpower rivalry and of the Cold War have helped transform or end the proxy wars that plagued Africa, Central America, and Asia for the past fifteen years or more. Drained of ideological or financial support previously furnished by the Americans, Soviets, East Germans, South Africans, and other East-West protagonists, conflicts such as in Mozambique—although still on extremely shaky ground—have been winding down. Others, notably in Namibia, El Salvador, Ethiopia, and Eritrea, may have achieved a semblance of prolonged peace. Even the traditional bulwarks against communism, the corrupt one-party dictatorships of Kenya and Zaire, have seen the carpet of outside support pulled out from under them. For many Third World peoples, peace negotiations, democratization, and self-determination have become commonplace.

The removal of the ideological veneer has allowed deeper ethnic, tribal, and clan struggles to surface. Business interests, often linked to various power factions (governments, guerrilla organizations, or thuggish armed bands), have become more visible. Civil conflicts are profitable arenas for arms trafficking, aid hijacking, and profiteering. Power, money, and personal greed, rather than self-determination and political freedom for the masses, were and are the pivotal forces behind many power struggles.

For years, it has proven to be far more convenient for the media to refer to these conflicts in terms of familiar themes: East-West rivalry, national interests, famines, and droughts. These were issues that the public could understand. But this terminology tended to mask the central causes of the desperate plight of many civilian populations. Ignoring or minimizing fundamental causes often has prevented the outside world from adopting appropriate solutions.

Perhaps the most glaring recent example is Somalia. After military dictator Siad Barre was ousted in January 1991, Somalia's principal predicament was bitter clan divisions, street fighting, rampant shelling, and food shortages. Massive famine had not yet gripped the country. When the world finally decided to lend its attention in early summer 1992, the conflict was largely portrayed by the media and many aid organizations as one of people in desperate need of food. It was the same old story as in Ethiopia seven years earlier. The public was shown images that Western audiences have come to expect of Africa: pathetic pictures of men, women, and children dying from hunger in a conflict. Little attempt was made to explain the deep-seated reasons behind the strife. The message was that food could save Somalia.

Only secondary consideration was given to the notion that clan rivalries, thuggery, and greed fueled the crisis. The possibility that the United States and the former Soviet Union might bear some responsibility for giving Somalia enormous arsenals of weapons during the superpower struggle in the region was conveniently forgotten. The chance that vast quantities of unprotected food might exacerbate and prolong the country's plight was considered too complicated for the public to understand.

The international community proceeded with its massive and media-driven humanitarian program, which eventually led to the December 1992 U.S.-led intervention in Operation Restore Hope. Sending food appealed to Western politicians and fed some victims. But the UN and the donor countries continued to ignore their real responsibilities: What was to be done with a nation that had fallen apart completely and was run by criminal, anarchic, and power-hungry bands, while thousands of civilians died? Although major network programs such as CBS's "60 Minutes" finally focused on the story, most coverage contributed little toward a better understanding of what was really happening.

"If you show poor starving victims the whole time, it kills the story," said Eva Varangu, foreign editor of "Sunday Morning," the Canadian Broadcasting Corporation's leading radio news program. "News is one thing, but the relief agencies are also at fault in pushing these disaster stories. Obviously, we should be looking at famine, but we should also be asking: What are 14-year-old kids doing with guns? Where have all these weapons come from? Why all this killing? What can we really do to stop it? That's what should be explained to the public." Few people in the West had any idea of what was going on. It was simply another African war, another country that had long since sunk into human desperation. "This is what Westerners think of Africa. A place constantly beset by wars, famines, droughts. A hopeless case," said Paul Van Slambrouk, deputy manager and international editor of the *San Jose Mercury News* in California.

False Portrayals and Archaic Images of Humanitarian Crises

What we are witnessing is the superficial and often inaccurate portrayal of devastating predicaments. Media in search of dramatic images or aid organizations intent on securing money can tragically misrepresent the real issues at hand.

During the 1984–1985 crisis in Ethiopia, gross misreporting of the situation contributed to tens of thousands of unnecessary deaths. Apart from organizations such as Boston-based Cultural Survival and Médecins Sans Frontières (MSF), few of the over sixty agencies in Ethiopia were prepared to speak out against forced population removals, political manipulation, and aid abuses by the Addis Ababa regime. For fear of jeopardizing their relief activities, respected international relief organizations preferred to lie to their constituents or remain silent. Many argued for more humanitarian aid to solve the crisis. Many news reports, often relying on aid agencies for information, referred to the situation as one of famine and drought, rather than a crisis severely aggravated by war, government repression, and aid manipulation.

International aid agencies that publicize selected aspects of emergencies for their own purposes are a familiar phenomenon to most experienced journalists covering humanitarian crises. A senior representative of World Vision, a U.S. relief agency operating in Ethiopia, told this writer, "You can't confuse the public with complex issues. Starving babies and droughts are something people can understand. But trying to explain corruption or aid abuses is not going to help our fund-raising and will only hamper our work."

Archaic but familiar themes also were used during the Gulf War. Much of the Western media seemed to be part of a government-orchestrated effort to present the conflict as a necessary evil to save the people of a small, helpless country from the Hitlerian dictatorship of Saddam Hussein. All the necessary themes to mobilize public opinion were in ample supply: freedom, dictatorship, self-determination, democracy, and Western oil interests.

At the same time, Liberians were being massacred by rampaging tribal thugs. Yet most of the epithets used by the allied coalition in Kuwait were forgotten, and Liberia's plight was largely ignored. A handful of journalists, diplomats, and relief workers worked at constant risk to their lives, but governments and editors saw the Gulf War as the only war worthy of attention. It was hard to explain to these "children of America," as many Liberians call themselves, that human rights sometimes are linked to oil supplies or strategic interests. For journalists in the Gulf, whether they were from the major European or U.S. networks or small-town newspapers, the forty other conflicts ranging from Sri Lanka to Sudan and El Salvador did not seem to matter.

Reporting the Third World: A New Dark Ages?

With the upsurge of increasingly bitter conflicts, the public debate over military intervention for humanitarian reasons has grown. These operations obviously pose major difficulties and are sown with minefields of their own. Sending in the troops, even under a UN flag, requires careful scrutiny. Somalia, unlike Kuwait or even Kurdistan, commanded no immediate apparent strategic interest (although the possibility of large-scale oil reserves has been an issue for a number of years). The U.S. intervention may have set a precedent for similar actions elsewhere.

Intervention is not the only possible response. It is not in the interests of Western countries to ignore turmoil. Already the influx of refugees and migrants fleeing war, economic turmoil, and poverty has had severe and hostile repercussions in host countries ranging from Germany and France to traditionally tolerant Canada. Groups such as the International Organization for Migration in Geneva are suggesting that it might be more effective, and less costly, to help resolve Romania's or Haiti's problems at the source.

There is a need for media with the foresight and resources to report such issues, and to encourage a more informed debate.

At best, international attention always has been reactive, short-term, and selective; at worst, it has been unrealistic or nonexistent. The sad reality is that most media and aid organizations do not consider it profitable to explain the complexities of most of the world's humanitarian disasters. The Somalias, Sudans, and Liberias will be tragic sideshows with little or no international attention. Only when a situation comes into vogue does the media go into reactive high gear. It is increasingly difficult to stimulate and sustain public awareness of a particular humanitarian crisis, while focusing on similar situations elsewhere. Unless the media assumes its full responsibility to inform with consistency, public awareness of events in Mozambique, Eritrea, Burma, Sri Lanka, or East Timor is bound to suffer.

Editors and producers offer many reasons for the decline in international reporting of humanitarian issues. For some, the problem is compassion fatigue. The public can take only so much. For others, the problem is cost. It is becoming too expensive for newspapers, magazines, and broadcasters to maintain consistent foreign coverage. For others, too, it is a question of priorities. Audiences are more interested in what goes on at home than in some faraway African or Asian country, where fighting and starving are commonplace.

Many editors interviewed in North America and Europe agree that the most dramatic change in international coverage has occurred since the late 1980s. Although certain regional newspapers such as the *Dallas Morning News*, the *Miami Herald* and the *Atlanta Constitution* have maintained their international coverage, they are a minority. Media organizations have either reduced their overseas reporting or placed greater emphasis on the former Soviet Union, Eastern Europe, and the Middle East, to the detriment of Africa. The *New York Times* also has begun emphasizing domestic coverage. "The end of the Cold War has affected foreign reporting in a big way," said Joelle Kuntz, deputy editor of one of Switzerland's most internationally oriented French-language newspapers, *Le Nouveau Quotidien*. "All the familiar conflicts or names of leaders, even countries, are gone. And not only readers find it confusing. It is difficult for journalists to keep up with all the changes."

As for television, producers and reporters lament that in-depth reporting on events from abroad has entered a veritable Dark Age. The three main U.S. networks have witnessed a fall in good international coverage, despite efforts by some to maintain standards and cover issues that deserve to be reported. Even influential anchormen such as Peter Jennings of ABC News and Dan Rather of CBS News, who are known to favor foreign reporting, find that they can go only so far with their emphasis on international stories. "Basically, what it comes down to is that nobody is interested in Africa unless we really have to do it. And then it's more likely to be South Africa or perhaps situations like Somalia or Ethiopia, where the networks feel morally obliged to do the story," observed senior NBC producer Joe DeCola.

Budgetary reasons or less air time are the constraints cited most by broadcasters. High-quality programs such as the "MacNeil-Lehrer News Hour," one of the first programs to run in-depth stories on Somalia before it became fashionable, face financial difficulties in getting self-produced segments on the air. As executive producer Les Crystal points out, MacNeil-Lehrer must rely heavily on inexpensive coverage from British television, freelancers, and other outsiders. "There are obviously reports that we would like to do, or feel we ought to be doing, but cannot because of lack of funding. In the case of Somalia, it is unfortunate that there was nothing done earlier by the media, given that the Americans and Russians helped provide most of the arms now killing so many people."

The Atlanta-based Cable News Network (CNN) offers extensive foreign coverage twenty-four hours a day around the world. While a substantial proportion of its programming is provided by Britain's Independent Television News (ITN) network, the programs present essentially a U.S. viewpoint. Its live broadcasts during the Gulf War also raised serious questions about the accuracy and independence of coverage that relies on on-the-spot reporting around the clock rather than more in-depth reporting and fact-checking. Because it is susceptible to manipulation by governments and individuals, CNN's approach may be far more insidious in informing the public than its news directors imagine.

With strong biases toward domestic coverage, major television news shows are broadcasting fewer international topics. WGBH's highly reputed "Frontline" program, while still dealing with international issues, appears to be seeking stronger U.S. angles on stories. Appropriate news, current affairs, and documentary slots, traditional outlets for airing humanitarian issues, also are disappearing on most major North American and European networks. Or they are broadcast at non-prime-time hours inconvenient for family viewing. "It is becoming increasingly difficult to keep up one's commitment to international issues," said Tony Burman, an executive producer of CBC-TV current affairs who has experience as a journalist in Africa. "Africa is basically an ongoing story and it gets very frustrating when there are limits to what you can report. Once you provide viewers with continuous intelligent coverage, their interest is reawakened."

Good current affairs programs along the lines of MacNeil-Lehrer or the United Kingdom's Channel Four News that broadcast segments of more than five or six minutes are becoming the exception. Even Britain's BBC and ITV, world leaders in documentary programming, are reducing their in-depth coverage of foreign news because of pressures to put on more commercially oriented shows. There are signs of an increase in entertainment-style current affairs segments, where the correspondent adopts greater importance than the subject, whether they are Kurdish refugees or shell-shocked Bosnians.

Some editors argue that times have changed. Audiences, particularly young ones, are no longer interested in television that provides in-depth analysis of complex issues, including humanitarian emergencies. They say television has to give people what they want. But the discrepancy between what network directors think their audiences want, and what the audiences themselves want, may be enormous.

"People who watch documentaries or currents events in which they are interested are more likely to watch the full program than other shows. I think there is a lot bigger audience for quality programming, whether for children or adults," said Jeffrey Carmel, editor of the monthly Latin American report, *Hemisfile.* Public concern over issues such as Ethiopia or Somalia demonstrates far more interest among readers and viewers for information on international issues than many editors believe.

Providing the Right Coverage: Whose Responsibility?

The deterioration of international news programming raises the question of the responsibility of the networks to provide more and better public interest programs at hours accessible to most audiences. Too many Western networks have been allowed to evade their legal and moral obligations to provide high-quality programming. This is an area where educational and humanitarian lobbies and concerned citizens could, and should, make themselves heard.

Some television networks are trying to entice broader audiences without appealing to the lowest common denominator. France's "Antenne 3," for example, has adopted a back-to-the-fifties style for its highly rated documentary program, "Zanzi Bar." Produced by a small group of independent filmmakers, the show has broadcast hour-long films on topics like the crack problem in Washington, D.C., or Beirut as seen through the eyes of local soccer teams representing different religious and ethnic groups. "Television network directors have become utterly obsessed by commercialism and other false criteria. They have forgotten that well-made documentaries are not only needed, but watched," said French filmmaker Christophe de Ponfilly.

Nevertheless, as even the most ardent advocates of documentary or current affairs programming will admit, they reach only limited audiences. Other media conduits also must be explored. A well-produced rock video dealing with humanitarian or environmental issues could provoke far more reaction among MTV audiences than a well-made documentary. One broadcaster exploring new avenues is Andy Kershaw, a Lancashire disk jockey specializing in "world music" on Britain's popular "Radio One." By combining music and his down-to-earth style of interviewing singers, relief workers, foreign correspondents, politicians, and street kids, Kershaw has stimulated a new awareness among young audiences for Third World issues.

Docudramas also can reach targeted audiences. The Hollywood film *The*

Killing Fields probably sensitized the public far more to the ravages of the Khmer Rouge in Cambodia than any documentary on the subject could have. Similarly, the Home Box Office feature "Sakharov" probably made a greater impact on the issue of human rights versus totalitarianism than various current affairs segments on the Soviet physicist and his wife. Even the popular U.S. adventure television series "MacGyver" has helped provide a form of public service by dealing with human rights and other humanitarian issues.

No Money—A Feeble Excuse?

The argument from many media people that sponsoring foreign correspondents or television crews is too expensive is often little more than a feeble excuse. Indeed, major organizations have been pulling out full-time correspondents and closing bureaus in recent years. ABC, CBS, and NBC have all severely reduced if not completely shut down their operations in Paris, once a major broadcast base with dozens of correspondents, producers, and researchers. All increasingly rely on stringers and independent producers for stories. Nonetheless, tight budgets need not harm coverage of international humanitarian issues. The use of freelancers can, in fact, make a lot of financial and logistical sense.

The problem is one of long-term perception rather than a shortage of money or correspondents. Organizations such as the BBC World Service, the *Economist*, or *Deutsche Welle* have managed to maintain good coverage of issues in spite of cutbacks. In many cases, the lack of commitment coupled with the poor use of available resources has been the most damaging. Many news organizations that are moaning about not having enough money for overseas coverage spent small fortunes on reporting the Gulf War and Somalia. Budgets were so massively overdrawn that little was left to finance reporting from other parts of the world. Was it really necessary to have over three thousand journalists, photographers, cameramen, presenters, and technicians covering the Gulf War? Or to have hordes of reporters on the beach to record the arrival of the Navy Seals in Somalia? Was the general public any better informed?

For conflicts such as the Gulf War, there was little room to show the real consequences of destruction. Many correspondents, some of whom patriotically identified with their own governments by referring to "our troops" or "our planes," helped perpetuate the myth encouraged by the military that this was a "clean" and "surgical" war. Experienced correspondents such as Jonathan Randall of the *Washington Post*, Robert Fisk of the London *Independent*, and William Dowell of *Time Magazine* all expressed dismay at the way "entertainment" journalists sought to ignore the real face of war. "Anyone who has covered a war knows that clean or surgical wars don't exist. People die in wars," said Dowell, who has reported in Vietnam, Afghanistan, and the Middle East.

Although foreign correspondents such as Randall had reported the plight of the Kurds for years, few editors or policymakers showed interest. Nor did they show much concern for what was happening in other parts of the Islamic world, where ramifications of the Gulf War were bound to be felt. Only when it became clear that the Kurds would be an important element in the pursuit of Western policy aims in the Gulf did media attention begin to focus on the Kurds in northern Iraq.

Armies of journalists are not needed to cover wars or humanitarian conflicts. Reporting from the Gulf and Somalia could have been far more effective, accurate, and honest had there been fewer and better fielded reporters and more sharing of resources. Many editors failed to realize that the world is going through a communications revolution and that different approaches are needed. Technology has improved but also severely diminished international coverage. During the Vietnam War, journalists could obtain highly visual "bang-bang" (action) footage of strafing helicopters or military engagements in the morning and have it shipped out by evening. Thus, the editor's and the public's concept of war was corrupted. Action imagery became imperative. But combat or aerial attacks are only a small part of the whole picture. The real effects of war—starvation, destroyed harvests, shattered houses or water supplies, children dying of exposure, or fleeing refugees—are often ignored because they present less graphic, if not less horrific, images.

During the Beirut and Gulf conflicts, satellite communications resulted in bombardments being shown live on television. In other wars, where satellite communications were difficult, such as Afghanistan or Kurdistan, coverage was severely restricted by lack of accessibility. When such bang-bang footage is not available, the story does not appear quickly and powerfully for viewers. "If it can't be done in three days, it hasn't happened," said one ABC producer commenting on the attitude of many network news editors.

The result is that journalists, particularly television cameramen, are under pressure to bring back spectacular images to satisfy network appetites. This coverage often neglects long-term effects like stunted development prospects, food shortages, land mines, or disease brought about by malnutrition. Most of the British, French, U.S., and other freelance film teams who have covered conflicts remained highly professional and honest in their reporting. Some, however, have taken questionable shortcuts to obtain dramatic but bogus footage for the connivance of certain networks.

Smaller Teams, Smaller Budgets, More Coproduction

Excellent television and print coverage can be accomplished with budgets far smaller than those of the 1960s and 1970s, when the networks thought nothing of chartering a 747 to fly out footage or taking over entire hotel floors. Today, two- or one-person crews are common. There also is a steady trend toward more coproduction with noncompeting networks such as the BBC, NBC, or Germany's ZDF. Aid agencies such as MSF, UNICEF, and the International Committee of the Red Cross occasionally become involved in the coproduction effort by purchasing footage or providing ground logistics.

News editors are usually suspicious of "propaganda" footage, no matter how well-meaning, provided by aid agencies, but they will readily coproduce with independents who make their own deals with aid organizations. Costs are thereby cut and discussion of complex issues has a better chance of getting on the air. There also are more efforts to produce international versions of documentaries, often with network producers editing their own film from material provided by another broadcaster.

Most of these initiatives come from production groups such as Woods Communications in Paris and New York or Frontline News in London. "It's quite simple," says Tom Woods, a U.S. producer who coproduces programs with the "MacNeil-Lehrer NewsHour," NBC News, and the French networks, and aid organizations ranging from UNICEF to the World Wide Fund for Nature (WWF). "No single entity has the money any more to cover a production on its own, particularly for supposedly obscure subjects such as Mozambique or Afghanistan. So you have got to put together your own package if you want to do any form of quality reporting."

Experienced independent producers such as British cameraman Peter Jouvenal of Frontline News usually try to hook up with a BBC, ZDF, or PBS correspondent for shoots in Afghanistan, Central Asia, or Somalia. "By working as a small team you are far more mobile, and your costs are low," said Jouvenal. As with a growing number of other independents, he uses professional Hi-8 video rather than the heavier and more expensive Betacam cameras.

Public Opinion—Playing the Lobby Card

Sensitizing public opinion also depends heavily on lobbies. Although some editors and producers deny that their decisionmaking is prompted by local pressures, they do admit that the interests of local constituencies remain an important factor in stimulating coverage, particularly for regional newspapers and broadcasters.

The interests of Florida's large and outspoken population of Hispanic readers have prompted the *Miami Herald* editors to improve coverage of Latin American and Caribbean affairs. For a long time, the Cuban population ensured regular coverage of the situation in Angola. On the other hand, Florida's growing population of Haitian exiles has not had much influence in news selection until recently.

In Britain and continental Europe, large communities with Ukrainian or

East European background remind editors of the need for more coverage of developments in their native regions. Expatriate Muslims, particularly Asians, are stepping up pressure for reporting on issues often neglected by European editors. While such interests have spawned a rise in local ethnic programming, only recently has greater general public awareness emerged through fairer coverage by the national networks.

Foremost among the Europeans in improving multicultural coverage and sensitizing the public to humanitarian issues are the Scandinavians. They have dramatically increased broadcasts aimed not only at different ethnic groups but at themselves. "The Scandinavians are miles ahead in this area, particularly in children's programming," observed Claire Frachon, a French specialist in European television programming. "They are trying to communicate to both immigrant groups and local communities by broadcasting films or programs in the original language and with subtitles. This way children will get used to the sound of foreign languages from an early age, a bit like music."

France, which has always pushed for assimilation rather than integration, has far to go with its concept of ethnic programming, but change is visible. Newspaper and television coverage of North Africa used to cater more to the interests of the *pied noir* community (French former settlers and residents from Algeria) than those of Muslim background, some of whom were already third-generation French. Reporters of North African (Arab) origin now often cover these stories.

Given that the decline in foreign reporting applies to Africa more than any other continent, there has been remarkably little pressure in either North America or Europe from the potentially enormous African and African-American lobbies. "We are constantly receiving letters from Estonians, Ukrainians, and Yugoslavs commenting on our coverage about Yugoslavia, Eastern Europe, and the former Soviet Union, but we have received virtually nothing from Africans," said one British ITV broadcaster of Arab Sudanese background.

In many respects, the apparent lack of voiced interest in the humanitarian predicaments of Sudan, Ethiopia, and Somalia reflects Africa's own inability to deal with divisive issues. The best example is the Organization of African Unity's (OAU) lack of action for the past two decades. The OAU has been outspoken toward pariahs like South Africa and Israel, but almost inert in confronting the massacres, repression, and corruption perpetrated by member African governments and guerrilla groups.

An estimated thirty million blacks live in the United States. Apart from their criticism of apartheid in South Africa, they have been unable to improve coverage of other African issues. Many black Americans, who now prefer to call themselves African-American, try to identify with a preslave heritage that has little to do with the Africa of today. In fact, their lack of interest in the plight of Liberians or Sudanese ravaged by war, oppression, or genocide has provoked animosity and bitterness among some Africans. "It is as if Americans . . . don't want to know about blacks killing blacks in Africa," said a Kenyan human rights lawyer. For numerous Americans, whether black or white, Africa still remains very much the "dark continent."

In Western Europe, where East European immigrants have been assimilated fairly well over the past two or three generations, one finds fewer references to Franco-Polish, Italian Armenian, or German Russian. In the United States, however, many people still refer to themselves as Irish American, German American, Italian American, or African American to proclaim their affinities with the old country. Such labels often are little more than romantic distractions. With the mixing of races and ethnic groups, such double-barreled epithets have about as much to do with modern-day Nigeria, Ireland, Germany, or Italy as do South African Afrikaaners with Holland or Huguenots with France. U.S. immigrants, regardless of origin, have become essentially American, far more than many might admit.

Nonetheless, ethnic lobbies can prove decisive in directing or sustaining public concern for humanitarian issues. This is particularly the case in the United States among America's newer immigrant groups, who have sought to support their former homelands in times of crisis. There is little doubt that many such lobbies have brought enormous pressure to bear on Congress and have prompted the media to react accordingly. Americans of Polish background have rallied to help Poland as have American Slavs, Armenians, and Ukrainians toward their own former countries or peoples during periods of natural disaster, war, or political repression. The Irish and Jewish lobbies are obviously among the most successful of these groups in the United States. It is no surprise that most major U.S. media maintain correspondents or bureaus in Israel, but only one or two, if any, in all of Africa.

New Approaches Through Media and Education

The failure of Americans to acquaint themselves with the problems of Africa lies up to a point with poor or superficial media coverage. But it also lies with inadequate basic education. A more direct approach to stimulate greater awareness of humanitarian issues, particularly among young people, would be to improve geography, history, and foreign language studies in schools. This should include social studies combined with current affairs, as some schools are doing. This instruction should stress different cultural and religious heritages rather than promote ethnocentric parochialism. In the case of black Americans, a better understanding of Africa might encourage a more genuine interest in the problems of this hapless continent. It might also contribute to helping blacks come to better terms with their cultural identity within the United States.

Part of the responsibility for stimulating public awareness of humanitarian issues lies with the relief agencies themselves. Too many aid organizations, whether the United Nations High Commissioner for Refugees (UNHCR), the World Health Organization (WHO), or the thousands of nongovernmental organizations, seek to promote themselves rather than the issues. Aid organizations need to recognize that without better media coverage, it will become more difficult to deal with Third World humanitarian crises.

Mozambique, Sudan, or Burma are in competition for the public's attention with Eastern Europe, the U.S. elections, or scandals in the British Royal Family. Media reporting is at a premium. It is the editors who need to be persuaded that better coverage is in the public interest, and could also increase circulation or ratings. A regional newspaper or television station, for example, could agree to provide broad coverage because a relief agency with local volunteers is involved or because a particular program is supported by a local interest group. Newspapers could report certain overseas stories as a matter of prestige or proclaimed public interest, or because a pop star or actress decides to promote the issue for a specific charity. The reasons are numerous but are all part of media strategies. Some agencies can help push issues that are not receiving coverage by helping bring members of the press into the field. The media claim to be wary of organized junkets, but relief organizations often are the only means for journalists to have access to crisis areas and to civilians caught in war. Aid groups can also help provide ground support in the form of vehicles, fuel, and communications.

Yet many aid organizations fail to understand the media. As some editors and development representatives agree, relief workers in the field should be briefed on the importance of the media and the need to cooperate whenever possible. Without public attention, there would be no fund-raising to help them in their work. At the same time, journalists need to understand that relief workers have a job to do as well. But all have an equally important role in putting the issues across to the public, and in the end, that is what matters.

Notes

1. Mario Bettati and Bernard Kouchner, *Le droit d'ingérence* (Paris: De Noël, 1987).
2. Unless otherwise noted, citations in this chapter are taken from interviews with the author in 1992.
3. Médecins Sans Frontières.

■ Part 2 ■
Military Force and Humanitarian Action

Commentary

THOMAS G. WEISS & LARRY MINEAR

The end of the Cold War has changed the face of world politics. New features include major alterations in the geography of the former Soviet Union and Eastern Europe, the breakdown of predominantly bipolar political relationships among states, the new importance of nonmilitary threats to national and international security, and the revitalization of multilateralism, with correspondingly expanded expectations of the United Nations.[1]

Breathtaking as these changes are, they are no more dramatic than the series of international military actions mounted in the erstwhile Second (or Communist) and Third (or developing) worlds to provide humanitarian assistance to those in need. For military and civil defense establishments to assist in natural disasters is not new, although the nature of cooperation has changed with the availability of underutilized NATO and Warsaw Pact resources.[2] In light of the altered political context, an effort is in fact now under way to codify and expand this experience under the auspices of the International Federation of Red Cross and Red Crescent Societies and the UN's Department of Humanitarian Affairs.[3]

What is unusual and of potentially enormous consequence for the global humanitarian economy of the future is the use of military force to ensure the delivery of aid on occasions when governments and insurgents prevent relief operations. Major initiatives in northern Iraq, Somalia, and Bosnia already have been undertaken in this decade in which foreign soldiers helped to ensure access to suffering civilians in spite of the reluctance or even hostility of local authorities. Each initiative has involved thousands of troops and

57

expenditures exceeding one billion dollars. While billed as unique, the peculiarities of each tend to blur over time. A series of initiatives, each presented as one-of-a-kind, soon constitutes a new genre of international action. The need to respond to human suffering was also a significant justification for major UN military operations in Cambodia and Mozambique. Such undertakings lead even skeptics to believe that armed humanitarian efforts may be far more prevalent in the future than in the recent past.

The most unusual event—undoubtedly a watershed and, in retrospect, perhaps more precedent setting than was understood at the time—followed passage of Security Council Resolution 688 in April 1991. Overriding early Iraqi government protests of the presence of elite forces of the United States, the United Kingdom, France, and the Netherlands deployed troops in Operation Provide Comfort, helping to rescue some one and a half million Kurds.[4] In due course, humanitarian activities spearheaded by troops from the allied coalition were handed over to the United Nations as the allied coalition continued its military monitoring of the area.

The fifteen hundred UN soldiers initially assigned to Sarajevo as part of the UN Protection Force in the former Yugoslavia (UNPROFOR) quickly proved inadequate to the task. In September 1992 the Security Council authorized adding at least five thousand more troops to protect humanitarian convoys and escort detainees in Bosnia-Herzegovina to safety. NATO initially sent sixty-five hundred soldiers from four member countries to support humanitarian activities in the area. Moreover, after months of discussion, a decision was made at the beginning of April 1993 to enforce a ban on Serbian overflights. This type of military action—whose justification, as it had been in Iraq, was at least partially humanitarian— indicated the expansion of plausible military options in the service of efforts to sustain civilians in times of war.

The third major event in the series took place in Somalia. The humanitarian protection activities of military forces in northern Iraq and Bosnia were upstaged—and reinforced—by the approval of Security Council Resolution 794, which led to the deployment of what eventually became some twenty-two thousand U.S. marines and ten thousand troops from some twenty other nations. This Unified Task Force (UNITAF) was more widely known under the Pentagon name, Operation Restore Hope. These activities were caused by the failure of only five hundred UN peacekeeping troops that operated under traditional rules of engagement to protect humanitarian operations.

At the end of March 1993, the Security Council continued its steady progression toward enforcing humanitarian access by authorizing twenty-eight thousand UN soldiers. This included a few thousand U.S. logistics troops left behind, who served for the first time under a UN general, as well as another two thousand soldiers held in reserve as a rapid strike force—under

U.S. command and control—to take over protection activities from the U.S.-led coalition. Scheduled to begin in May 1993, the United Nations Operation in Somalia (the second phase of UNOSOM) would be the largest, most expensive, and most ambitious UN operation to date. Also for the first time, the UN Secretary-General would command directly a military force deployed under Chapter VII of the UN Charter. The Security Council has empowered UNOSOM to use whatever force is necessary to ensure access to suffering civilians and to disarm Somali warlords who refuse to surrender their arms.

In view of the recurrent authorization of UN or UN-related troops for humanitarian support roles in one conflict after another, it had become difficult by early 1993 to argue that precedents are not being set. Nevertheless, the resolution authorizing action in Somalia goes to great lengths to maintain the fiction—so dear to many developing countries that fear legitimizing the concept of military intervention and to wealthier countries that might be asked to underwrite these activities—that the situation in Somalia is somehow unique. The rapidity of the change to a more assertive approach is particularly noticeable because only a few years earlier the modest idea of assigning peacekeepers a humanitarian support role had been controversial.[5]

Chapter 4, the first in Part 2, is "Humanitarian Intervention" by James O. C. Jonah, a lifetime international civil servant who since 1992 has been UN Under-Secretary-General for Political Affairs. As head of the African and Middle Eastern components of the UN's Department for Political Affairs and previously in charge of the UN's Office for Research and the Collection of Information, Jonah has been intimately involved with monitoring complex emergencies and attempting to effect political solutions. He spearheaded UN efforts in 1991–1992 to negotiate a solution to Somalia's violence, served as an emissary after the deportation of Palestinians to southern Lebanon by Israel in late 1992, and has carried out other troubleshooting missions over the years on behalf of the Secretary-General and Security Council.

Jonah lives up to his reputation for candor by using the word "intervention" in his chapter, which normally makes diplomatic hairs stand on end. While the concept of intervention is in the air these days and a frequent topic of discussion in diplomatic circles, even UN Secretary-General Boutros Boutros-Ghali studiously avoided the term in answering the Security Council's call for a new vision of the UN's future activities in international peace and security.[6] Jonah not only uses the term but embraces it while assessing the current evolution of international norms and suggesting processes and structures for this new day and age.

International relations consist of many efforts to influence the behavior of states, and each effort constitutes intervention in their domestic affairs. Jonah, however, employs a narrower and perhaps more analytically useful approach. He limits the concept of humanitarian intervention to military actions undertaken to guarantee humanitarian access with the approval of the

Security Council but against the expressed wishes of a state. Somalia provides the gist for his reflections about attempting to negotiate with those who had utilized food as a weapon in their power struggle after the departure of Siad Barre in January 1991. The resulting conflict claimed an estimated three to five hundred thousand lives, jeopardizing the lives of some two million more Somalis by starvation and war.

In addition to employing greater unity in its use of humanitarian intervention, the current international debate would benefit from identifying the terms and preconditions to trigger these actions. Jonah's view is that decisionmaking and accountability for interventions need to be clearly vested in the United Nations, whatever the modalities of implementation. While the lack of a UN military capacity made a U.S.-led coalition the only real option for Somalia, the UNITAF undertaking gained political significance and legitimacy from the UN's blue fig leaf.

Jonah's concentration on Somalia spotlights humanitarian intervention in circumstances in which there is no governmental authority—what international lawyers would label *res nullius*. The earlier UN-authorized military intervention in northern Iraq took place without governmental consent, although the reluctant consent of Iraqi authorities was subsequently extracted to permit UN guards to help secure humanitarian operations, with allied troops and airpower to back them up from Turkey. The presence of UN troops in Bosnia has been resisted by virtually all parties at one time or another.

Whether the situation is one of anarchy, acquiescence, or resistance, recent international actions put states on notice that major violence against their own populations no longer will be considered exclusively a matter of domestic jurisdiction. The rights of civilians in times of war increasingly are viewed as not being matters of sovereign discretion. Access no longer depends exclusively on decisions of local authorities but is subject to more generally agreed international standards. Boundaries are becoming more porous and more subject to international intervention, if not yet altogether irrelevant.[7]

In short, as the world moves from the Cold War to the post–Cold War era, sovereignty as traditionally understood is no longer sacrosanct. The age-old balance between state assertions of sovereignty and international expressions of solidarity with those who suffer has begun to shift perceptibly in favor of those in need. Operations such as Provide Comfort and Restore Hope and many crossborder operations mounted by nongovernmental organizations, and even a few governments in places like Eritrea and Tigray, indicate that humanitarian action precedes codification in international law. Human life takes precedence over artificial legal constructs that are used to justify using food and medicine as weapons by belligerents, whether they are recognized governments or insurgents in armed opposition.[8]

Philosophers and theologians have agreed over the years that no state or authority has a right to starve or abuse its own people with impunity. This idea is gaining fresh ground among some analysts as well as practitioners. The international community is groping toward what the French government has trumpeted for some time: *le droit d'ingérence*, or the right to intervene.[9] The international community usually seeks, however, to win the consent of political authorities rather than to override them. To declare that sovereignty is in a subsidiary position to humane values and that the international community can resort to military action to enforce this hierarchy frames the issue in starker terms than those used comfortably by many governments and analysts.

Governments and would-be governments increasingly understand that claims of sovereignty are sometimes judged by how responsibly it is exercised. Sovereignty devoid of humane values increasingly appears illegitimate: "Use it responsibly or lose it." The international community has chosen, at least in northern Iraq and Somalia, not to finesse the issue of the relative value of sovereignty in a head-on clash with humanitarianism. This vigor makes more likely appeals to governments to exercise their sovereignty more responsibly.

The two remaining chapters in Part 2 explore from different perspectives the implications of the increasing use of military force for humanitarian action and actors. In "Armed Relief," John Mackinlay provides reflections based upon his career as a former British military officer who served as an observer in the Sinai, as well as in many overseas postings as a regular infantry officer. His firsthand experience as a peacekeeper has been enhanced by recent analytical work undertaken as director of the project entitled "Second Generation Multinational Operations" at Brown University's Watson Institute.[10] His research involved visits in 1992 to UN peacekeeping operations in the former Yugoslavia, Cambodia, northern Iraq, and Kuwait.

Based on recent deployments of multilateral military forces to meet humanitarian exigencies in war zones, Mackinlay foresees a rapidly expanding role for such operations. He analyzes a number of possible uses that vary in the extent of force and the numbers of troops involved. The low end of a range of options involves actions such as positioning troops to forestall an eventual humanitarian catastrophe—for example, the deployment in December 1992 of a UN battalion in the former Yugoslav republic of Macedonia to avoid another Bosnia. An option involving greater application of force is represented by the provision of troops to escort the transport and delivery of food in Bosnia. At the high end of policy choices are efforts such as Operations Provide Comfort and Restore Hope in Somalia.

Mackinlay argues that in order to cope with a new world disorder characterized by levels of violence and unrest resulting from micronationalisms undreamed of by the framers of the UN Charter, the increased reliance upon military forces in support of humanitarian action is very probable. However, a number of questions need to be asked about the deployment of forces in this context. Are troops able to be trained to deal with highly volatile security situations? Will they be able to function in highly politicized circumstances without being drawn into the conflict, either by choosing sides or being perceived as choosing sides? To what extent will the task of protecting humanitarian operations entail basic police and law enforcement functions (e.g., weapons confiscation)? What are the terms of engagement regarding the authority of the troops to take preemptive as well as defensive action? Should new guidelines be developed for UN troops specifically with humanitarian support functions in mind?[11]

In Chapter 6, "Relief Operations and Military Strategy," Gayle E. Smith scrutinizes how the activities of belligerent military forces affect the work of humanitarian organizations. For more than a decade, she has worked closely with relief organizations in the Horn of Africa and counseled governments on aid and development issues. She is currently based in Addis Ababa as a consultant to nongovernmental organizations and adviser to the present transitional government in Ethiopia. Her wealth of practical experience in Ethiopia, the Sudan, and Somalia is enriched by familiarity with other regions as well. She is known for her analytical rigor and candor.

Smith advances the thesis, growing out of her own experience, that the success of humanitarian interventions directly correlates with the ability of practitioners to understand military strategy and creatively adapt their activities accordingly. If they fail to do so, relief activities are likely to redound unduly to the military advantage of one or another belligerent, compromising the evenhandedness of humanitarian agencies and in effect making them parties to the conflict and its outcome.

Where Mackinlay describes what he views as the largely positive interaction between outside troops and the humanitarian operations that they support, Smith sees local militaries as purveyors of violence and wreakers of human suffering. At the same time, she urges humanitarian groups to move beyond hand-wringing to greater vigilance in protecting their own activities against manipulation and abuse. She elaborates some preliminary rules of the game to guide private agencies operating in close proximity to military forces in times of war.

Relying more and more upon outside military forces to sustain civilians and protect aid workers in times of war is not without critics. NGOs are divided about a greater role for the world's militaries in the global humanitarian economy of the future. There is even debate among parliaments and within defense establishments. Some welcome logistical and other resources that the military provide; others note the often high price tag. Some see the addition of a greater element of coercion as helpful in creating humanitarian space in civil strife settings; others hold that voluntariness is at the heart of humanitarian action and that there is no substitute for painstakingly negotiating access to those in need. Some want to harness otherwise underutilized military forces; others believe that doing so will strengthen the already disproportionate influence of the military in some societies.

Discussions and conferences, journal articles and books these days are examining the "alternative uses of military forces," an objective indicator that militaries around the world are, from a self-interested point of view, looking for ways to protect their budgets from the post–Cold War scalpel.[12] What could be better insurance against parliamentary cuts than the demonstrated need for assistance from the military in sustaining suffering civilians in a growing number of natural and man-made disasters?

A conference organized in December 1992 by the International Federation of Red Cross and Red Crescent Societies and the UN's Department of Humanitarian Affairs was held in facilities in Brussels provided by the North Atlantic Treaty Organization. NATO Secretary-General Manfred Wörner had just presided over a meeting of defense ministers who had pronounced themselves ready to do "what is necessary" in Bosnia if the UN requested it. During the same week, the U.S.-led Operation Restore Hope began deploying troops to Somalia. Wörner opened the meeting by announcing to assembled representatives of civilian and military institutions that "this is another NATO from the one that you have known." In April 1993 NATO agreed to enforce a United Nations–ordered no-fly zone over Bosnia-Herzegovina, the first NATO military operation out-of-area based upon humanitarian imperatives in support of the United Nations.

Pressing military resources into the service of humanitarian objectives becomes more attractive in light of the growing "humanitarian gap"—that is, the shortfall between the burgeoning demands for relief and the resources available to be committed quickly to sustaining civilians during war. In this context, the use of military and civil defense assets to help victims may be welcomed. At the same time, some argue in favor of reducing the size of post–Cold War military establishments rather than retooling them for new duties. In any event, the determining factor should be the real requirements of disaster victims and not merely the availability of resources. Discussions about applying excess military capacity should be demanded in order to ensure that these resources are used efficiently and appropriately.

Along with the dangers of a supply-driven use of the military are concerns about the militarization of civilian aid programs and of civil society. It is difficult to imagine a positive contribution from heavily armed and repressive militaries of many nondemocratic countries. The use of military resources is as expensive as their deployment is swift. Moreover, it is dangerously easy for the public to confuse an immediate and simple infusion of logistical help with the far more complex and arduous tasks of getting a war-torn society permanently back on its feet. Since resources are scarce, allocations for military relief could occur at the expense of civilian institutions and channels. The issue of demilitarization would seem at least as pertinent for advancing the cause of humanity as any increased reliance upon military forces in emergencies.

The three chapters that make up the second part of the book examine different aspects of military force in support of humanitarian action. Since the international community also can apply economic force to advance humane objectives, a word about nonforcible sanction may be useful.

Economic sanctions, like many other policy tools theoretically available during the Cold War, have suddenly become a viable policy option in its aftermath. Economic sanctions are usually seen as the first and least violent form of enforcement to reverse threats to peace, to be followed, if necessary, by the application of military force. In spite of their recent use in Iraq, Haiti, Libya, Cambodia, and the former Yugoslavia, very little has been determined about their utility in achieving humanitarian goals or their sometimes negative humanitarian consequences. Previous research largely has concentrated instead on the utility of sanctions as a foreign policy tool of the United States and on their economic consequences.[13]

Two pertinent challenges related to impact and applications emerge from the recent experience of the international community as documented in the field research of the Humanitarianism and War Project.[14] First, can the application of economic sanctions serve humanitarian objectives when they cause serious hardship among civilian populations? As suggested by the Gulf War, the political strategies adopted, the economic sanctions imposed, and the military force authorized by the Security Council each created hardships for civilian populations. Moreover, each also complicated the ability of the UN's own agencies to provide relief to civilians caught in the conflict and undermined their credibility.

Could a better approach have been used to minimize the impact on vulnerable civilians? Several possibilities come to mind. Before the Security Council decides on economic or military enforcement action, the views of UN organizations with humanitarian competence should be given serious consideration. UNICEF and the World Food Programme, for example, are well situated to warn against, anticipate, and monitor such consequences, especially for vulnerable groups who suffer most under sanctions.[15] The UN Secretary-General also could be authorized to request an advisory opinion of the International Court of Justice regarding the nature of and restrictions applying to the use of military force in order to reflect adequately concerns related to proportionality and the protection of humanitarian values.[16] If the Security Council decides to proceed with a given action, governments should be obliged to provide resources to the UN system so it can respond fully to the humanitarian consequences. None of these possibilities was explored during the Gulf crisis.

The second challenge regarding economic sanctions relates to the timing of an associated deployment by a UN or UN-authorized military force. Enshrined in the UN Charter and practice is the assumption that economic sanctions should be tried first, and only when they fail should collective military action be undertaken. Suffering civilians in Serbia and Haiti in 1993 occasioned by such sanctions provide compelling reasons to rethink this conventional wisdom.

A vigorous and preventive deployment of UN peacekeepers to Bosnia-Herzegovina might have obviated the subsequent need for economic pressure on Belgrade and Serbian irregulars. The need to avoid deploying large numbers of troops to prevent disaster contributed to the Security Council's decision to send preventive UN soldiers to Macedonia in December 1992. An earlier military enforcement action to restore an elected government in Haiti might have entailed far less suffering for the civilian population than extended sanctions.

As with the first triad of essays, the three authors here raise a number of issues requiring further analysis and reflection:

1. "Humanitarian intervention" has become a household term, albeit one whose imprecision generates great public confusion and political controversy. From the standpoint of international law, the concept is an oxymoron: providing truly humanitarian assistance itself does not constitute an unfriendly act. Greater precision therefore would require speaking instead of military action in support of humanitarian activities. To what extent would a clearer definition result in greater consensus and less resistance to assertive international action in support of those in need?

2. The term "new interventionists" has been applied to those who recommend that the international community become more assertive in dealing with massive violations of humanitarian and human rights. While it is widely assumed that such interventionism would deploy military force as needed, some who recommend a more assertive role see the need for a more creative mix of policy instruments, perhaps including—but by no means limited to or starting from—the application of military force. What instruments are available and what mechanisms can be devised to assure that the entire array of possible policy options is used in a timely and consistent manner?

3. Many who are reluctant to see military force assume a larger role in the future international humanitarian economy believe that the problems creating recurrent human suffering need to be addressed by other means. At the same time, it is undeniable that humanitarian action is undertaken sometimes as a palliative or a surrogate for stronger action. Even the deployment of troops to protect humanitarian operations can be a substitute for the direct use of force against the belligerents. What precautions can be devised to protect humanitarian action from abuse as smoke screen or symbol?

4. The effectiveness of humanitarian action in some circumstances may be enhanced by its association with military force. However, while some prefer that the force be multilateral in character, action by individual

governments or multinational coalitions has often proved more effective than action undertaken by the UN. In fact, multilateral action is caught in a vicious circle. The UN is not entrusted with its own independent military capacity by governments who then argue that the UN is demonstrably unable to mount effective military-support operations. What can and should be done to break the circle?

5. As humanitarian personnel from civilian organizations interact more regularly with military officials, a conflict of cultures becomes apparent. Even when certain objectives converge, military and humanitarian institutions use different methods of decisionmaking, approaches to accountability, operational styles, and relationships with local populations. To what extent will effective international efforts to deal with armed conflicts in the post–Cold War era require bridging these cultural divides? To what degree should the humanitarian culture be adopted to become more compatible with the military, or should the major accommodation be on the side of the military?

6. The use of force can make a positive contribution toward the advancement of humane values, including ending a given conflict. But humanitarian action devoid of coercion also can be a contribution to peace. Agreements extracted from warring parties to cooperate with international aid efforts have offered openings to negotiations that have addressed the roots of conflicts. Does granting military coercion a larger place in the international humanitarian economy risk preempting or sidelining efforts to resolve conflicts through consensual means? How can humanitarian relief play an even more significant role in fostering confidence building, peacemaking, and peace building?

7. Regarding the consequences of economic sanctions on vulnerable civilian populations, largely visceral reactions toward their positive and negative use to date reflect preferences rather than data or analysis. What factors should enter into the search for principles and ground rules underlying decisions on the international use of economic coercion as a response to war or injustice? From a humanitarian standpoint, what objective criteria should be considered before economic, or military, action is undertaken?

Notes

1. For a discussion, see James N. Rosenau, *The United Nations in a Turbulent World* (Boulder: Lynne Rienner, 1992); and Thomas G. Weiss (ed.), *Collective Security in a Changing World* (Boulder: Lynne Rienner, 1993).

2. For a discussion of this assistance, see Hugh Hanning, *Peaceful Uses of Military Forces* (New York: International Peace Academy, 1976); and Assembly of the Western European Union, "Role and Contribution of the Armed Forces in the Event of Natural or Other Disasters in Peacetime," document 960, November 7, 1983.

3. See documentation prepared for a meeting at NATO headquarters,

"Workshop on the Use of Military and Civil Defense Assets in Disaster Relief," Brussels, December 14–15, 1992.

4. See Thomas G. Weiss and Kurt M. Campbell, "Military Humanitarianism," *Survival* 33, no. 5 (September/October 1991): 451–465.

5. See Thomas G. Weiss (ed.), *Humanitarian Emergencies and Military Help in Africa* (London: Macmillan, 1990); and Leon Gordenker and Thomas G. Weiss (eds.), *Soldiers, Peacekeepers, and Disasters* (London: Macmillan, 1991).

6. Boutros Boutros-Ghali, *An Agenda for Peace* (New York: United Nations, 1992).

7. For a set of essays about these matters, see Gene M. Lyons and Michael Mastanduno (eds.), *Beyond Westphalia? National Sovereignty and International Intervention* (Berkeley: University of California Press, forthcoming 1993).

8. For an elaboration of these issues, see Jarat Chopra and Thomas G. Weiss, "Sovereignty Is No Longer Sacrosanct: Codifying Humanitarian Intervention," *Ethics and International Affairs* 6 (1992): 95–118; Larry Minear, "Humanitarian Intervention in a New World Order," *Overseas Development Council Policy Focus* 1 (1991); and Barbara Hendrie, "Cross-border Relief Operations in Eritrea and Tigray," *Disasters* 13, no. 4 (1989): 351–360. For a discussion of the extent to which the military option has become plausible within the United States, see Raymond W. Copson, "The Use of Force in Civil Conflicts for Humanitarian Purposes: Prospects for the Post–Cold War Era," *CRS Report for Congress*, document 92-899F, December 1992. For a more skeptical view of the overextension of both the United States and the United Nations, see Stephen John Stedman, "The New Interventionists," *Foreign Affairs* 72, no. 1 (1992/93): 1–16.

9. See Mario Bettati and Bernard Kouchner, *Le droit d'ingérence* (Paris: Denoël, 1987); and Bernard Kouchner, *Le Malheur des Autres* (Paris: Odile Jacob, 1992).

10. See John Mackinlay, *The Peacekeepers* (London: Unwin Hyman, 1989); and John Mackinlay and Jarat Chopra, "Second Generation Multinational Forces," *Washington Quarterly* 15, no. 3 (Summer 1992): 113–134, and *A Draft Concept of Second Generation Multinational Operations* (Providence: Watson Institute, 1993).

11. See James N. Rosenau, *Turbulence in World Politics* (Princeton: Princeton University Press, 1990); Augustus Richard Norton, "The Security Legacy of the 1980s in the Third World," in Thomas G. Weiss and Meryl A. Kessler (eds.), *Third World Security in the Post–Cold War Era* (Boulder: Lynne Rienner, 1992): 19–34; Lawrence Freedman, "Order and Disorder in the New World," *Foreign Affairs* 71 (1991/92): 20–37; Morton H. Halperin and David J. Scheffer, *Self-Determination in the New World Order* (Washington, D.C.: Carnegie Endowment, 1992); Daniel Patrick Moynihan, *Pandemonium: Ethnicity in International Politics* (New York: Oxford University Press, 1993); Joel Kotkin, *Tribes: How Race, Religion, and Identity Determine Success in the New Global Economy* (New York: Random House, 1993); and *Ethnic Conflict and International Security*, special issue of *Survival* 35, no. 1 (Spring 1993).

12. See, for example, Colin L. Powell, "US Forces: Challenges Ahead," *Foreign Affairs* 72, no. 5 (Winter 1992/93): 32–45.

13. One recent exception is Lisa Martin, *Coercive Cooperation: Explaining Multilateral Economic Sanctions* (Princeton: Princeton University Press, 1992). For a more traditional treatment, see Gary Clyde Hufbauer, Jeffrey J. Schott, and Kimberly Ann Elliott, *Economic Sanctions Reconsidered: History and Current Policy* and *Economic Sanctions Reconsidered: Supplemental Case Histories* (Washington, D.C.: Institute for International Economics, 1990), which updated *Economic Sanctions in Pursuit of Foreign Policy Goals* (Washington, D.C.:

Institute for International Economics, 1983). See also David A. Baldwin, *Economic Statecraft* (Princeton: Princeton University Press, 1985); and Theodore Galdi and Robert Shuey, *U.S. Economic Sanctions Imposed Against Specific Countries: 1979 to the Present* (Washington, D.C.: Congressional Research Service, 1992).

14. See Larry Minear and Thomas G. Weiss, "Groping and Coping in the Gulf Crisis: Discerning the Shape of a New Humanitarian Order," *World Policy Journal* 9, no. 4 (Fall/Winter 1992): 755–788.

15. The impact of economic sanctions on vulnerable groups seems akin to that of structural adjustment programs. For a discussion of the latter, see Richard Jolly and Ralph van der Hoeven (eds.), *Adjustment With a Human Face—Record and Relevance*, special issue of *World Development* 19, no. 12 (1991).

16. This suggestion was made by Boutros Boutros-Ghali in *An Agenda for Peace* (New York: United Nations, 1992): para. 38–39. For a further discussion, see Thomas G. Weiss and Jarat Chopra, *UN Peacekeeping: An ACUNS Teaching Text* (Hanover: Academic Council on the UN System, 1992): 41–42.

■ 4 ■

Humanitarian Intervention

JAMES O. C. JONAH

In recent years the issue of humanitarian intervention has gained great prominence in international affairs. The many studies and discussions on this issue predated the events and aftermath of the Gulf conflict.[1] Scholars and practitioners have been searching in recent years for solutions to the problem of the use of food as a weapon, for which there was evidence in the Horn of Africa, particularly in Sudan.[2] The problem gained greater prominence after the Gulf War, particularly with respect to the Kurds in northern Iraq.[3]

The winning coalition that drove Iraqi forces from Kuwait faced a dilemma after the Gulf War. One consequence of the war was the plight of Kurdish refugees languishing in northern Iraq in inclement weather. Public opinion in the coalition countries called for action to protect the Kurds from Saddam Hussein. The issue of their protection led to immediate debate in the Security Council. Aware of the difficulty of obtaining from the Security Council a clear commitment for humanitarian intervention, some coalition members, such as the United Kingdom, took the lead in instituting an exclusion zone in northern Iraq. This took the form of statements by the coalition members that Iraqi aircraft would not be permitted to fly over certain parts of northern Iraq, as well as the creation of an enclave where the Kurdish refugees were located.

These policies and actions highlight the issue of national sovereignty, which has bedeviled past efforts to promote the concept of humanitarian intervention. Most small- and medium-size states, particularly in the Third World, have expressed concern at the way the concept of humanitarian intervention has been applied in Iraq. They fear that this precedent could be used in the future as a pretext for old-fashioned political and military intervention in weak states.

Theory and Practice of Humanitarian Intervention

These concerns have led to an effort to better define the conditions under which humanitarian intervention could be practiced. In interviews with representatives of member states at the United Nations and in discussions at various seminars, there is no objection to humanitarian intervention where there is overwhelming evidence that many people are starving and those involved in the conflict are deliberately preventing the international community from delivering assistance to those who need it.

There is a consensus that under such conditions efforts must be made to overcome obstacles and to override the objections of the warring parties. There is also a consensus that these efforts should not be carried out unilaterally—either by one country or a coalition of countries—but that such a situation should be brought to the attention of the international community to obtain a clear mandate for humanitarian intervention. But it has not been easy to win the support of the Security Council for actions of this nature. Most members of the Security Council have few qualms about undertaking humanitarian intervention where it is clearly warranted, but two or three members, including one permanent member, remain skeptical about the concept of humanitarian intervention.

It is equally true that for the membership of the United Nations as a whole, a majority of member states are not inclined to accept the concept of humanitarian intervention. This became clear in 1991 at both the Economic and Social Council (ECOSOC) and General Assembly sessions when the issue of creating a humanitarian "supremo" within the United Nations was debated. This high-level official would have the authority to undertake humanitarian interventions on behalf of the international community. Another reason for the creation of this post was to ensure better coordination among the United Nations agencies and programs providing humanitarian relief.[4] But underlying the contentious debate that lead to the adoption of Resolution 46/182 was the assumption that the high-level official, acting under the authority of the Secretary-General, would be able to promote and undertake humanitarian intervention.

The experience of the United Nations in bringing humanitarian relief to vulnerable groups in conflicts has had mixed results. When UNICEF, under the leadership of James Grant, succeeded in negotiating "corridors of tranquillity" to allow the delivery of relief supplies in the Sudan, some people believed that perhaps an appropriate solution had been found.

In fact, the initial success of the corridors of tranquillity became a model. It was applied in Angola and Mozambique, and was attempted in Iraq. But as a practical matter, the corridors of tranquillity have not worked as anticipated. Warring parties still can prevent the delivery of humanitarian relief. In these circumstances the only option available to the United Nations has been to conduct difficult negotiations on the ground with the parties to the conflict who are preventing delivery. The delivery of supplies remains vulnerable to disruption by parties who want to prevent relief flights or limit access to areas of need. There have been numerous instances in which planes and trucks carrying relief supplies have been fired upon, with casualties for local and international personnel. The corridors of tranquillity have not worked satisfactorily, and debate has continued on what should be the proper response of the international community to humanitarian emergencies in time of conflict.

The events in Bosnia-Herzegovina and the former Yugoslavia have spotlighted the issue of humanitarian intervention. After the exclusion zone was instituted in Iraq without direct United Nations involvement, Prince Saddrudin Aga Khan worked out an arrangement with Iraqi authorities for the deployment of five hundred United Nations guards to help with humanitarian activities in northern Iraq. Even though these arrangements do not involve humanitarian intervention, they have been discussed in those terms. In fact, the prince cited the Memorandum of Understanding of April 18, 1991, with the Iraqi government, under which the five hundred United Nations guards operate on Iraqi territory, as a "better option" than the exclusion zone. However, since the guards can operate only with the approval of the Iraqi government, this does not solve the problem of humanitarian intervention.

This shortcoming became clearer when the Memorandum of Understanding expired near the end of 1991. It then was necessary for the United Nations to negotiate a new Memorandum of Understanding since the Iraqi government had exercised its sovereign right to propose new elements, which caused difficulties for the United Nations. Difficult negotiations ensued, and it was only in mid-October 1992 that agreement was reached in the form of a new Memorandum of Understanding, which provided for three hundred United Nations guards to be stationed in northern Iraq. The new memorandum initially provoked a strong reaction from the U.S. government, which said the new agreement made too many concessions to the Iraqi government. It is clear this approach has not resolved the problem of humanitarian intervention.

The Case of Somalia

There has been much discussion about the best way to provide humanitarian relief to Bosnia-Herzegovina, but the major debate over humanitarian intervention has focused on Somalia. Humanitarian intervention in Somalia directly confronts the question of the defense or violation of state sovereignty. The tragedy of Somalia is that there is no central government, or any government at all in the normal sense of the term. Instead, there are local warlords and warring factions. It is difficult even to talk about sovereignty in Somalia. Partly because of this, the Security Council has not found it easy to deal with this matter.

The Security Council sees two aspects to the problem. The first is that involvement by the Security Council becomes difficult without a request from a sovereign government. Despite the compelling need for intervention, some members of the Council are reluctant to become enmeshed in civil conflicts without it. In the case of Somalia, a way around this obstacle was the creation of a legal fiction in the form of a letter from the Somali chargé d'affaires in New York who, in reality, represented no one.[5] Nevertheless, this provided the basis for action by the Security Council when it adopted Resolution 733 on January 23, 1992. Legal purists were satisfied by being able to point to the request from a government although, in fact, none existed. It was also necessary to emphasize the international dimension of the problem. This maneuvering provided a platform to allow the Council to offer humanitarian intervention.

After the overthrow of the Siad Barre regime in January 1991, and throughout that year, humanitarian relief efforts in Somalia were frustrated by the deliberate actions of the warring parties to prevent relief supplies from reaching their enemies. In addition, total anarchy reigned in the country, leading to pervasive insecurity, which stopped delivery of relief supplies in all parts of the country. There was evidence in 1991 of widespread malnutrition among such vulnerable groups as children, women, and the displaced, but there was no evidence of mass starvation. The most pressing issue was how to secure conditions under which United Nations agencies and nongovernmental organizations (NGOs) could distribute humanitarian assistance to vulnerable groups. The unpleasant option was to negotiate with clan leaders and elders.

The United Nations also concentrated on negotiating a cease-fire in Mogadishu, where fighting had been so intense that delivery of supplies was halted in November 1991 until a new cease-fire was arranged on March 3, 1992. This cease-fire involved General Mohammed Farah Aidid of the United Somali Congress and Interim President Ali Mahdi Mohammed. It did not, however, solve the problem posed by the many armed gangsters roaming the city. The proliferation of weapons among the youth became a problem not only in Mogadishu but also throughout the country.

How to tackle the problem of armed gangs became a pressing matter. Two approaches were tried. The UN approach was to apply the concept of humanitarian intervention in the context of a peacekeeping operation. This took the form of a proposal by the Secretary-General to the Security Council, after negotiations with the warring parties, to provide five hundred United Nations peacekeeping troops to protect the delivery of relief supplies.[6] The troops were to be provided by Pakistan. The support of the warring parties was to be obtained before this force could be deployed. It was also understood that the five hundred soldiers would not maintain law and order in Mogadishu, but would only protect the convoys delivering supplies to the vulnerable groups. The Security Council adopted Resolution 751 on April 24, 1992, and accepted the approach proposed by the Secretary-General.

This was progress, but the approach still did not meet all the requirements of humanitarian intervention. This became clear when General Aidid initially refused to allow fifty unarmed military observers to wear military uniforms. It took four months of negotiation before he consented and five months before he agreed to the deployment of the five-hundred-troop peacekeeping contingent. And it still was not possible to reach full agreement with General Aidid and the belligerents on all issues regarding the deployment of peacekeepers. The issue of how to assist the most vulnerable groups remained.

Another approach was used by some NGOs and especially by the International Committee of the Red Cross (ICRC). The Red Cross position was ambivalent. Throughout 1991 the Red Cross was the only major international relief organization bringing supplies to the people of Somalia. The Red Cross had initially negotiated with the clan leaders and elders to involve them in the distribution of relief supplies. The Red Cross was skeptical of the UN approach of employing security forces to protect those distributing relief. It believed this approach might aggravate the security problem.

When General Aidid prevented deployment of the five hundred United Nations troops, the option of hiring local armed security agents gained currency. The agents were called "technicals" and were paid to provide protection. The widespread use of technicals raised serious ethical questions. There is evidence that the technicals became, in effect, a protection racket. Some began looting, and only a small percentage of relief supplies reached those most in need. Full deployment of the United Nations peacekeeping force would not have solved the problem of the technicals, as experience showed. In Mogadishu, the technicals refused to allow the Pakistani peacekeeping contingent to disembark unless the technicals were assured of continued employment and given uniforms.

In view of the deteriorating situation in Somalia, where the level of human suffering was extremely severe, the Secretary-General was determined to chart a new course. In his report to the Security Council on July 22, 1992, he proposed a zonal approach, in which four zones would be created, each linked to a port.[7] The four zones were: the northwest (Berbera), the northeast (Bossasso), the central rangelands and Mogadishu (Mogadishu), and the south (Kismayo). The Secretary-General also proposed the deployment of three thousand more peacekeeping troops to help protect convoys. This was accepted by the Security Council in Resolution 775 on August 28, 1992.

This was a feasible plan on paper, but its implementation was impeded by General Aidid's refusal to accept deployment of the peacekeepers. The UN again had to negotiate with the clans. It reached an agreement for the deployment of a Canadian battalion in Bossasso, and serious efforts were made to reach agreements for deployments in Berbera and Kismayo. The delay in fielding the UN force demonstrated that the international community had not yet solved one of the basic problems of humanitarian intervention. Debate began anew on whether the United Nations should override the objections of General Aidid and other warring forces and intervene by force to ensure the delivery of relief. In the Security Council there was widespread recognition that a deteriorating security situation warranted forceful UN intervention.

However, the Europeans posed a crucial question: Who would provide the troops? If European troops were used to intervene, would this not revive charges of neocolonialism? So the Council seriously considered using non-European forces. Contacts were made with some African countries, and they indicated that they would provide forces if asked to do so by the Security Council.

The tragedy of Somalia has led the Organization of African Unity (OAU) to rethink basic approaches. Before the conflict in Somalia, African states would have been most reluctant to allow outside forces to intervene in internal conflicts on the continent. This is most evident in the Sudan. There is now a discernible change of viewpoint. At the OAU meeting of foreign ministers in Addis Ababa in February 1992 and at the summit in Dakar in July 1992, African states were prepared to sanction intervention in situations such as Somalia. A paper prepared by OAU Secretary-General Salim Salim tackled this issue head-on. Since that time there has been no major opposition by African states to UN intervention in Somalia that is aimed at the delivery of humanitarian relief.

History may recall that Somalia represented the real test of the ability of the international community to implement the concept of humanitarian intervention. World leaders in key countries clearly understood that the deplorable situation in Somalia could not be allowed to continue. Humanitarian intervention became a pressing option that could take one of two forms. The first would be the deployment of UN forces in Somalia on the understanding that they could act against any faction, even General Aidid, that obstructed the delivery of relief. This would not necessarily fit the classic definition of humanitarian intervention because there was considerable evidence that many Somalis, including some warlords and leaders such as Ali Mahdi, welcomed a UN force. The question was how the Security Council would go about authorizing such a force, and whether a heavily armed military force would be used to suppress attacks by warlords and other armed groups. There obviously would be casualties. It would be necessary to weigh the pros and cons of such a venture.

The second possibility, which was quietly reviewed and discussed in the media,[8] would be the assumption by the UN of full responsibility for Somalia by declaring a trusteeship on the basis of the United Nations Trusteeship system. The world organization presumably would be in charge of the country for a few years; it would deal with the humanitarian emergency, create conditions for normal development activities to resume, and organize elections to return power to a legitimate government. This would be a step beyond the model of Cambodia, where the UN exercises its authority in a number of fields but is not in complete control, as would be the case with a trusteeship.[9]

It is always difficult to separate the political and humanitarian actions of the international community when discussing humanitarian intervention. One inevitably merges with the other. In Somalia the United Nations has not been able to keep the two apart. For example, the United Nations can be criticized for not taking the initiative to intervene politically before December 1991, when the Secretary-General finally approached the Security Council. But it is less valid to criticize the UN for slow action on the humanitarian side of the issue. Shortly after the fall of the Siad Barre regime, the UN initiated humanitarian assistance in parts of Somalia where the security conditions were better. The UN could be faulted for showing inordinate concern for the security of its staff, but not for ignoring the problem.

A Comparison with Liberia

It is instructive to examine the situation in Liberia to demonstrate what could have happened in Somalia during 1991. In Liberia, too, a tragic and chaotic situation had developed without much attention from the outside world. It had been perceived early on as a domestic problem, even though the conflict sent many Liberian refugees to neighboring countries, which were and are ill equipped to care for them.

The breakdown of law and order aggravated the situation and resulted in malnutrition and starvation. As in Somalia, a lack of security had impeded the delivery of humanitarian relief. Significantly, as the international community stood by and ignored the problem, the Economic Community of West African States moved to fill the vacuum. The deployment of its peacekeeping force, ECOMOG, was initially criticized, but with the passage of time, it came to be regarded as a good example of regional arrangements that can help provide stability.

Humanitarianism in Somalia—The Ideal Test Case

Recent developments show that Somalia is an ideal test case for the concept of humanitarian intervention. This chapter has pointed out factors that discouraged humanitarian intervention in Somalia. However, events during the closing days of November 1992 focused attention on the need to take dramatic action. The trigger was the irresponsible firing, by one of the warlords, on a relief ship loaded with food for Somalia. This followed occurrences of kidnapping and looting, as well as deliberate attacks on members of the Pakistani battalion that the Security Council had sent to Somalia.

Another major consideration was the convergence of views between UN headquarters and its operation in the field in Mogadishu on the need to take firm action to ensure unimpeded delivery of assistance. Shortly after the new special representative of the Secretary-General, Ambassador Kittani, arrived in

Somalia, elements of the Pakistani battalion occupied the international airport in Mogadishu. They stood their ground against threats from General Aidid and an actual exchange of fire. This was the first UN demonstration of its determination not to yield to threats.

It may be appropriate at this juncture to respond to concerns frequently raised by African members of the Security Council. They have asked why the Secretary-General did not discuss with the Security Council the difficulties encountered on the ground following the agreement by the Council in April of 1992 to dispatch five hundred peacekeeping troops to Somalia along with fifty unarmed military observers. (This force was later increased to a total of thirty-five hundred peacekeeping troops, but they were not deployed.)

The Secretary-General had not, in fact, returned to the Council to describe the difficulties UN forces and humanitarian agencies were facing. This was inevitably compared to the promptness with which the Council was informed of problems in Bosnia, which led the Council to attempt remedial action. In fact, it would have been difficult for the Secretary-General to go to the Security Council when his representative in Somalia, Ambassador Sahnoun, was appealing for more time to negotiate with the warlords in order to facilitate United Nations operations on the ground.

The new special representative in his first report was able to pinpoint very quickly some major obstacles: utter chaos in the city and the increasing reluctance of warlords to permit United Nations relief operations. At the same time, roaming armed gangs had stepped up their banditry. It was increasingly evident that only a small portion, 20 to 30 percent, of relief supplies was reaching the most vulnerable groups. The entire population was threatened with starvation. Furthermore, the Secretary-General and the United States government reached the same conclusion at the same time, from different perspectives and without any special exchange of information. During the closing months of 1992, senior U.S. officials were on the ground in Somalia and they witnessed the degradation and anarchy in the country.

The accepted wisdom before that time had been the rather facile assessment that difficulties were due mainly to the lack of coordination among UN agencies and infighting among senior officials. The real problem was the irresponsible behavior of the warlords and armed gangs who were benefiting from the plight of their fellow citizens. The warlords and gangs were in effect running protection rackets and reaping enormous foreign exchange profits that they used to purchase more weapons.

The Secretary-General concluded, in a letter to the Security Council dated November 24, 1992, that despite its best efforts the UN's approach in Somalia simply was not working: "I cannot conceal from the Security Council that the situation is not improving and the conditions which have developed in Somalia since the fall of the previous regime make it exceedingly difficult for the United Nations operation to achieve the objectives approved by the Security Council."

A major bottleneck was trying to win the consent of the "local authorities" for the full deployment of the thirty-five hundred peacekeeping troops authorized by the Security Council. In some cases the local authorities had reneged on their consent. Troop-contributing countries were getting impatient, since they needed precise information to plan for the dispatch of their soldiers. The Secretary-General concluded that the Security Council should seriously consider adopting Chapter VII provisions. This was the first unambiguous proposal for humanitarian intervention in Somalia. A similar review was being undertaken in Washington. Within hours, the congruence began to surface between the approach emerging from the United States and the actions being contemplated by the Secretary-General.

These parallel views of the situation would have had limited impact had consensus not developed at the same time in the Security Council for a change of direction. Media coverage of the deplorable situation had concentrated the minds in the Security Council so that it was ready for a dramatic change in policy. When the Secretary-General briefed the Security Council informally on November 25, 1992, he did not hesitate to say that he sought drastic action. The Secretary-General received almost unanimous support from members of the Council. The concept of humanitarian intervention was accepted grudgingly by only one or two council members. None dissented from the conclusion that provisions of Chapter VII should be applied. The major difficulty was how these provisions should be implemented. The Security Council asked the Secretary-General quickly to prepare different options to address the problem.

Although a conceptual breakthrough regarding humanitarian intervention had occurred, even its supporters were wary of the two previous models for United Nations action in similar situations. The first model was the Korean War, in which the Security Council, acting under Chapter VII, had called upon the United States to lead a collective security force. Under this model, the United States and other allied forces fought under the UN flag, but the world organization had little or no control over the allied forces.

The second model was the Gulf War. Under the terms of Resolution 687 in 1991, the Security Council, without naming any particular country, called upon countries allied with Kuwait to remove Iraqi troops then occupying Kuwait. The coalition forces led by the United States did not fight under the blue United Nations flag. The UN exercised no command over them. There was no mechanism for the Security Council to determine if excessive force was being applied or to end the operation. Key provisions of Chapter VII that would have enabled the Security Council itself to undertake military action had not been implemented. These provisions pertain to agreement among member states to immediately supply forces for enforcement action (Article 43), and for the effective functioning of the Military Staff Committee to assist the Council in military matters (Article 47).

The Secretary-General faced a formidable task. If he failed to provide acceptable options, the breakthrough for the concept of humanitarian intervention would fail to materialize or be rendered meaningless. In a letter dated November 29, the Security Council was presented with five options. The first was to pursue the existing course with greater vigor and intensity. The second was for the United Nations to withdraw its military forces and let the humanitarian agencies negotiate the best feasible arrangements with the local warlords and factions. Under the third option, United Nations Operation in Somalia (UNOSOM) was to undertake a show of force in Mogadishu to create conditions there for the safe delivery of relief supplies. The fourth option was a countrywide enforcement operation by a group of member states with the authorization of the Security Council. The fifth option, which the Secretary-General noted would be "consistent with the recent enlargement of the Organization's role in the maintenance of international peace and security and which would strengthen its long-term evolution as an effective system of collective security," would be an enforcement operation carried out under United Nations command and control.

The deliberations of the Security Council were remarkable. All members focused on the three options that involved the use of force or ignored Somali sovereignty. The two options that did not call for the use of force got little attention. In light of past doubts and hesitations that had plagued efforts to mount humanitarian intervention, this determination among members of the Council was refreshing. No member was prepared to tolerate the deplorable situation leading to mass starvation. A number of member states seized upon the assessment of the Secretary-General that there was no Somali government or reliable local authority from whom the United Nations could obtain consent for its operation. Actually, this was not a point at issue, since operations under Chapter VII of the Charter do not require consent of a government even if one exists. The Charter is clear that Article 2 (7) cannot be invoked once an enforcement action under Chapter VII has commenced.

The major debate—some would say controversy—revolved around which of the three options calling for the use of force would be acceptable to the Council. There was a general inclination to adopt the fifth option, since it provided for United Nations command and control of unified forces. Most members of the Council, however, understood that the fourth option was the only realistic one. United Nations peacekeeping forces in many parts of the world have encountered enormous difficulties, and many are operating on somewhat shaky ground. A major obstacle to the effective implementation of the fifth option was the lack of enough credibility to ensure enforcement in operations under UN command and control. A reluctant consensus developed in favor of the fourth option, but with safeguards in addition to those already enumerated by the Secretary-General in his letter of November 29.

The nonaligned caucus in the Security Council was faced with a dilemma. They wanted to see a speedy humanitarian intervention in Somalia to save its starving people. At the same time, they were reluctant to turn over the operation to unified or coalition forces that would not be under UN command and control. The nonaligned caucus therefore took the lead in formulating proposals to make the operation more of a partnership between unified forces and the United Nations.

In sharp contrast to the Gulf operation, the United States and its allies also wished to proceed with the full support of the United Nations, partly because the objectives in Somalia were not strategic, but humanitarian. It was therefore comparatively easy to obtain agreement on proposals formulated by the nonaligned caucus. But Washington would not compromise about the commander of the unified forces, who had to be an American. This was not a major sticking point, since the nonaligned caucus readily agreed that the command and control of the military forces ought to lie with the United States. Its concern was to ensure that the political dimension would be the direct responsibility of the United Nations. This, they believed, could be ensured by highlighting the political role of the Secretary-General. This approach was acceptable to Washington. It formed the basis for the compromise resolution adopted unanimously by the Council as Resolution 794 (1992),[10] which led to the deployment of the Unified Task Force (UNITAF).

Conclusion

This chapter has discussed humanitarian intervention from a rather narrow perspective. Most commentators tend to consider gross violations of human rights among the grounds for justifying humanitarian intervention. Here, however, humanitarian intervention was justified on the basis that innocent civilians had been deliberately starved by the actions or inactions of belligerents. When evidence is overwhelming that people are dying because of the deliberate obstruction of humanitarian assistance, the international community has the obligation to intervene to assure that relief reaches the victims.

This narrow concept of humanitarian intervention is not directly linked to the pursuit of peaceful solutions to a political crisis, although that could be one of the beneficial outcomes of such an intervention. While there have been other examples defined by the media as instances of humanitarian intervention, Somalia has been isolated as the most credible example. Any Security Council decision to *enforce* an agreed solution should not be considered as a form of humanitarian intervention. Such actions should be seen, rather, as political intervention in the context of Chapter VII of the UN Charter. There is an important distinction between intervention and involvement. There also are many instances in which the United Nations and the international community could be involved or take part in finding solutions to crises that do not involve intervention in the legal sense. This distinction is important because popular commentary tends to use the words "intervention" and "involvement" almost interchangeably.

The appeal of the Secretary-General to the Security Council for intervention under Chapter VII of the Charter was based on the humanitarian needs of Somalis. The lack of a government complicated the delivery of humanitarian assistance. The failure to deliver such assistance quickly and effectively could have resulted in far greater human tragedy, and the Security Council agreed that humanitarian intervention was justified. U.S. involvement in Somalia was justified solely on the basis of humanitarian concerns. Presidents Bush and Clinton have made strenuous efforts to emphasize that the United States was not taking part in an enforcement measure in Somalia, and was not primarily responsible for brokering a political settlement. This reinforced the distinction previously made between purely humanitarian intervention and the search for peaceful settlements.

It is worthwhile to note the initial difference of views between the Secretary-General and Washington over the linkage between disarmament of the Somali warlords and the technicals, and the need to attain the "secure environment" called for by the Security Council in Resolution 794. This difference in perception is not necessarily linked to the process of achieving a peaceful settlement. Before the adoption of Resolution 794, the Security Council had given the Secretary-General a mandate to promote national reconciliation in Somalia. In a sense, the UN has two main objectives in Somalia: to ensure the delivery of humanitarian assistance for which intervention has become necessary, and to encourage Somalis to reach an agreement on national reconciliation that is not directly linked to humanitarian intervention.

The important question is to what extent humanitarian intervention hinders or helps the search for a political solution to the crisis in Somalia. The Secretary-General and perhaps the international community as a whole share the view that humanitarian intervention will resolve the issue of suffering and starvation by ensuring the delivery of relief supplies to the Somali people. Furthermore, it could indirectly weaken the ability of the warlords to use food as a weapon. To the extent that humanitarian intervention results in the disarmament of warlords and the technicals, it could weaken their grip on the Somali people and provide the basis for a broader search for a political solution, which could involve not only the warlords but also intellectuals, elders, women's groups, and other professional interests.

During the early months of 1993, a related question was whether the withdrawal of UNITAF would harm the UN's ability to deliver humanitarian assistance. This question weighed heavily on the Secretary-General and caused him to not move too quickly to the transition from UNITAF to a United Nations command. His aim remained to avoid a descent to the point that warranted humanitarian intervention in November 1992. In the intervening period, considerable progress was made. Common ground emerged between the Secretary-General and UNITAF on how to proceed to the transition, perhaps in phases.

There is considerable confidence that arrangements being worked out will not result in a deterioration of the situation, and that continued U.S. support will be assured. It is also possible that any new resolution of the Security Council that sanctions the transition will assure that UNOSOM II has the equivalent authority of UNITAF under Chapter VII of the Charter. There will also be enhanced efforts to establish a link between efforts to promote national reconciliation and peace to reconciliation and development, in order to reduce a recurrent need for humanitarian assistance. However, protracted and complicated negotiations are still required. No quick solution is expected.[11]

Humanitarian intervention in Somalia has also been used to begin creating viable institutions to maintain law and order and to contribute to national reconciliation. Attempts have been made to revive the local police force as the first building block to reestablish institutions needed for national reconciliation.

Impact on Sovereignty

The narrow basis that was used to justify humanitarian intervention in Somalia is essential. At the United Nations, developing countries remain extremely uneasy about the concept. Member states want to maintain the sanctity of sovereignty. In the case of Somalia, the use of food as a weapon and the ensuing human suffering persuaded member states that humanitarian intervention, which in essence violated sovereignty, was necessary. This decision was eased by the lack of a government and by the intensive and widespread media coverage of the tragic plight of the Somali people. Only in similar situations, which will be extremely rare, can one foresee the international community's violating the concept of sovereignty again. As the case of Bosnia demonstrates, violations of human rights by themselves will not be sufficient for the international community to violate the concept of sovereignty.[12]

The Future of Humanitarian Intervention

While a conceptual breakthrough has been made in efforts to promote humanitarian intervention, it is important to ask whether this represents a watershed. Many members of the Security Council, as well as outside commentators, have argued that Somalia represents a unique situation. People have noted its unique features: the absence of a government or local authorities, rampant banditry, the proliferation of weapons among bands of armed gangs, the criminal exploitation of starving people for profit, and the emotional response to the Somali tragedy throughout the world because of massive and graphic daily coverage by the media, particularly television. In a sense, Somalia should warrant total support for humanitarian intervention. The fact that hundreds of thousands had died of starvation and nearly a thousand more were perishing daily three months into the operation could not be tolerated.

However, Somalia also has raised a host of questions. What should be the duration of humanitarian intervention in such a situation? This issue has been bedeviled by the concern of the United States public and media to not become bogged down in a quagmire, as many believed happened in Vietnam. Is it enough, as stated in Resolution 794, that the unified forces will have completed their mission when "a secure environment for humanitarian relief operations" has been attained? In his letter of November 29, the Secretary-General noted the need to remove at least heavy weapons from Somalia. At what point should humanitarian intervention revert to a normal peacekeeping operation, which implies the consent and cooperation of local authorities, including warlords? The Security Council skirted this issue by giving the Secretary-General, in operative paragraph 6 of Resolution 794, wide discretion regarding the deployment of the peacekeeping forces previously authorized for Somalia.

Launching a humanitarian intervention operation in Somalia raised the question of a similar type of intervention in Bosnia-Herzegovina. The prevailing view is that Somalia's uniqueness limits any lessons for Bosnia. The operation in Somalia is considered militarily feasible and will not be overwhelmingly costly. In Bosnia the terrain is quite different, and a much larger force would be required. Even then the chances of success would be problematical. Moreover, the absence of a government does not apply to Bosnia.

In Bosnia the issue is not primarily starvation, but rather the massive violation of human rights through ethnic cleansing, systematic rape, and the like. For this reason it has proven more difficult to reach international consensus on the appropriate international response. The debate is largely over how to enforce decisions to prevent the violation of human rights, not over how to ensure the delivery of humanitarian assistance to prevent mass starvation. There is therefore great reluctance to undertake a Somali-type operation in Bosnia. While this would suggest that a lot more must be done to formulate a general global policy on humanitarian intervention, at least the Security Council has taken a formal decision in support of humanitarian intervention.

Notes

The views expressed in this chapter are those of the author and do not necessarily represent the position of the United Nations.

1. There is by now a large literature on the various dimensions of humanitarian intervention. A wide range of views can be found in the six articles on "The Use of Force in the Post–Cold War Era" in the *Denver Journal of International Law and Policy* 20 (Fall 1991) and in David J. Scheffer, Richard N. Gardner, and Gerald B. Helman, *Post–Gulf War Challenges to the U.N. Collective Security System: Three Views on the Issue of Humanitarian Intervention* (Washington, D.C.: United States Institute for Peace, 1992). For a particularly

skeptical view, see Stephen John Stedman, "The New Interventionists," *Foreign Affairs* 72, no. 1 (1992/1993): 1–16.

2. See Larry Minear et al., *Humanitarianism Under Siege: A Critical Review of Operation Lifeline Sudan* (Trenton: Red Sea Press, 1991).

3. See Thomas G. Weiss and Kurt M. Campbell, "Military Humanitarianism," *Survival* 33, no. 5 (September/October 1992): 451–465; and Larry Minear and Thomas G. Weiss, "Groping and Coping in the Gulf Crisis: Discovering the Shape of a New Humanitarian Order," *World Policy Journal* 9, no. 4 (Fall/Winter 1992–1993): 755–788.

4. General Assembly Resolution 46/182.

5. United Nations document S/23445/February 20, 1992.

6. United Nations document S/24480/August 24, 1992.

7. United Nations document S/24480/July 22, 1992.

8. See *Reuters* report, September 20, 1992, "Trusteeship Needed in Somalia, British MP Says." The interested reader is also referred to Gerald B. Helman and Steven R. Ratner, "Saving Failed States," *Foreign Policy* 89 (Winter 1992–1993): 3–20.

9. The Paris Accords, which specify the role of the United Nations, can be found in document A/46/608 - S/23177/October 30, 1991.

10. For a review of developments in Somalia following the adoption of Security Council Resolution 794, see the most recent report of the Secretary-General to the Security Council contained in document S/25168/January 26, 1993.

11. The informal preparatory meeting on national reconciliation held in Addis Ababa in January 1993 achieved a measure of success, but the ad hoc committee established at that meeting by the Somali factions in attendance has not reached agreement on issues assigned to it by the Addis Ababa meeting. The ad hoc committee failed to resolve the issue of broader participation or the agenda of the meeting on national reconciliation to take place in mid-March in Addis Ababa.

12. For the views of the Secretary-General on the evolution of sovereignty, see Boutros Boutros-Ghali, "Empowering the United Nations," *Foreign Affairs* 71, no. 5 (Winter 1992/93): esp. 98–99.

■ 5 ■
Armed Relief

JOHN MACKINLAY

In 1989, while the consequences of glasnost were taking effect in the Security Council and increasing the effectiveness of the United Nations, few international lawyers, military officers, and UN officials believed that human suffering on its own would become the basis for intervention. Even fewer supported the use of military forces to protect humanitarian relief convoys.

However, in the next three years, multinational forces under the UN were deployed to northern Iraq, Bosnia, Somalia, and Cambodia with a variety of humanitarian support tasks. This unexpected surge of activity softened the previously hostile public attitude toward military participation in humanitarian relief and helped define a more practical role to allow these forces to use their capabilities. But it also compelled the military to work closely with some reluctant partners among international and nongovernmental relief agencies. The mutual gap in cultures and perceptions diminished the effectiveness of international humanitarian efforts and, above all, cost lives.

This chapter urges a common approach to the use of military assistance to protect future humanitarian operations. The role of the military as relief convoy protectors must be defined, and should lead to a code of conduct for the use of force in these special circumstances. There is also a critical need for a global network of training centers where staff from UN agencies, NGOs, and the military can study this common approach and overcome mutual antipathy.

Cold War Skepticism

The cultural baggage of Vietnam[1] and the negative aspects of the massive armies that characterized the Cold War created an ugly stereotype of the military. Its image was that of a monolithic organization with dumb, brutalized conscripts, particularly in the minds of the humanitarian relief community. This was especially true in the United States, where a number of officials had started careers with relief and development agencies in the 1960s as an alternative to conscription. Through their involvement in Third World conflicts, they were exposed to armies that lived up to their worst expectations of the ugly military. The possibility of using military force to assist in the delivery of humanitarian relief was viewed in these circles with disquiet.

This intuitive feeling of hostility was pointedly expressed at a conference held at Niinsalo, Finland, in October 1989, attended by relief officials and military officers. The summary of discussions noted that only "the most dramatic expansion of tasks would include the use of military force to ensure that disaster relief arrives in affected regions. Unless there was a remarkable provocation and an equally unusual degree of consensus among governments, intervention would be highly unlikely."[2]

In addition to the negative attitudes from the humanitarian community, there were practical reasons why, in many instances, military assistance was a bad option. Even military presence was an unwelcome impediment. Intergovernmental and nongovernmental relief officials found their long-standing impartial status and credibility with local armed factions beginning to erode because of their association with an outside military force, even of foreign troops manifestly concerned only with assisting relief work.[3] Negotiating the conditions of relief delivery became more difficult, as motives became suspect and relationships with local factions became adversarial.

In financial terms, foreign military assistance was costly. Their land, sea, and air transport systems were too sophisticated for the simple task of relief delivery. Military pilots and crews, although highly skilled, insisted on rigorous servicing and safety standards, which sometimes worked at cross purposes with delivery plans. Sustaining military relief operations in a hand-to-mouth economy caused local inflation and food shortages that extended well beyond immediate relief targets. In cases where military logistics were used for relief purposes, aid workers complained of overkill.

For example, the delivery of large quantities of culturally or nutritionally unsuitable field rations tended to create rather than solve problems. Drugs administered in good faith by army medics interfered with the priorities of local medical authorities, and when the supply was stopped, it left patients without natural resistance or with the prospect of completing the treatment with an appropriate alternative medication. In the longer process of recovery, the military provision of temporary accommodation and field supply of power and water to local communities tended to retard incentives for local authorities to restore their own facilities. Moreover, the use of local labor in the process of restoration had a therapeutic and training benefit that was overlooked by military planners who preferred to use their own engineers and technicians.

Because of its transitory presence, the military often lacked the local knowledge needed to plan and distribute relief effectively. In short tours of duty military officials were unlikely to develop the necessary depth of contact and experience to overcome this problem. Their outlook and professional training did not equip them to assess overall relief needs in depth. Relief organizations needed to analyze relief needs, assess the most vulnerable locations, and develop a relief plan identifying appropriate food, shelter, and medical support. This required expertise outside of the military, in the international humanitarian community.

Learning from Experience

Three years after the harsh judgments at Niinsalo, it is now possible to detect a change in attitude toward military involvement in humanitarian relief. This turnaround should be seen in the context of a vast change in global politics and security structures after the Cold War, which has been discussed in this book and elsewhere.[4] The collapse of the Soviet empire released a surge of violent energy among multiethnic states in its former republics and throughout the Third World. The resulting conflicts tore apart integrated communities and caused widespread population movements. An estimated eighteen million new refugees and internally displaced people were recorded in 1992. At the same time, growing international confidence in the UN encouraged the Security Council to act more boldly in dealing with internal conflict. Humanitarian imperatives became the overriding cause for action.[5] An unprecedented number of interventions took place, in which the military's help with security, logistic support, and convoy protection was an essential factor in the overall humanitarian responses.

Turkey/Northern Iraq 1991
Of the estimated 1.7 million Kurds who fled Saddam Hussein's anticipated reprisal in the spring of 1991, four to five hundred thousand headed north to the Turkish border. The swiftness of their exodus, their inaccessible assembly sites on the border, and hostile weather turned their sudden arrival into a huge and abrupt disaster. The situation developed so quickly that the humanitarian relief community was unable to organize a response before large numbers of Kurdish refugees began to die. Using an existing NATO infrastructure, marine battalions from the United Kingdom, France, Italy, Netherlands, and Spain were organized with the U.S. Marine Corps under a U.S. command system reconstituted from NATO assets held in Europe. Having established a relief and rehabilitation plan with the Turkish authorities, they were able to respond so swiftly that by the time civilian agencies, especially the UN, had mobilized it was almost over and there was no sense in changing the management structure.[6]

Croatia-Bosnia 1992
After fighting spread to Bosnia-Herzegovina, access to Sarajevo and other besieged cities became difficult. Security Council Resolution 776 extended the existing peacekeeping operation's (UNPROFOR) mandate beyond

monitoring the original peace process to supporting and protecting humanitarian relief activities. This was spearheaded by the UN High Commissioner for Refugees (UNHCR). In Ms. Ogata's own words:

> Meeting these emergency needs UNHCR has had to turn to the military especially for logistic support. . . . UNHCR's airlift operation and land convoy system are provided to a considerable extent by military teams from donor governments. Working under UNHCR supervision as part of a civilian humanitarian effort, they have made a crucial contribution to saving the lives of thousands of displaced people. The airlift to Sarajevo in particular has attained a symbolic value far beyond the mere distribution of relief. . . . Security conditions on the ground left us with little choice and we have had to receive military protection for our convoys.[7]

Cambodia 1992

Although the cease-fire between the warring factions has been "more honour'd in the breach than the observance," there is nevertheless a workable level of security in the 95 percent of Cambodia still held by the former government or Cambodian People's Armed Forces (CPAF) troops. The unique characteristic of the United Nations Transitional Authority in Cambodia (UNTAC) in its postdisarmament phase is the vast range of its civil responsibilities. These include the interim administration of provinces, protection of civil rights, rehabilitation, and the oversight of government departments and the civil police. In this phase the military plays a largely subordinate role. Its primary role has been to organize and train the embryo structure of civilian mine clearance teams, restore essential links in the national road system, and provide an element of security for national elections. Moreover, military UN logistics provide a vital structure for the day-to-day functioning of the peace process. Officials and election staff move freely in the remote areas using UN military communications and local transport by air, land, and internal waterways. Military logistics provide power, water, and medical cover for the remotely deployed UN civil agencies.[8]

Somalia 1992

Against the background of a total breakdown of law and order, about twenty-two thousand U.S. armed forces were deployed to several base areas in Somalia with another ten thousand composite multinational contingents, including units from the NATO, African, and Pacific regions. Before their arrival, local warlords had withheld relief supplies of food as a weapon to reinforce or extend their territorial influence and secure their local position. The task of the Unified Task Force (UNITAF) has been to intervene and create conditions for the uninterrupted delivery of relief supplies. Although the initial phase has been successful and supplies have been resumed in most areas, it remains to be seen to what extent the problem has become manageable over the long term.

Finding a New-Era Image

The highly visible manner in which this body of recent experience was presented to the public challenged the negative Cold War stereotype of the military and suggested the need for a reappraisal of military capabilities. Except in Cambodia, the media attention, or CNN factor, that caused politicians to respond to the tragedies of 1991–1992 continued to deliver a blow-by-blow account as the relief process began to unfold on the ground. Public opinion in the troop-contributing countries grew more supportive of the UN and more appreciative of military participation. Apart from minor abuses that accompany a large and variously disciplined body of troops, the military element in these operations generally behaved well.

Incidents such as the well-orchestrated NGO protest in Phnom Penh against sexual harassment by UN soldiers in restaurants[9] have been overshadowed by good publicity and a general sense of appreciation. For Ms. Ogata, a significant development from this period has been "the increasing collaborative relationship between the humanitarian and the military [in which] UNHCR has had to turn to the military especially for logistic support."[10] The Cold War image of the military as an ugly monolith was being gently replaced by a more realistic appreciation of modern professional armies and their capabilities, which have gradually become the norm in peace-support operations.

At the most senior level of the military and humanitarian connection, relations have worked quite smoothly. Interviews with senior executives in the humanitarian relief community tend to indicate a warmer attitude toward military participation.[11] But at lower levels and in the field, there is still a frisson of suspicion and rivalry, particularly among older relief officials whose formative experiences date from the Cold War period. They found military units inflexible, junior staff unresponsive to requests for assistance, and the decisionmaking hierarchy hard to penetrate.

For their part, military headquarters and host governments sometimes were exasperated by the unprofessionalism of many relief agencies. In the case of Turkey, government officials were overwhelmed by the arrival, in most cases too late, of over two hundred NGOs and agencies. Only a tiny number of the estimated ten to eleven thousand relief workers who found their way to the border area could communicate with local Turkish officials. Some behaved with unforgivable arrogance toward local authorities and Turkish relief staff.[12] Not many were self-sufficient in logistics, transport, or internal radio communications; they demanded the use of these, as a right, from NATO military units. This behavior prompted the widespread response that in future large joint ventures, emergency relief personnel must be fewer and better qualified.[13] Some agency officials said the military interfered with their "humanitarian space" and that it was preferable to discontinue their relief function rather than invite the problems of military protection.

The mutual aversion and misunderstanding between humanitarian relief workers and military officers in the field acted against a well-conducted relief effort. In many cases, substantive, if petty, reasons justified feelings of frustration on both sides. But in a group of like-minded operators striving to achieve a common purpose, these minor irritations should have been firmly set aside, and a more sincere effort should have been made to accommodate the idiosyncratic behavior of ill-suited partners in the interests of making the international effort succeed. However, in relief operations where external humanitarians—civilian and military alike—came burdened with a sense of rivalry and mutual disaffection, tiny infractions became enlarged, and even turned into reasons for withdrawing cooperation.

Defining a Humanitarian Role for Military Forces

In spite of friction in the field, at the national and international levels the military has been fortunate in its experiences with interagency rivalries. Each of the case studies, except Cambodia, has had such a compelling reason for military assistance that the military's presence, tasks, and role in coordination have been largely accepted. Although its relationships with the other components have varied, in each case the imperative for security gave the military an overriding position. The central question, eloquently posed by Ms. Ogata, is: "Should military protection of humanitarian convoys be regarded as a temporary aberration, or should new codes of behavior be established to ensure ways of military activities in accordance with humanitarian principles and practice?"[14]

The answer is twofold. One hopes that the heavy demand for military protection and involvement in relief delivery is temporary. In the longer term the civilian expertise of UN agencies and NGOs on humanitarian matters, vastly superior to the military's, once again will predominate in emergencies. But in contemplating the landscape of global violence today and its development in the immediate future, further requirements for external military assistance seem likely. Although a code of behavior is essential, a more immediate priority is for the military to define its role in humanitarian relief operations and establish how it should relate to the other components in the matrix of humanitarian relief.

In considering cases of humanitarian relief, the familiar matrix of host country/UN agencies/NGOs must now be enlarged to include military assistance. Although each component will maintain its own mandates and operational styles, thereby creating a tension with the other three, they must all work together if the international response is to produce the best result for the victims. Recent field experience shows they may follow selfish interests in some cases, to the detriment of the mission.

The host government, if there is one, is usually concerned with maintaining its sovereignty. This will be threatened by the demand for free movement of third-party ships, aircraft, vehicles, and media in large numbers.

Some have agendas oriented more toward donor or sponsor constituencies than toward the plight of victims. They demand intrusive access to the most sensitive areas and issues. And the host government may also have its own, sometimes adversarial relationship with the disaster victims.

The tug-of-war between UN agencies and NGOs usually revolves around who should coordinate the relief plan during hostilities, decide on priorities, and stipulate who is to do what. The preeminent UN organization, or lead agency, will strive to achieve the role of coordinator by establishing a partnership with the host government and sometimes with the armed opposition. NGOs will often seek to exercise their independence, at times challenging the guidelines of the overall plan, to establish their own areas of responsibility; some have better relations with the armed opposition than with the government.

The military are naive newcomers to this otherwise familiar mix of internecine institutional rivalry. With assured funding and deployed in what is for them a low-priority role, they have less at stake. Their selfish interests usually focus on maintaining the integrity of their command structure, the security of military personnel, and the efficient use of their equipment. They will be reluctant to relinquish control of their assets on a piecemeal basis, even for an obvious task. They will avoid unconditional subordination in an assistance role, particularly if this would expose them to what they would regard as unreasonable demands by humanitarian agencies or a host government.

An examination of recent cases, while limited, suggests that the unchallenged role of the military is to protect relief operations but not to become involved in distribution. In Turkey's hostile terrain, bad weather and speed of delivery favored a military coordinating structure in addition to its protective role. In Bosnia, where local infrastructures are more developed, the problem concerns military protection; there, setting priorities and coordinating relief is a matter for the UN lead agency, UNHCR. In all cases there is a real need for both the military itself to be clear about its precise role in the matrix of actors, and for the other institutions to accept it in that function. Its role would fall into three levels or categories: national security, local security, and emergency logistics.

National Level Security
The strategic delivery of humanitarian relief supplies relies on a host nation having secure and serviceable ports and air terminals. In some cases this will require securing their approaches and, if possible, protecting civil transport from standoff attacks by portable surface-to-air missiles and heavy weapons. Some ports and airfields will need to be improved or even upgraded to receive unusually high tonnage over a short period of time. Effective traffic control and the management of cargo handling and unloading facilities will be essential factors in a successful buildup of assets for relief. The security of

the approaches to these national installations is a sophisticated military function that may involve the presence and coordination of combat aircraft and warships. Where hostile missiles and heavy weapons systems threaten sea lanes and air corridors, some form of electronic direction-finding capability will be essential. Unless selected items of strategic intelligence are released to the military protection force, it may become impossible to provide reliable early warning of impending attacks and the position and capability of hostile weapon systems.

Local Security

After the strategic lift is safely completed, cargoes need to be marshaled into a secure storage area before being redistributed for local delivery. Military assistance may be needed for the security of these areas. The protection of convoys will be the most demanding and hazardous task for the military. In a long-standing war zone where weapons have become widely distributed among factions and the local population, food convoys will be the prey of a diverse range of potential looters. Their motives may be military, political, or purely venal. Individuals, local gangs, and elements of the armed factions will challenge convoys by using mines, overt roadblocks, ambushes, sniper fire, and vicarious standoff attacks from long-range weapons. Sometimes there may be no motive for an attack except aggressive display. Military engineers and ordnance disposal experts will be needed to maintain and improve roads and bridges and to disable mines. The protection of VIPs and UN personnel traveling on duty will also be a time-consuming military task.

Emergency Logistics

In countries that have an inherently weak infrastructure or in cases where vital installations have been neglected or destroyed, emergency logistic support may be provided by outside military forces. This is not primarily for the victim community, but to allow the effective functioning of the relief agencies. Support may include: communications; local transport by air, land, and internal waterways; heavy lift equipment; freight handling facilities; shelter; field power systems; and potable water.

Using Force

With a few exceptions, the military can be lumped together in its general acceptance of the fairly obvious protection role that has emerged from recent experience. If protection becomes a sine qua non for the continuation of relief, in the matrix of actors the military has an unchallenged capability. The delineation of a military role that sits comfortably with other institutions should be relatively straightforward, but it leads at once to a much tougher problem. In the execution of their tasks at national and local levels, military assistance units in their protection role are likely to be challenged. An effective response is crucial to their continued success and credibility. How the members of future military protection forces interpret their role is complicated, and has a direct bearing on their acceptability to other actors in the matrix.

Two different approaches seem to be emerging. The defense forces of Europe and the doctrinally similar armies of the British Commonwealth approach the question from a long background of operating with the consent of a substantial element of the local population. In a small way this may be due to domestic influences of national law that proscribe carrying personal weapons and curtail the right to self-protection by force of arms. More significantly, it is influenced by postwar military experience either as peacekeepers in UN forces or in counterinsurgency.

The benefit of fostering substantial local consent to their presence and role was that they did not have to utilize the larger force levels needed in a more substantially opposed, worst-case scenario. In the past, when faced in a third-party peacekeeping role with a major opposition, they would withdraw. The net effect of this concept is that these armies have, in spite of some notable aberrations, developed a concept of operations that is largely geared to winning and sustaining the element of consent. This involves a constrained approach to using force. Tough measures and the actual use of weapons are preceded by an escalating series of warnings and negotiations. In their view, the use of firearms has had a very short-term benefit, and the price for shooting it out is usually paid in the long term by those who have to continue to operate in the areas disaffected by a violent military response.

The other approach comes from nations where it is more common to carry and use weapons for personal protection in the home. More significantly, these nations may not have had much military experience of peacekeeping or low-level counterinsurgency. The limitation of operating with consent from the local population and the effort needed to sustain that consent play a smaller part in contingency planning. On the ground, troops tend to get tougher quicker. Firing for effect is a more frequent option, and results seem to be immediately satisfying and effective. Continuing to operate in the same locality on a long-term basis can become more dangerous for the unprotected members of humanitarian agencies and government. Relations with belligerents become adversarial and security becomes a nationwide problem.

Although elements from both camps have participated successfully together in peacekeeping forces, the UN has never faced the problem of merging the two opposed concepts into a single doctrine. In the past peacekeeping did not often require the use of force except in isolated incidents. The military lessons from the Congo, if there were any at all, did not manifest themselves as part of a UN doctrine. In Lebanon and to some extent in Cambodia, where the use of force is also prevalent, the UN has avoided standardization by tacitly condoning a federal approach.[15] Within its own area of operations, each battalion carries the weapons it deems necessary for the task. Sometimes these are different. For example, battalion A, deploying with medium mortars and armored vehicles, may be next to battalion B, which is deployed only with sidearms. Recently in Somalia and Bosnia, where force has been used frequently, the clash of doctrines to some extent has been postponed by the fortuitous grouping of European contingents in Bosnia and the U.S.-led force in Somalia.[16] Nevertheless, tensions have surfaced at the U.S. proposals to use air power to enforce the Bosnian no-fly zone.

Among battalions, and in spite of UN standard operating procedures, reactions vary, and some battalions return fire more readily than others. So far the loose federation of opposed doctrines operating together within the same force has not caused a serious reversal of a UN peace process. But in the future, particularly in the protection of humanitarian relief where military forces are certain to be challenged, the effects may be more damaging. The actors in the matrix must know from which camp their military partners come, because their approaches to using force and fostering consent from belligerents may have consequences for civilian humanitarians.

Preparing for the Future

If military protection of relief operations is becoming a more likely contingency, there is now a requirement for military staff and their relief partners to prepare themselves for joint operations in the next generation of international military operations.[17] It would greatly improve the chances of reducing interagency rivalry and misunderstanding at the highest levels if the governments that regularly provide this type of military assistance could agree on a universally accepted definition of the military's role. They should take care to develop their manifesto within the realistic margins of relief protection, as outlined above. Experience and military limitations show that this role should not extend into the aspects of planning and distribution in which NGOs and UN agencies are preeminent.

After establishing a role, there is need for a doctrine of implementation. The UN and the humanitarian relief community will have to reconcile, in a workable and common approach, the varying national concepts for the use of force. The code of conduct that emerges from this process must take account of legal and ethical factors, as well as the wide divergence of views between the humanitarian relief community and the military. Within the military itself there will be at least two different schools of thought. The whole process of development is sure to take some time. Some thought is required for an interim formula that provides the pragmatic basis for a working relationship, but recognizes the need for a more effective long-term solution. Once a code emerges, it should be recognized, promulgated, and continuously reviewed by the UN at the highest level.

However successful the code of conduct, there will remain cultural differences between the military and humanitarian relief institutions. These will continue to degrade and disable the best-planned operations. The narrowly experienced professional military officer with his authoritarian sense of institutional priorities will continue to conflict with relief workers who, having perhaps spent months or years working in the host country before the military arrival, may feel a sense of turf invasion. This rivalry is exacerbated at a more senior level when civilian officials and military officers are thrown together in crisis for the first time and may not at first develop a workable modus operandi or personal relationships.

There is an obvious need for a common approach and a greater sense of community among players in future relief operations. The development of a code of conduct that delineates the responsibility of the primary agencies is essential. Study of this approach at international or UN training centers would erode cultural and professional differences and develop a much stronger sense of community among humanitarians, military or civilian. Military staff, UN agencies, NGOs, and government officials must study and map out a common code of conduct. In the more relaxed circumstances of a training exercise, they could iron out differences. Multidisciplinary training centers are needed, where the idiosyncratic approaches of different institutions can be reconciled, and where lessons from recent experience also can be captured. Developing relationships at these centers and learning the culture of other important actors will provide students—who in reality are the technicians and decisionmakers in future crises—with experiences to counteract adversarial attitudes in operations. An international alumni may emerge to overcome at least some of the fundamental problems that beset relief workers and their relationships with an assisting military force.

Notes

1. See Richard A. Melanson, *Reconstructing Consensus: American Foreign Policy Since the Vietnam War* (New York: St. Martin's, 1991), and *"This Will Not Be Another Vietnam": George Bush and the Persian Gulf War* (Providence: Watson Institute Occasional Paper no. 9, 1992).

2. Leon Gordenker and Thomas G. Weiss (eds.), *Soldiers, Peacekeepers and Disasters* (London: Macmillan, 1991): 7. The general subject matter also appeared in an earlier volume; see Thomas G. Weiss (ed.), *Humanitarian Emergencies and Military Help in Africa* (London: Macmillan, 1990).

3. Gordenker and Weiss, *Soldiers*, 11.

4. See Thomas G. Weiss (ed.), *Collective Security in a Changing World* (Boulder: Lynne Rienner, 1993); and Thomas G. Weiss and Meryl A. Kessler (eds.), *Third World Security in the Post–Cold War Era* (Boulder: Lynne Rienner, 1991).

5. Sadako Ogata, "Refugees and World Peace," speech delivered at United Nations University at the ICRA/ACUNS Symposium, Tokyo, January 7, 1993, 4; Christopher Greenwood, "Is There a Right of Human Intervention?" *World Today* 49, no. 2 (February 1993): 39.

6. This account is derived from the unpublished version of Franca Brilliant,

Frederick C. Cuny, and Victor Tanner, "Operation Provide Comfort: A Study of Lessons Learned for the Office of Foreign Disaster Assistance and US Army Civil Affairs."

7. Ogata, "Refugees and World Peace," 13.

8. See Jarat Chopra, John Mackinlay, and Larry Minear, *United Nations Authority in Cambodia* (unpublished Watson Institute paper).

9. *Phnom Penh Post*, October 11, 1992, 2 and 12.

10. Ogata, "Refugees and World Peace," 12.

11. In addition to speeches like Ms. Ogata's, the author found a degree of unanimity on this question in his field work following the Kurdish crisis in Ankara and Teheran among senior officials from UNDP, JUSMAT, and the relevant foreign ministries of Turkey and Iran.

12. Interview with a senior official in the Department of International and Economic Organizations, Ministry of Foreign Affairs, Ankara, May 22, 1992.

13. Brilliant, Cuny, and Tanner, "Operation Provide Comfort," 37. This was also a major theme in Larry Minear, U.B.P. Chelliah, Jeff Crisp, John Mackinlay, and Thomas G. Weiss, *United Nations Coordination of the International Humanitarian Response to the Gulf Crisis, 1990–92* (Providence: Watson Institute Occasional Paper no. 13, 1992); and Larry Minear and Thomas G. Weiss, "Groping and Coping in the Gulf Crisis: Discerning the Shape of a New Humanitarian Order," *World Policy Journal*, 9, no. 4 (Fall/Winter 1992–93): 755–788. See also R. M. Connaughton, "OP Haven—Some Thoughts and Lessons," UK Ministry of Defense, internal report, August 1, 1991.

14. Ogata, "Refugees and World Peace," 14.

15. Different approaches are referred to in Connaughton, "OP Haven," 17: "Rules of Engagement. These were also different but sufficiently harmonized not to be of major concern. The British rules were less aggressive than the American."

16. "Boy's Death in Somalia Tests Uneasy US Role," *New York Times*, February 20, 1993, p. 1. This report explores the problem of overreaction by the U.S. Marine Corps in Somalia and cites several fatal shootings that resulted.

17. Humanitarian contingencies are one of many such challenges. See John Mackinlay and Jarat Chopra, "Second Generation Multinational Operations," *Washington Quarterly* 15, no. 3 (Summer 1992): 113–131; and *A Concept for Second Generation Multinational Operations 1993* (Providence: Watson Institute Occasional Paper no. 15, 1993).

■ 6 ■

Relief Operations and
Military Strategy

GAYLE E. SMITH

The world has witnessed in recent years a dramatic increase in disasters affecting developing countries. In most cases, armed conflict caused sufficient human dislocation to warrant an international response. At the same time, armed conflict impedes delivery of assistance, and humanitarian aid can be simultaneously a tool of war and an object of war.

The response of the international community to disasters linked to armed conflict has been diverse. In southern Sudan, for example, the UNICEF-led Operation Lifeline Sudan provides assistance in insurgent-held areas of the country with the approval of the Khartoum government. The failure of the former Ethiopian government to acknowledge the existence of insurgent-held areas during that country's famine in 1984–1985 led to crossborder operations from the Sudan into guerrilla-held areas of Ethiopia. In northern Iraq, the former Yugoslavia, and Somalia, the collision of war and human need has resulted in the deployment of military forces to protect humanitarian efforts.

The response of the international community mostly has been inadequate. In many cases, the immediate relief needs have been met, but then the need for humanitarian intervention has often reemerged. In these cases, either the original conflict continued or the fundamental economic problems underlying the disaster were not solved. In few cases, if any, has a humanitarian response contributed to resolution of the conflict or the demilitarization of the disaster zone. Few international relief operations have increased local civilian capacity to manage disasters and hold contending armies accountable.

This chapter argues that relief practitioners should study military strategy and then plan their interventions to prevent the intersection between conflict and relief work from exacerbating the plight of civilians. The increasing use of military forces to protect relief workers in conflict-born disasters, and the use of a "humanitarian protection force" in Somalia, may be appropriate, given the prevailing circumstances. The increasing use of military forces to administer or protect relief programs also points to the inability of the international relief system to cope with human crises in the midst of conflict.

Most major human disasters unfolding now are accompanied by conflict. Any effective relief intervention must acknowledge this from the outset. If not, the relief system will fail, and no alternative will remain but to increase the use of weaponry. Military forces have advantages in these cases, such as a distinctive logistical capacity and the ability to hold warring parties accountable (by increasing the incidence of force). But the international relief system also can increase its ability to provide logistical support and promote greater accountability.

A prerequisite to improving the international aid community's management of conflict-born disasters is coordination. Relief agencies frequently fail to work in tandem, but instead compete for resources and responsibility. The various agencies of the international humanitarian community will become effective only when they abandon the pretense of cooperation for an acknowledgment of their differences and a willingness to collaborate.

Neutrality and Evenhandedness

The principles of humanitarianism require unobstructed loyalty to civilian populations and political impartiality. These goals are often translated to mean that international aid providers must remain neutral in an armed conflict. The desire for neutrality often is the impetus for assuming a nonpolitical role.

While external aid providers should not take partisan political stands (except, perhaps, in extreme cases such as Nazi Germany and Khmer Rouge Cambodia), providing aid in a conflict is, in its impact and implications, an extremely political act. If the political environment surrounding humanitarian operations is disregarded, there is a high risk that relief work by outsiders will intensify conflict or fall victim to manipulation by one or more parties to the conflict. Neither is in the interests of the civilian populations to which the international humanitarian community is responsible.

If effective humanitarian responses are to be achieved, external interventions, particularly those that bring food or other necessities of survival, will directly affect the balance of power in the conflict. As such, genuine neutrality cannot be achieved if neutrality is interpreted to mean noninvolvement. What can be achieved is an informed intervention that, if carefully designed and undertaken, can result in fairness and balance. The shift in thinking—and in the identification of goals—from neutrality to balance is crucial to the success of future humanitarian work in armed conflicts. For this shift to take place, it is necessary to understand that humanitarian principles are rarely, if ever, the priority of the parties to a conflict.

Although the recent human crises in Sudan, Ethiopia, and the Gulf have triggered an international debate on the issue of food as a weapon, the denial or provision of sustenance to civilians has been a tactic of war for centuries. While this phrase has gained currency in recent years, food is rarely a weapon. Instead, it is a tool that contending armies use to influence the balance of power. Hunger is the weapon; the provision of food to counter hunger is a means of gaining support. The seminal writings of Sun Tzu in *The Art of War*, written almost three thousand years ago, point to the deliberate use of food to achieve military victory. Military theorists have studied the gains to be made by employing sieges or blockades against populations loyal to the enemy.

More recent history points to other significant examples. During the Israeli invasion of Beirut in 1982, the distribution of food, water, and other relief goods in the besieged city was blocked by the Israeli Defense Forces (IDF). In an unpublished study of the use of food as a weapon conducted for Bread for the World, Research Director Marc Cohen points to many examples, among them the denial, by President Herbert Hoover, of food to areas of Hungary under Communist control in the early part of this century, and the use of hunger as a weapon of control by the Indonesian military in East Timor in 1979.

Cambodia provides a striking example of the manipulation of humanitarian assistance by a party to conflict. The Khmer Rouge reestablished itself with the help of resources provided by the international community that had been intended for civilian victims of the Vietnamese invasion and famine that followed. The former Mengistu government of Ethiopia used relief aid to lure civilians into government-held areas from guerrilla zones, and it restricted the flow of aid into rural areas administered by the opposition.

Contending armies and donor governments have used and will continue to use food and other types of relief as political and military tools. The U.S. Food for Peace program was designed not to alleviate world hunger, but to gain influence and reduce U.S. agricultural surpluses. President Carter imposed a grain embargo against the Soviet Union in retaliation for its invasion of Afghanistan. The Reagan administration provided relief to the Ethiopian regime in 1984–1985 after deliberately withholding it until severe famine conditions ensured that the aid would have the greatest political influence over Mengistu. In Somalia—clearly today's most extreme example—relief supplies have become the currency of an internal conflict.

Many of the world's aid providers, including NGOs, are neither bound nor guided by a desire to exert political influence by providing humanitarian assistance. Despite a genuine humanitarian intent, they are vulnerable to becoming enmeshed in the use of food as a weapon. Their assistance can—and often will—be used as an instrument to achieve political and military ends by belligerents. They also run the risk of being used as instruments for political influence by "backdonors," such as bilateral government agencies that want to influence the balance of power through the use of humanitarian assistance.

These stark realities do not mean that NGOs cannot achieve their goals of loyalty to civilians or political impartiality. However, NGOs and other external aid providers must recognize that any form of intervention in a conflict will have a political impact and will affect the balance of power. While they may be able to profess humanitarian intent, no external body providing assistance in an armed conflict can claim neutrality. To do so is to deny the political environment in which aid operations are undertaken.

What can be achieved is evenhandedness, defined as follows by Peter Davies, the former executive director of the U.S. NGO consortium InterAction: "to provide assistance in such a manner that none of the parties to conflict is able to accrue undue military advantage." While evenhandedness can help reduce the exploitation of humanitarian assistance, it can also help aid providers engage in dialogue with warring parties. Agencies that can demonstrate that they are providing equal access to all civilians can argue humanitarian principles with far greater credibility than can an agency pursuing a biased approach.

Achieving evenhandedness requires that the international community undertake several deliberate steps in forming and applying relief responses in armed conflicts. These include:

1. effective coordination with a view to a division of labor;
2. the analysis of links between the emergency, the conflict, and the prevailing economic situation;
3. an analysis of military strategies and possible connections between those strategies and provision of external assistance; and
4. specialized training in how to operate in armed conflict.

While emergency assistance can be used for political or military manipulation, it also can be used to mitigate conflict and to stabilize underlying economic disruptions. A corollary to resisting the manipulation of aid for military advantage is a goal of promoting stabilization and easing conflict. For many humanitarian aid providers, this may be perceived as an overtly political and inappropriate form of intervention. But if aid providers assume that their role is to treat the manifestations of human emergencies as well as the causes, then mitigating conflict is a laudable goal.

Finally, there are limitations to striving for evenhandedness in such cases as Somalia, Bosnia, Sudan, and Ethiopia. In places like these, sustained relief can prolong conflict, or unbiased actions can risk maintaining conditions that led to the original conflict. These critical considerations underscore the need for international relief practitioners to confront the political environment where they operate. Where evenhandedness may sustain conflict, it is necessary to make a political determination based upon a humanitarian goal. Means of evaluating such decisions are addressed later in the chapter.

Division of Labor

In most disasters caused by conflicts, aid becomes overtly politicized at two levels. On the ground, belligerents employ the assistance received (or not received) for their political and military ends. At the level of the international community, allocation of assistance often is determined by political imperatives.

Each of the three tiers of the international aid system responds in a different manner. Most of today's conflicts are not state-to-state, as was the case during much of the post–World War II era, but are internal. The United Nations is occasionally restricted from applying equal standards to the parties to a conflict. The structure of the UN requires it to respond to the needs articulated by member governments that, in many conflicts, are a party to that conflict. This structural bias toward the state may mean that UN operational agencies cannot enter nongovernment-held areas of the disaster zone, as in Ethiopia in 1984–1985. In other cases, it may mean that the UN must create an alternative approach acceptable to the host government at war, as in the case of Operation Lifeline Sudan. In all cases, it means that the UN is restricted in its attempts to operate impartially.

The second tier, bilateral aid agencies, often responds to emergencies on the basis of foreign policy objectives. This tendency is reinforced in armed conflicts where the donor government is likely to have a political position on the war itself. This may mean that assistance is provided in an unbalanced fashion; civilians on one side of the battle lines may be favored over civilians on the other side simply because the donor government wants one side to gain military and political advantage.

The NGO community, the third tier, is least likely to be impeded by the politicization of aid. Unrestricted by mandate and unfettered by foreign policy goals, NGOs can and do provide the most impartial channel of aid. However, the NGO community is hindered by a number of factors. It has far less influence than its larger and more powerful counterparts within the international aid community. In some cases, NGOs depend on politically motivated bilateral donors for assistance. The NGO community is uncoordinated, both in policy and operations, and has little understanding of or training in the realities of war.

In an ideal scenario, the international response to conflict-based disasters would be based on a deliberate division of labor. The UN would respond in the areas and in the fashion dictated by its mandate. Bilateral aid agencies would respond according to governmental policy imperatives. The NGO community, with its greater flexibility, would fill the gaps. Coordination would be undertaken jointly by the three tiers, but not centralized solely through the UN. This sort of "response mapping" could help ensure that all civilians—whether they live in government- or opposition-held areas—received equal access to assistance. In many cases, including Southeast Asia,

Sudan, and Ethiopia, this division of labor was done in an ad hoc manner. Civilians did not receive equal access, and thousands, if not millions, may have died unnecessarily.

Linking Cause and Effect

Linkage is the second area that needs greater analysis. Disasters arising from conflicts have visible roots in those conflicts. In the Third World, both disasters and conflicts often are rooted in economics. As Fred Cuny[1] and Randolph Kent have written, most Third World disasters occur because populations are economically vulnerable to "disaster agents," such as drought, floods, disruption of the agricultural cycle, or local conflict. It is not these agents that cause the disaster, but rather the economic vulnerability of much of the developing world's population.

Conflict often emerges from economic disparity. While many conflicts are expressed in ethnic or religious terms, long-running conflicts in the Third World often evolve from the struggle over control of resources. In many cases, resources—natural resources, export commodities (and thus foreign exchange earners), or external assistance—are controlled by a minority at the center. The increasing vulnerability of the majority gradually lends itself to rebellion, and sometimes armed conflict, aimed at the center. This economic factor also expresses itself in local conflicts, which may arise from disputes over wells or grazing land or from competition between migratory and host populations over limited resources. Conflict is also waged over terrain, not only because the goal of battle is to expand control over more territory, but also because territory provides access to economic resources. In the southern part of the Sudan, for example, the first targets of the renewed war in 1983 were not government garrisons or weapons depots, but an oil exploration site and a major water-resource development project.

Many disaster theorists argue that effective disaster response must address underlying economic factors, and not simply provide survival assistance, thus protecting the economic status quo. Disaster responses to conflicts should address economic factors; in doing so, however, the relationship between external intervention and the conflict grows deeper, and the involvement of outside aid agencies in the conflict becomes clear.

The challenge is not to plan relief programs in isolation from existing economic, political, and military factors, but rather to place the programs in their proper context. Traditionally, design and implementation of relief has been divorced from the dynamics of conflict and economic disruption. Recognizing that the need for relief emerges from these background conditions implies a need for policies and programs that address those conditions.

Analyzing Military Strategy

The linkage between disasters and war, and between disaster response and the outcome of conflict, is clear when military strategy is examined. Many humanitarian aid providers would argue that analyzing military strategy is the work of intelligence experts and army officers. Aid providers must understand military strategy because their assistance will, in every case, become part of that strategy. Ensuring that their assistance does not permit accrual of military advantage by either side requires understanding how that assistance fits into military strategy, and identifying ways of reducing political impact or ensuring that the impact helps ease the conflict. If external assistance is seen by any party to conflict as a potential tool in its politico-military strategy, then aid providers must know enough to ensure that they are neither manipulated nor used unwittingly to affect the balance of power.

Evaluating the military strategies of warring parties requires examining five dimensions of war: logistics, geography and demography, economics, politics, and the social domain. Each of these is most applicable to conflicts that involve a conventional army pitted against a guerrilla movement, or the classic insurgency-counterinsurgency model. However, they also contain lessons for conflicts bordering on anarchy, such as in Somalia and Liberia, and to local conflicts, although this latter category has its own particular dimensions.

One aspect of the role of the state versus the role of an insurgency must be considered before an evaluation begins. While both the state and an insurgency can manipulate humanitarian assistance, most often the state assumes a defensive position in a conflict (the protection of its authority), while an insurgency assumes an offensive position (the expansion of its authority via the erosion of state superiority). This molds the approaches undertaken by each party.

Logistics

Logistics, particularly transportation and communications, are crucial to any military strategy. In the case of insurgent warfare, the goal of the government or conventional force usually is to keep infrastructural systems open and accessible. The objective of the insurgency is to restrict transportation and to disrupt communications. It is rare for a guerrilla force to gain control over infrastructure sectors; conventional forces often have air power that prevents guerrillas from monopolizing primary transport systems. At best, a guerrilla force might achieve temporary (often nighttime) access, or develop an alternative transportation system.

Communications systems in most developing countries are sufficiently centralized to prohibit a guerrilla force from seizing and using them; the guerrillas' objective, however, is to prevent the government from using them effectively. In some cases, such as the Mozambique National Resistance (RENAMO) in Mozambique, the guerrillas' objective has been to destroy government-controlled infrastructure. In cases such as Eritrea and Ethiopia, guerrilla forces generally protected infrastructure on the assumption that they would need it when they assumed power.

Both internal and external relief providers depend on national infrastructure to implement programs. In most developing countries, relief operations can rely only rarely on alternative systems, although separate communications or transport systems sometimes are established. While this may be advantageous to a relief community trying to separate itself from a conflict, the creation of distinct relief systems also allows government forces to exploit existing national systems for the purposes of conflict. This was the case with the Ethiopian airlifts in 1984–1985. The use of externally provided planes to air-drop food allowed the central government to use its own military and civilian planes to support the war and the forced resettlement program, rather than to divert some of those resources to relief work.

The logistical dimension of conflict thus has serious implications for aid providers, since the same roads and bridges that carry relief goods also are used by contending armed forces. Governments must keep transportation systems open to ensure that national marketing and distribution do not collapse, and to allow the movement of military supplies and troops. To a guerrilla force, impeding the ability of the government to maintain economic functions or undertake military maneuvers is crucial. It is common for guerrilla forces to attack roads and main transport arteries, and for governments to use the cover of relief convoys, which are less likely to come under attack by the enemy, to move military equipment.

The logistics of war have many implications for the aid community. The systems they use often are for military purposes and may become military targets. A second and perhaps more troubling consideration is that in a large relief program it often is necessary to expand infrastructure and to reinforce road and air transport systems and communications networks. When this is undertaken through official channels, the government benefits from infrastructure expansion, and the insurgency acquires more targets. In those few cases when infrastructural services in a guerrilla-held area are expanded for relief work, the results are reversed, with the added advantage to the guerrilla force that it acquires infrastructural systems where none may have existed before.

Geography and Demography

The goal of belligerents is to control, or gain control of, territory. Particular areas will be active war zones and may be totally inaccessible to the external aid provider. Some of these are sufficiently strategic to either or both combatants that they will change hands regularly. Aid providers should identify these key areas and design their own systems for delivering supplies to them so that aid delivery is, as far as possible, independent of the control of belligerents. If this is done, assistance to populations in need can be secured and will not require that control remain constant.

The objective of a government army is to maintain control, which can be difficult because in most developing countries state access to remote rural areas is usually limited even in times of peace. A guerrilla army may pursue one of two options. It may carve out a base area, which it actively and exclusively administers, while launching hit-and-run attacks that limit government control over adjacent areas. In this case, large regions may emerge as no-man's-lands controlled by neither government nor guerrillas, which can change hands regularly, even daily. A guerrilla army may also try to control and administer a wider region, or entire territory, defined on a national or economic basis. In this case, a larger nongovernment-held area may emerge, and an alternate form of governance may develop. In either case, government armies generally are confined to urban areas, while insurgencies concentrate their forces in the countryside.

When an emergency exists and civilian populations suffer from extreme hardship, aid can become a vehicle for the expansion or consolidation of territory. The agent that can deliver assistance often becomes the agent of the government or administration. This was demonstrated in Ethiopia in 1985, when the Addis Ababa government negotiated the Food for the North Initiative, which was implemented by two U.S.-based NGOs. The aim of the initiative was to deliver assistance to what were described as contested areas of war-torn Eritrea and Tigray. Several sites were identified, all urban and all controlled by the central government. Most were, in fact, government military garrisons. The Addis Ababa regime agreed that food could be supplied to these areas, which were tightly surrounded by guerrilla units and thus largely inaccessible to relief convoys.

Shortly into the implementation of the initiative, the western Eritrean town of Barentu was captured from the government by the Eritrean People's Liberation Front (EPLF). As government forces retreated, so did the NGO in charge of relief delivery. Consequently, the civilians in Barentu were not assisted, although limited supplies were provided through the EPLF's own channels. Some weeks later, the EPLF withdrew from Barentu and government forces returned; almost immediately, relief facilities were reestablished.

What happened in Barentu had two effects. The dependence of the relief system upon government control of the town meant that civilians were cut off from assistance when Barentu moved into rebel hands. Since government forces could allow relief distribution when they controlled the town, while the EPLF was less able to do so, the stature of the government was enhanced. The message to civilians was that they would be assisted if the Ethiopian army was present, but not if the EPLF entered the city. Many

Eritrean civilians interpreted this as discriminatory and highly political. Had a system allowed aid delivery to Barentu independent of both the Ethiopian government and the EPLF, civilians would not have fallen victim to fluctuations in the military situation.

External aid agencies must be aware that while military battles may determine the operational areas of conflict, outside assistance is the secondary tool with which the administrative and political control of those areas is consolidated. As such, aid agencies should conduct the mapping exercise described below and follow guidelines to ensure that the aid delivery system is independent of military strategies. This is particularly important in the no-man's-land that changes hands regularly.

Understanding the civilian population is crucial. One of the central tenets of guerrilla insurgency and counterinsurgency strategy derives from the military philosophy of Mao Ze-dong, who likened his guerrillas to fish in the sea. For parties to a conflict, control over populations is critical. Guerrillas try to keep civilian populations inside the areas under their control and make it difficult for them to live in enemy territory. The provision or denial of relief is a tactic to control civilian movement.

Forced migration is another tactic to control people. Policies employed by the Khartoum government in the Sudan in 1986 triggered the rural-to-urban migration of hundreds of thousands of southern Sudanese, who were lured north from areas controlled by the Sudanese People's Liberation Army (SPLA) by food kept in government-administered cities. Some years later, a change in government in Ethiopia forced an end to SPLA use of Ethiopian refugee camps as a rear-base area, and this provoked the migration of over 150,000 southern Sudanese refugees from Ethiopia back into southern Sudan. In northern Ethiopia in 1984, the Tigray People's Liberation Front (TPLF) organized the movement of 200,000 civilians into neighboring Sudan to resist the government's policy of forcibly conscripting or resettling Tigrayan civilians who entered government-controlled feeding centers.

Migrations in most conflict-based emergencies may seem spontaneous. Often, however, these migrations have political and military causes and designs. As such, they often can be predicted, and sometimes prevented. It is crucial for aid providers to handle this problem for two reasons. Any mass migration will generate emergency needs and further expansion and complication of the relief effort. Mass migrations usually involve rural dwellers who abandon their ability to produce and are thus rendered dependent on the external aid system.

The Economic Dimensions

There are many economic dimensions of strategy. One common consequence of war is that transport and marketing are disrupted. At the same time, able-bodied producers are removed from production—particularly in the agricultural sector—with serious effects for the agrarian family. Civilian needs often increase, and both purchasing and selling prices for locally produced goods are affected, often hurting the civilian population. In many cases, production is also disrupted, either by direct attack, military occupation, or out-migration.

Two other factors are central to the economic aspects of war. One of the most significant to aid providers is the supply of food for belligerents' armed forces. Armies are made up of producers who, for the duration of conflict, are nonproductive. Armies rarely feed themselves. They depend upon national resources or local populations for their survival. It is not in the interest of an army aiming to gain popular support to demand that civilians provide them with food, particularly when those civilians are suffering. As such, externally provided assistance becomes a potential source of sustenance for armed forces.

Aid providers also are concerned with targeting versus protection of economic resources. In extreme cases, such as Mozambique and Somalia, economic infrastructure has been targeted and destroyed. When air power is used, croplands and other economic installations under enemy control become targets, as in the allied coalition's air war against Iraq. In only a few cases— where an insurgency, for example, defines a protracted struggle and includes an economic agenda in its own political strategy—are economic resources protected.

Most of the world's armies, whether conventional government forces or guerrilla insurgencies, adopt a short-term perspective; their goal is to defeat the enemy. As such, the long-term implications of destroying infrastructure and ruining economies are rarely, if ever, taken into account. Perhaps the best example can be taken from the Gulf War. The destruction of Iraq's economy and infrastructure may have undermined Saddam Hussein and clearly contributed to forcing the retreat of the Iraqi army from Kuwait, but the devastation that was wreaked upon Iraq generated short-term emergencies and ensured that the governance and economic development of Iraq will be difficult tasks for any regime that may take power in Baghdad in the future.

The economic dimensions of war pose large questions for humanitarians. The argument has been made that emergency assistance should be provided within a developmental framework, directed, as far as possible, toward decreasing the economic vulnerability of target populations. This can be achieved many ways, including market interventions and support for development programs. However, every dollar of assistance provided for nonemergency activities raises the stakes. The expansion of a road network— for marketing or relief purposes—may increase the logistical capacity of one of the combatants; the erection of schools or clinics may enhance the political and social standing of the force governing the area.

The Politics of War

The political dimension of war is obvious from the stated political objectives of each party. Politics at this level does not necessarily affect the external aid provider unless, for example, the stated goal of a combatant is genocide, or unless the external aid provider chooses to pursue advocacy.

Many NGOs adopt policies of advocacy, particularly regarding human rights, justice, and peace. Even when public positions are stated in a nonpartisan fashion, belligerents are likely to interpret advocacy as support for themselves or the enemy. So advocacy positions must be articulated carefully. Even in times when donor agencies do not deliberately take public positions of support for one of the parties, their involvement in a conflict may be construed as such. During the 1984–1985 famine in Ethiopia and Eritrea, for example, neither multilateral nor bilateral agencies worked in the opposition-held areas of the famine zone. The NGOs working in these areas thus provided information to the wider relief community that was not available from other sources. The provision of this information often was perceived as politically motivated. Crossborder operations can require consultation with antigovernment forces; in El Salvador, this communication was perceived as an act of collaboration by the government.

Most aid providers avoid adopting a public stance on the political problems underlying human disasters. This often is necessary because warring parties may interpret public statements as directed against them, and take action against the agencies involved. Most aid agencies attempt discretion when addressing human needs in armed conflicts. While this often is advisable, an important distinction must be made between discretion and silence. During the Ethiopian famine, for example, the needs of civilians in opposition-held areas were not articulated at major meetings of UN, bilateral, and NGO donors at the height of the crisis, partly because of sensitivity to the government of Ethiopia and fear of reprisals. The regime was able to hold the aid community hostage and ensure that a veil of silence shrouded the unofficial side of the famine. Civilians living on the wrong side of the lines paid the price. A similar scenario is developing now in the former Yugoslavia.

Most pertinent to the aid provider is the issue of political legitimacy. The eruption of a human crisis in the midst of armed conflict produces international attention. War gives belligerents an opportunity to gain international support. In these cases, parties will vie for international recognition and political legitimacy. This is particularly true for nongovernmental opposition forces, which, with few exceptions, are not recognized by the United Nations or other members of the international community. This has been true recently throughout the Horn of Africa, where liberation movements have gained international status. They have gained status not because their claims or demands have been accepted, but because they became active players in international relief operations.

The government seeks to demonstrate to the international community that it remains the legitimate authority in all areas of the country, or that the armed opposition cannot survive. This is often untrue, but armies rarely admit losses. In Ethiopia the Mengistu regime did not publicly concede there was a war in the country until three years after the major famine of the mid-1980s; the Sudanese government admitted to loss of territory in southern Sudan through its endorsement of Operation Lifeline.

In the battle for legitimacy, the provision of assistance from the outside often is used to prove the point. By their actions, relief providers endorse the parties to a conflict. External aid agencies should try to provide assistance evenly to areas under the control of belligerents at the outset of an intervention. They must avoid expanding the legitimacy of one of the parties by providing assistance that will allow it to increase the size of its territory. This can be achieved through the mapping exercise outlined below.

Second, relief agencies must ensure that they adopt equality in managing the inevitable incidents that arise in wars. Roads are blocked, bridges are blown up, and relief personnel come under attack. Each party to the conflict will use incidents precipitated by other belligerents to prove its own legitimacy. So it is essential that the aid community treat all similar incidents the same way. This is difficult because guerrilla forces sometimes are viewed more closely than governments. In cases where the central government is viewed as particularly odious or in extreme violation of human rights standards—such as in the Sudan—looser standards may be applied toward the armed opposition. The inability of the UN to publicly condemn a member government can lead to further imbalance.

Social Arena

In the social arena, parties to a conflict pursue twin goals: to capture the "hearts and minds" of the civilian population, and to undermine the credibility of the enemy in the civilians' eyes. The use of propaganda, which rarely affects the aid provider directly, is very pertinent on the ground.

The battle for hearts and minds may intersect with relief operations in three ways. Most significant is the provision of resources; the armed force that provides assistance to local populations is likely to be regarded with more loyalty than a force that cannot. Second is the use of resources to pacify local populations, as in Guatemala. Pacification is different from stabilization, which may be attempted in order to reduce armed conflict or economic disruption. The goal of pacification is inherently political, seeking to meet people's needs in a limited way to quell their support for an enemy force that is attempting to organize them on the basis of those needs.

The third and most repugnant social dimension of war is the use of terror. A contending army shows civilians they cannot afford to support the enemy. This has happened in Peru, where Shining Path has executed countless civilians as collaborators to undermine support for the government. In Ethiopia army units entering recently captured villages often raped women or tortured members of civilian councils organized by the armed opposition.

Relief operations and military strategy intersect on at least five levels. The challenge to external aid providers is to ensure that intersection remains clear, and that no one gains undue military advantage. The external aid provider can achieve this in four ways.

Preventing Undue Military Advantage

Decentralization and Accountability
The primary obstacle to delivering assistance in war zones often is the conflict itself. Every component of the relief operation becomes vulnerable to political manipulation or abuse. Civilians suffer, and in the worst cases, the conflict escalates. The most effective way to counter this trend is to devolve responsibility and accountability to the civilians themselves.

If civilians have ownership over relief or development programs, they will protect them. During the war in Ethiopia's northern Tigray region between 1975 and 1991, civilians defended clinics and schools against the Ethiopian army. In Somalia local NGOs have experienced far fewer cases of looting than their nonlocal counterparts have. Local citizens, particularly elders, can exert influence over the Somali militias better than outsiders can. Attacking forces are less inclined to assault a locally owned or managed operation than one owned and run by non-Somalis.

Increased local management of disasters is likely to enhance protection of relief operations, and also to have a positive effect on the belligerents vying for the hearts and minds of civilians. A local community is more likely to condemn a military unit that destroys its own grinding mills than one that attacks the headquarters of an international relief organization.

Devolving disaster management to the local level also empowers communities in their struggle against the forces competing for power. Civilians are transformed from victims to participants. The only successful effort to negotiate the conduct of the relief effort in Ethiopia (the Southern Line Operation conducted by the Joint Relief Partnership and the Relief Society of Tigray) was conducted between nonmilitary Ethiopian organizations. Because of their relative control over relief programs, they were able to exert influence over the warring parties.

Increasing local capabilities also serves the economic interests of both the host country and the international community. Relief programs that are designed and managed on the basis of local realities often are more effective than those forged externally. The ability of local communities to manage their own disasters directly reduces the scope of external intervention. Local accountability can also help demonstrate transparent motives, which is important to the external aid provider. In any situation of conflict, the actions of outsiders are viewed with suspicion by the parties to the conflict. Transparency of intentions can counter this danger.

Training
Often neither field nor headquarters staff of international relief agencies has enough specialized training in disaster management. Training can and should be enhanced in three areas. These include logistics, economic theory and practice, and military theory and practice. Both planners and field workers attempting to reduce human suffering in the heat of a conflict should understand basic military principles and the fundamental tenets of strategy and tactics. Moreover, they should be able to identify weapons. Placing an untrained person in the field without this knowledge may jeopardize his or her life. Programs designed without due consideration of military factors also are unlikely to achieve the balance described above.

There is a need for a course in disaster management in conflicts that pertains to all aid providers. This course would be a prerequisite for designing approaches and serving in the field. Besides covering the basics of military theory and practice, such a course should include extensive study of the many cases of sustaining civilians in times of war. Course curriculum should concentrate on managing the intersection of aid and conflict in each of the areas outlined above.

Mapping
The goal of mapping is to reduce the negative impact of military strategies on relief operations and to achieve greater balance in delivery. Its objective is to overlay an operational plan on what is essentially a military map. Conducting this exercise when planning an emergency operation allows relief providers to identify means of sustaining civilians in all areas, including those areas that may require negotiations between the aid community and belligerents. These negotiations, if effectively linked to political efforts undertaken by other members of the international community, can provide the basis for easing and resolving the conflict. To be effective in its application, mapping requires far more coordination within the NGO community, and between that community and bilateral and multilateral agencies, than exists now.

The first step in a mapping exercise is to identify three distinct types of operational areas: government-controlled zones; insurgent-controlled zones; and no-man's-lands administered by neither side. Most conflicts are likely to include each of these types.

The second step is to define access. In a best-case scenario, such as Operation Lifeline Sudan in 1990, the host government will endorse international humanitarian access to populations outside its areas of control. In more problematic cases, such as Ethiopia during 1984–1985, the host government may deny the existence of conflict and deny access. In the worst-case scenario, such as Somalia in 1991–1992, there may be no central authority. Defining access requires determining which parties control these areas and what logistical systems must be used.

It is important to identify means of access that will not allow one party to gain access through relief operations to the territory of its enemy. Government facilities should be the source of access to government-held areas, and opposition elements should be the source of access to the areas they control. It is important to identify operational areas as they exist at the moment of outside intervention.

The division of labor approach then should be applied so that international aid providers are assigned to the areas they are best suited to serve. Planners then must identify areas requiring full cooperation among all aid actors and capable of generating negotiations between the external aid community and the warring parties. These include:

- no-man's-lands controlled by neither of the contending armies;
- points considered strategic by warring parties, such as garrisons, major urban centers, and economic installations;
- active battle sites; and
- trouble spots where a number of factors may combine to allow for potential violence—these may include refugee camps, tense areas adjacent to battle sites, or major aid or logistical installations (warehouses, ports, major roads).

For each of these areas, ideal access must be determined by identifying those aid providers with the greatest technical ability to meet human needs. In a best-case scenario, the aid community would identify these areas and then present belligerents with plans for serving them. If the aid community is not to be manipulated, in negotiations it must show a united stance on the part of multilateral, bilateral, and NGO donors, regardless of their distinct areas of operation.

In all areas it is also necessary to identify mechanisms for accountability and to find ways of providing local communities with greater participation and ownership. These mechanisms may include local NGOs or traditional community organizations such as, in the case of Somalia or eastern Ethiopia, the elders.

The final phase of the mapping exercise involves a review of each of the five components of military strategy outlined above. An analysis should be done of potential points of intersection between relief operations and logistics, geography and demography, economics, politics, and social trends. Identifying ways in which relief programs might be manipulated allows planners to find a means of countering the manipulations. If, for example, aid planners suspect it is in the interest of one of the parties to move a civilian population, either by force or political manipulation, greater assistance to that specific population could be a countermeasure. If a government proposes the expansion of a communications network for relief purposes, but also may use the system to achieve military ends, the whole relief community, rather than the government, could manage that system.

Rules of the Game

If division of labor and mapping are applied, the ability of the aid community to establish the rules of the game is enhanced. This is because efforts are being made to reach all civilians without manipulating operational borders; the relief community can speak with a single voice; and the community is clearly conveying to belligerents that it is not subject to manipulation, but that it understands the situation on the ground.

The rules of the game will be different for each situation, but three are likely to apply at all times, and should be established at the outset of operations. First is the articulation of a stated position on the response to offenses such as attacks on relief convoys or personnel, or the deliberate destruction of infrastructure required for relief work. The aid community should emphasize that it would treat all incidents with equality, whether committed by the government or the armed opposition forces, and that it would respond decisively. Responses may include the exertion of greater control by the aid community over operations (as opposed to relying on government or opposition structures) or public statements that may affect the struggle for political legitimacy.

The second rule concerns negotiation methods. The international community should negotiate with one voice and not be vulnerable to divide-and-conquer tactics. Where the contending forces are unwilling to meet for relief work negotiations, appropriate intermediaries must be identified. In order to gain their confidence, each warring party may be given the right to veto one (but no more) of the proposed negotiators. At the outset, the points of immediate negotiation (e.g., access to no-man's-lands) should be made clear and, if necessary, be made a condition for intervention. If possible, the aid community should require regular meetings to discuss issues in need of consideration.

The third rule of the game pertains to public statements. While individual agencies retain the right to speak out as they see fit and according to their own institutional objectives, the aid community also must make clear to both parties that it will make regular statements regarding the conduct of the relief operation. These statements should be comprehensive and endorsed by each of the three tiers of the aid community.

Additional Considerations for the Aid Provider

Besides conducting the mapping exercise and establishing the rules of the game, the international humanitarian community can mitigate the extent to which it is affected by military strategy by bearing the following in mind:

1. No belligerent is likely to embrace international humanitarian

principles; while belligerents may give lip service, their goal is to win a war and to allow what are perceived as reasonable civilian and economic losses. Expectations should be reduced to realistic levels, and attempts to promote humanitarian principles should be conducted incrementally.

2. To limit external dependence and prevent spillover emergencies, one of the overall goals of a relief operations should be to predict and prevent mass migrations.

3. With a view to reducing the need for international relief, promoting development, and enhancing accountability, efforts should be made to devolve responsibility for the relief effort to local communities.

4. To ensure both transparency and balance, aid agencies should use standard approaches for monitoring international assistance. These should be applied equally to all warring parties.

5. Concrete plans should be developed for response options to areas that may change hands during the course of battle.

6. Rather than using a violations approach, whereby assistance is withheld on the basis of breaches of humanitarian standards, aid should be allocated on an incentive basis. Assuming that in every conflict relief assistance will become a target of war, the focus should be placed upon progress rather than upon infractions.

7. Efforts should be made to demilitarize war zones. This can be achieved by offering armed individuals economic incentives that are otherwise unavailable. This approach is most effective when attempting to reduce the availability of arms to noncombatants or looters, as in the case of Somalia, rather than when attempting to disarm warring parties. The latter can be achieved only by a comprehensive demilitarization program endorsed by all belligerents.

8. In planning relief distribution systems, all efforts should be made to provide civilians with assistance in the areas in which they live to ensure that politically motivated migrations are not triggered.

9. Humanitarianism should assume that every action undertaken will be perceived politically by, and likely have political impact upon, the parties to the conflict.

The Hard Reality: When It's Time to Take a Stand

The pursuit of evenhandedness can reinforce the objective conditions that gave rise to war. At the same time, provision of assistance to both or all parties also may artificially prolong the conflict. The aid community may need to make what is essentially a political judgment about the use of its assistance. In some cases, all external assistance should be withdrawn to induce the warring parties to cease hostilities. This, however, is usually impractical, since it is unlikely to bring about the desired results and civilians suffer the immediate consequences.

Limiting the extent to which external aid reinforces the roots of conflict may mean pressuring all belligerents to seek a negotiated settlement. In other cases, such as Somalia, the donor community may choose to employ force, and assume total responsibility for the management and implementation of relief. In cases where the actions of one party are clearly the primary cause of conflict and of the denial of humanitarian rights to civilians, aid agencies may allocate their assistance accordingly. Contrary to the principle of evenhandedness, the purpose in this situation is to favor one party.

Taking such an approach has serious implications for those wishing to pursue humanitarian goals. Surely, the defense of civilians against the wrath of Nazi Germany would have been sufficient cause to allocate assistance with partiality. In today's world, the international humanitarian community faces a similar challenge in the former Yugoslavia and, in the eyes of many, in the Sudan. Undermining a profane force, however, also means strengthening its opposition. Making this decision requires that the risks and benefits be weighed and that the character of the force that would receive the advantage be evaluated with a view to the following:

1. Purpose: Is the aim of the movement or government in question to defend or to challenge the conditions that led to the conflict?

2. Approach: Is the movement or government in question implementing an alternative political system while it wages war, or is it simply challenging or defending the status quo?

3. Recruitment: Are the combatants being forced to fight, or are they fighting voluntarily?

4. Civil-military relations: What sort of relationship does the force in question maintain with civil society? Is it a top-down or organic relationship?

5. Accountability: Does civil society exercise any leverage over the force in question? Does it have at its disposal any mechanisms for holding that force accountable?

6. Independence: Is the local relief system sufficiently autonomous from politico-military forces to limit manipulation?

7. Economic: How does the force in question sustain itself economically? To what extent does it draw upon and drain local or national economic resources? Do its actions or policies disrupt or enhance production?

The answers to these questions necessarily will be colored by subjective political, moral, and possibly religious views. As many conflict-born disasters have made clear, there are moments in history when the application of the adage "not to decide is to decide" translates into life or death for suffering civilians. Those moments require facing hard realities and taking bold action.

Notes

1. See Frederick C. Cuny, *Disasters and Development* (New York: Oxford University Press, 1984); Frederick C. Cuny, Barry N. Stein, and Pat Real (eds.), *Repatriation During Conflict in Africa and Asia* (Dallas: Center for the Study of Societies in Crisis, 1992); and Mary Ann Larkin, Frederick C. Cuny, and Barry N. Stein (eds.), *Repatriation Under Conflict in Central America* (Washington, D.C.: Center for Immigration Policy and Refugee Assistance, 1991).

■ Part 3 ■

Humanitarian Institutions: A Look to the Future

Commentary

THOMAS G. WEISS & LARRY MINEAR

Having reviewed key values and processes, we now turn to explore in more detail the emerging institutional shape of the world's new humanitarian order. This examination is particularly timely as attention in the wake of the Cold War is focused on changes needed to assure greater responsiveness from the world's humanitarian machinery. Discussions about the shape of the evolving humanitarian order[1] must be situated firmly within the context of international law. There is a well-established right of access to humanitarian assistance and a well-established right for impartial aid organizations to provide this assistance. In the codification, evolution, and dissemination of humanitarian law over a period of 125 years, the International Committee of the Red Cross (ICRC) has played the central role.

A fitting start is Michel Veuthey's "Assessing Humanitarian Law." For the last two decades, Veuthey has monitored closely discussions by the international community of humanitarian law and practice. His duties as a staff member of the Geneva-based ICRC have included regular attendance at United Nations debates in Geneva and in New York. The recent grant of observer status to the ICRC by the UN General Assembly was an acknowledgment by governments of its importance as an institution and as a contributor to international policy and action on humanitarian affairs.

Writing from his own point of view, Veuthey presents the body of humanitarian law already agreed upon and ratified by states. He makes particular reference to the Geneva Conventions of 1949 and the Additional Protocols of 1977 that elaborate the rights and responsibilities of political authorities and humanitarian organizations. He also describes the ICRC's efforts to monitor compliance with existing law and provide humanitarian assistance and protection to civilians when warfare breaks out within countries. He examines in depth the set of implementation mechanisms that have been agreed upon and sometimes utilized by states.

Veuthey points out, however, that legal safeguards are insufficient to sustain civilians during armed conflicts, or even to equip humanitarian organizations to provide sustenance. As many analysts have noted, the conventions and protocols are not as "hard" a law as the domestic law of most countries that is adjudicated in the courts and backed up by specific enforcement. Humanitarian law is "softer," and it is implemented or not in the actual behavior of soldiers and government officials.[2] However useful in circumscribing inhumane practices by governments and insurgents, warring parties often ignore international strictures that they see as contravening their immediate interests. The Independent Commission on International Humanitarian Issues concurs. Many governments take "a rather relaxed view regarding compliance with humanitarian norms," the Commission has stated. "Political considerations prevail over humanitarian requirements and humanitarian concerns are used to further political aims."[3] Breaches of legal obligation often are not counteracted swiftly and firmly.

It is also true that the rights to receive and provide humanitarian assistance are less fully elaborated, less clearly monitored, and perhaps also less widely respected than are individual civil and political rights.[4] Some experts therefore have suggested that it is premature to speak of a humanitarian "regime," since a regime requires a detailed set of obligations and system of enforcement, including penalties. Some scholars argue that the use of regime analysis might help bridge the analytical gap between existing legal texts and behavior;[5] some practitioners would counter that what is needed is less analysis and more political will to enforce existing provisions.

What makes Veuthey's description so useful is that it provides a historical backdrop for the evolution of international law more generally. The Covenant of the League of Nations, adopted in the wake of World War I, was silent about the legal obligations of states in the humanitarian sphere. After the searing experience of World War II, however, governments made several landmark decisions that laid the groundwork for the evolution and acceptance of greater humanitarian responsibilities. The UN Charter, adopted in 1945, and the Universal Declaration of Human Rights, enacted in 1948, have come to be seen as milestones in the redefinition of sovereignty in relation to humanitarian responsibilities.

The most common interpretation of the UN Charter emphasizes the role of domestic jurisdiction in the often-cited paragraphs in Article 2. The negative protections afforded states against interference in their domestic affairs, however, exist in tension with their positive obligations in the area of human rights. The first words of the Charter's Preamble are: "We the

Peoples of the United Nations determined . . . to reaffirm faith in fundamental human rights, in the dignity and worth of the human person, in the equal rights of men and women." Other articles, in particular 55 and 56, specify the critical importance of values and a "universal respect for, and observance of, human rights." In this perspective—and developments in recent years have highlighted it—states in joining the United Nations place key domestic policies and practices within the realm of international scrutiny.

Particularly since the end of East-West rivalry, the international community has embraced sovereignty more circumspectly, including outside humanitarian relief, when national authorities prove unable or unwilling within their own borders. Even the current UN Secretary-General, whose responsibilities make him acutely aware of the sensitivities of sovereign states, acknowledges that "the centuries-old doctrine of absolute and exclusive sovereignty no longer stands, and was in fact never so absolute as it was conceived to be in theory. A major intellectual requirement of our time is to rethink the question of sovereignty."[6]

The Security Council since April 1991 has pronounced itself clearly on the subject of the implementation of humanitarian values, in a manner that is distinct from the behind-the-scenes diplomacy that is the ICRC's hallmark. As mentioned earlier, Resolutions 688 and 794 authorized the use of military force to guarantee humanitarian space in northern Iraq and Somalia, when local authorities refused to respect international norms. The second decision demonstrated far more consensus. While the former received the support of only ten Security Council members (three others voted against, two abstained), the vote for the latter was unanimous. Many decisions on the former Yugoslavia also have inched toward more drastic outside action to sustain imperiled civilians.

Moreover, humanitarian law consists not only of the Geneva Conventions and Additional Protocols but also of the decisions of the General Assembly, as well as evolving international practice. Within the General Assembly—the world's quintessential political forum—recent discussions about the tensions between sovereignty and humanitarian access suggest a continuing evolution toward more progressive norms. In 1988 the General Assembly adopted Resolution 43/131, which recognized the rights of civilians to international aid and the role of NGOs in emergencies. In 1990 General Assembly Resolution 45/100 reaffirmed these rights and specifically endorsed the concept of corridors of tranquillity to facilitate the work of humanitarian agencies. In 1991 General Assembly Resolution 46/182 requested the UN Secretary-General to create the position of an emergency assistance coordinator to work with governments and insurgents to provide more effective humanitarian assistance. This resolution draws no distinction between victims of natural and man-made disasters; only the tacit "consent" of authorities rather than their "request" is required to activate a UN response.

Following from recent General Assembly debates and adding political weight to existing legal safeguards was the creation in early 1992 of a Department of Humanitarian Affairs. The major purpose of the new unit is to assure greater coordination and effectiveness of international activities. The terms of reference provided by the General Assembly, however circumspect and carefully crafted, contain evidence of a more assertive humanitarianism.

This evolution in law and practice leads to divergent conclusions about future steps. Some join Veuthey in his conviction that the essential missing ingredient in the humanitarian regime of the future is not new conventions or protocols, but greater fidelity by belligerents to existing law and more vigorous engagement by the international community. Others indicate that it is essential, both in raising international consciousness and in ameliorating the behavior of belligerents, to simplify and codify existing law so that warring parties understand their obligations and comply, particularly during civil wars. Veuthey and his ICRC colleagues concede that the existing provisions to protect civilians in internal wars are far weaker than the comparable protection for soldiers and victims of interstate conflict.

In any case, they are dissatisfied with the international capacity to provide humanitarian assistance. This is the subject of the final two chapters, which contain thoughtful reflections by two seasoned practitioners regarding the structural inadequacies and existing capacities of the international delivery system. Frederick C. Cuny, who elaborates his vision of "Humanitarian Action in the Post–Cold War Era," is a planner who founded and heads INTERTECT, a professional disaster management consulting firm based in Dallas, Texas.

Cuny has been involved in many emergencies over the last two decades. Indeed, the *Wall Street Journal* has referred to him as "Mr. Disaster." At the time of the Providence conference in December 1992 to review the chapters in this volume, he was advising the U.S. government about humanitarian strategies to deal with the crisis in Somalia. The revisions to his chapter were sent from Zagreb, where he was working under dangerous conditions to arrange fuel and firewood deliveries to Sarajevo and accelerate the pace of relief activities in eastern Bosnia. He has sought throughout his career to make use of his on-the-spot activities and written reflections to improve international efforts. His recommendations for Operation Restore Hope in Somalia were informed by his experience with Operation Provide Comfort in northern Iraq, and his views on airdrops into Bosnia by his experience with the use of the military in humanitarian support in both Iraq and Somalia.

The book concludes with James Ingram's "The Future Architecture for International Humanitarian Action." Chapter 9 reflects a distinguished career in international relief efforts, first as an Australian diplomat and head of Australia's bilateral aid organization and then as the chief executive officer of the World Food Programme. While Ingram presided over enormous growth in UN food aid programs, he viewed the organization's task not only as that of the world's principal food logistician but also as a focal point for reflection about food aid, food security, and food management challenges. Ingram now directs the Australian Institute for International Affairs.

Where Veuthey argues for greater use of existing institutions, Cuny and Ingram urge a radical overhaul of the international humanitarian delivery system. They question the ability of the United Nations as a whole, and the organizations that make up the UN system in particular, to deal adequately with the growing number of conflict-related emergencies in the post–Cold War era. Cuny calls for a drastic revamping of the UN system to respond effectively to massive population displacements caused by internal wars. Rather than being localized in developing countries, these crises will take place increasingly in nontropical countries of the former Soviet bloc. They also will involve a growing number of Muslims, whose cultural background is vastly different from that of the majority of outside aid workers and institutions.[7]

To cope with the growing challenge, Cuny proposes harnessing available military resources and pooling existing international nongovernmental organizations and specialized UN agencies under the aegis of a new UN Organization for the Victims of Armed Conflict. He has little patience with turf battles among relief officials or with the current confusing array of overlapping and sometimes nonexistent mandates. He readily criticizes bureaucrats—governmental, intergovernmental, and nongovernmental alike—for ineptitude and waste in dealing with the suffering caused by armed conflicts. In spite of past criticisms, he still sees no realistic alternative to the significant remodeling needed to create a new super organization that should improve the prospects for effective humanitarian action.

Ingram's analysis and recommendations range well beyond remodeling existing United Nations institutions. He goes against the tide of conventional wisdom in arguing that the UN cannot and should not be the centerpiece of future efforts to sustain civilians. He has concluded that the world organization is inherently unable to act with the impartiality necessary for effective relief in situations in which its member governments face challenges from armed insurgents. This is a surprising conclusion for a senior UN official who negotiated access for food shipments to places such as the port of Massawa in northern Ethiopia. However, he believes that his negotiations would have been equally successful as a non-UN official with similar political support.

Ingram pairs his views about the negative impacts of the UN's political orientation with sharp criticism of its management culture and the lack of professional orientation among its relief specialists. Rather than thorough reform of the world organization—there are clearly changes that he would like to see implemented immediately in the United Nations—he calls instead for the expansion and internationalization of the ICRC. While he favors having the UN continue to coordinate natural disasters, he urges that the ICRC be charged with orchestrating the global response to complex emergencies and delegating specific tasks to UN organizations and international NGOs as necessary.

One of the themes that recurs in these last three chapters, and is implicit in the previous six, concerns the proper relationship between humanitarian action and politics. The growing concern of the UN General Assembly and Security Council with relieving the urgent suffering of civilians more effectively is undeniably positive after the long dark humanitarian night of the Cold War. Offsetting the value of this higher visibility is the reality that geopolitics still dictates that some suffering in some countries will command the attention of the United Nations more than in others. Similarly, the implementation of humanitarian activities may benefit from added international political and military pressure emanating from the Security Council. At the same time, experiences in the Gulf and the former Yugoslavia demonstrate that humanitarian activities sometimes lose in integrity and effectiveness when associated with coercive strategies by the international community.

Another recurring theme concerns the international division of labor needed to sustain civilians in war zones more efficaciously. An improved humanitarian architecture for the future will require as its foundation a clear understanding of what each kind of humanitarian organization does best. Each of the main types of external humanitarian organizations (bilateral, UN, nongovernmental, ICRC) and their internal counterparts (governments, armed opposition groups, local NGOs) have made indispensable contributions to a more effective international humanitarian economy. It also seems clear that the edifice of the future will need to be tailored to the demands of the post–Cold War era, which include tensions within geographic borders, massive population displacement within and across state frontiers, and a growing role for nonstate actors.

The highly divergent views about institutional reform among the three authors in Part 3, however unsettling, may still be helpful in navigating uncharted waters. The fact that all three have hands-on experience in many institutions and are knowledgeable about a broad range of national and regional contexts requires that their views receive analysis and reflection. The continuing in-country research of the Humanitarianism and War Project, and a book to be published next year with that title,[8] will seek to provide data and recommendations for this ongoing process.

As with the first six chapters, these last three chapters raise additional questions for study:

1. In the current rash of humanitarian crises around the world following the Cold War, the behavior of belligerents is a daily affront to the conscience of the civilized world. Gross, calculated violations of human rights and humanitarian law are perpetrated routinely in spite of the provisions of existing international law. What sorts of educational and political strategies

could be devised to hold warring parties more effectively to their acknowledged obligations?

2. Those who oppose the creation of new humanitarian law argue that the problems faced today reflect not the absence of clear legal obligations but rather the unwillingness of governments to meet their agreed commitments and to keep them. What mechanisms—international and national, governmental and private—could be devised and implemented during the early post–Cold War era to assure greater accountability?

3. The largest number of persons affected by major humanitarian emergencies are now Muslim, while the vast majority of external humanitarians organizations and personnel are not. To what extent should the international community seek to stimulate the growth of Muslim organizations to meet these needs? To what extent can existing institutions become more attuned to the needs of civilians caught in war zones and more appropriate in their responses?

4. Given the plethora of institutional humanitarian actors—governmental and nongovernmental, international and indigenous, specialized and generalist—what sort of coordination should be expected in the evolving international humanitarian economy? Should some authority be created that would be able to direct activities more decisively, or should voluntary cooperation in coordination efforts be the maximum expected? Would it be more useful to seek better coordination within the individual institutional families (e.g., among UN organizations or among NGOs) rather than across the full range of actors? What personnel policies could be used to improve the professionalism of humanitarians?

5. While they figure increasingly in the rhetoric of decisionmakers and international solutions, with few exceptions regional organizations have been remarkably absent from the security and humanitarian arenas.[9] To what extent are these organizations able realistically to contribute to more vigorous humanitarian action? What can the international community do to strengthen their effectiveness?

6. The work of the UN's Department of Humanitarian Affairs, recommended by the General Assembly in December 1991 and created by the Secretary-General in early 1992, will be reviewed by governments in late 1993. What does the experience in the early chapter of its existence suggest about the changes needed for the future? Should attention be given to the creation of a coordination or oversight mechanism outside of the United Nations?

Notes

1. See Larry Minear and Thomas G. Weiss, "Groping and Coping in the Gulf Crisis: Discerning the Shape of a New Humanitarian Order," *World Policy Journal* 9, no. 4 (Fall/Winter 1992): 755–788.

2. See David P. Forsythe, "Choices More Ethical Than Legal: The International Committee of the Red Cross and Human Rights," *Ethics and International Affairs* 7 (1993): 136.

3. Independent Commission on International Humanitarian Issues, *Winning the Human Race* (London: Zed Books, 1988): 71–72.

4. See David P. Forsythe, *The Internationalization of Human Rights* (Lexington: Heath, 1991); and Jack Donnelly, *Universal Human Rights in Theory and Practice* (Ithaca: Cornell University Press, 1989).

5. See Stephen D. Krasner (ed.), *International Regimes* (Ithaca: Cornell University Press, 1983).

6. Boutros Boutros-Ghali, "Empowering the United Nations," *Foreign Affairs* 72, no. 5 (Winter 1992/93): 89–102.

7. See Sohail H. Hashini, "Is There an Islamic Ethic of Humanitarian Intervention?" *Ethics and International Affairs* 7 (1993): 55–74.

8. Larry Minear and Thomas G. Weiss, *Humanitarianism and War: Reducing the Human Cost of Armed Conflict* (Boulder: Lynne Rienner, forthcoming 1994).

9. See Neil S. MacFarlane and Thomas G. Weiss, "Regional Organizations and Regional Security," *Security Studies* 2, no. 1 (Autumn 1992): 6–37.

■ 7 ■
Assessing Humanitarian Law

MICHEL VEUTHEY

Humanitarian law is as old as warfare.[1] Every people, civilization—even animals—observe restraints in their use of violence within groups. These restraints, imposed by the need for survival, now are extended to all peoples and nations with the universal ratification of the main instrument of international humanitarian law, the four 1949 Geneva Conventions on the protection of war victims, and the recognition of the customary character of the 1907 Hague codification of the laws of war by the International Military Tribunal in Nuremberg and the International Court of Justice. Humanitarian law is rooted in the history and traditions of humankind. It is part of the future as an essential safeguard for survival.

Yet, parties to conflicts—governments and insurgents alike—seem to breach every day a new rule against civilian populations, prisoners, and even against humanitarian organizations. With ethnic cleansing, the aim of war is not victory but annihilation and extermination. The international community reacts slowly or not at all to practices verging on genocide. Conventions, protocols, declarations, agreements, and resolutions are mocked. Existing humanitarian rules and principles should be better understood, promoted, implemented, and vigorously enforced.

This chapter contains three sections. The first defines international humanitarian law. The second treats implementation mechanisms, which are commonly thought to be the weakest part of the international efforts to sustain victims of war. The third section summarizes the overall effectiveness of humanitarian law as a contribution to humanitarian action.

Humanitarian Rules and Principles

International humanitarian law can be defined as the principles and rules that limit the use of violence during armed conflicts. Its goals are to spare persons not directly involved in hostilities (such as wounded and sick, shipwrecked, prisoners of war, civilians, and medical and sanitary personnel); spare the objects necessary for survival; and limit the effects of combat violence to the amount proportionally necessary for war.

There are many written and customary rules of international humanitarian law. The most important treaties, which provide the basis for this discussion, are the four 1949 Geneva Conventions on the protection of war victims[2] and their two 1977 Additional Protocols.[3] Together, those six instruments of international law number more than six hundred provisions. There are other related instruments: the 1907 Hague codification on the laws of war; the 1925 Geneva Protocol for the Prohibition of Gas Warfare; the 1948 Genocide Convention; the 1954 Hague Convention on the Protection of Cultural Property in the Event of Armed Conflict; and various universal and regional human rights instruments, as far as they are applicable in situations of armed conflicts.[4] There are also pertinent disarmament instruments: the 1976 UN Convention Prohibiting the Hostile Use of Environmental Modification Techniques; the 1980 UN Convention on Prohibitions or Restrictions on the Use of Certain Conventional Weapons; and the 1993 UN Convention on the Prohibition of the Development, Production, Stockpiling and Use of Chemical Weapons and on their Destruction.[5]

The aim is not to make more codifications, but to implement existing rules. What is needed is not more humanitarian law, but more humanitarian spirit and more political will to enforce existing rules. To cite but one example, Common Article 3 was drafted in Geneva in 1949 to protect victims of noninternational armed conflicts. Its provisions could still save hundreds of thousands of victims on all continents.

The fundamental characteristics of humanitarian law are threefold: it is not subject to reciprocity; victims cannot give up their rights; and it is consistent. Reciprocity often has caused traditional restraints to warfare[6] and is a very powerful factor for the actual application of humanitarian law in the field. Nevertheless, reciprocity cannot be a condition for denying victims their rights. Humanitarian law is not subject to approval by both sides and should be applied unilaterally. Moreover, the absolute character of protection is guaranteed in the Geneva Conventions against any subsequent agreement waiving or lowering the level of protection among parties to the conflict, including a peace treaty.

Finally, humanitarian law has no double standards. Libyan POWs in U.S. hands in Chad are entitled to the same conventional guarantees as U.S. troops in Iraq. Precedents are important. Consequently, the lack of reaction to attacks against civilians in Bosnia and elsewhere set dangerous precedents. The bombing of civilian populations in Guernica and Nanking were preludes to the bombing of British, German, and Japanese cities during World War II.

Implementation Mechanisms

Implementation mechanisms[7] are provided in both the 1949 Conventions and the 1977 Additional Protocols: the 171 High Contracting Parties, the ICRC, the United Nations, and the International Fact-Finding Commission. It is useful to examine each of these in more detail, especially because implementation commonly is assumed to be one of the main weaknesses in public international law. This section concludes with a consideration of implementation efforts by regional and nongovernmental organizations, as well as other factors influencing application, particularly public opinion.

The High Contracting Parties

According to Common Article 1 to the 1949 Geneva Conventions and to Additional Protocol I of 1977, States Party undertake "to respect and ensure respect for those instruments in all circumstances."[8] They have a double responsibility that is individual and collective. States are responsible for their own behavior (as a party to a conflict or as a neutral country), their own authorities (in time of peace and in time of conflict, including for the prosecution of grave breaches), and for the behavior of other States Party, allies, or third countries. In the case *Nicaragua vs. USA,* the International Court of Justice noted that the United States was obliged to respect and ensure respect for the conventions, an obligation that did not derive from the conventions themselves, "but from the general principles of humanitarian law to which the Conventions merely give specific expression."

There are a number of ways for a government to fulfill responsibilities: promoting awareness of international humanitarian law; unilaterally or multilaterally denouncing violations of international humanitarian law; supporting humanitarian organizations; preventing violations of humanitarian law in bringing political, financial, or other pressure on those parties violating the law; prosecuting violators, or at least making known publicly that those persons would be unwelcome in any capacity on their territory; and assuming the mandate of a Protecting Power.

The Protecting Power, according to Article 2 of Protocol I, is "a neutral or other State not a party to the conflict which has been designated by a party to the conflict and accepted by the adverse party and has agreed to carry out the functions assigned to a Protecting Power under the Conventions and this Protocol." Liaison among belligerents through diplomatic or other channels, the provision of relief assistance, and visits to prisoners of war and civilians are possible actions. Widely used during the two world wars, the mechanism of the Protecting Power has only rarely and partially been used after it became mandatory in the four 1949 Geneva Conventions: in Suez in 1956 between Egypt and the United Kingdom; in Goa in 1961 between India and Portugal; and between India and Pakistan in 1971. In the Falklands/Malvinas conflict, Brazil and Uruguay played a very useful role in the transfer of wounded and the release of prisoners of war, but as neutral countries and not as Protecting Powers. Protecting Powers still are needed, and could have been instrumental in supporting the other implementation mechanisms of humanitarian law in such places as the Middle East, the former Yugoslavia, and in other international conflicts.

Dissemination (especially training and educating the armed forces) on humanitarian law is one duty of the High Contracting Parties according to the 1949 Conventions. In 1977 Protocol I reinforced this obligation in Article 83, and elaborated on the duty of commanders in Article 87 and the need for legal advisers in Article 82.

Prosecuting violators of humanitarian law is also one obligation of the High Contracting Parties. Each of the four 1949 Geneva Conventions contain specific provisions on penal sanctions: parties take legislative measures "to provide effective penal sanctions for persons committing, or ordering to be committed, any of the grave breaches." This includes searching for violators and bringing them to trial. The list of grave breaches varies. Some are mentioned in all four conventions (willful killing, torture or inhumane treatment, willfully causing great suffering, serious injury to body or health). The First, Second, and Fourth Conventions include destruction and appropriation of property as a grave breach; the Fourth Convention mentions unlawful deportation or transfer, unlawful confinement, and taking hostages.

The list of grave breaches was supplemented in Article 85 of Protocol I in 1977 to include attacks against persons and objects. Mutual assistance in criminal proceedings is underlined with the possibility of extradition. These texts were supplemented by Article I of the Convention on the Prevention of the Crime of Genocide: "genocide, whether committed in time of peace or in time of war, is a crime under international law which they [the States Party] undertake to prevent and punish."[9] General Assembly Resolutions 3(I) of February 1948 (Extradition and Punishment of War Criminals) and 170 (II) of October 1947 (Extradition of War Criminals and Traitors) reaffirm the obligation to extradite persons who have committed crimes under Article 6 of the Charter of the Nuremberg Tribunal. Article I, paragraph 2, of the Declaration on Territorial Asylum states that "the right to seek and enjoy asylum may not be invoked by any person with respect to whom there are serious reasons for considering that he has committed a crime against humanity."

The ICRC

The four 1949 Geneva Conventions on the protection of war victims require ICRC delegates to pursue several tasks in all cases of international armed conflict:[10] visit and interview prisoners of war and civilian internees; provide relief to civilians affected by armed conflict; search for missing persons and forward family messages to prisoners of war and civilian internees; offer its good offices to facilitate the institution of hospital zones and safety zones and localities; receive applications from protected persons; and undertake other humanitarian activities, subject to the consent of the parties to the conflict. According to Common Article 3 of the 1949 Geneva Conventions, in the case of an armed conflict not of an international character, the ICRC only may offer its services to the parties to the conflict.[11]

The statutes of the International Red Cross and Red Crescent Movement, adopted in 1986 by the Twenty-Fifth International Conference of the Red Cross specified the roles of the ICRC. The first is to maintain and disseminate the fundamental principles of the movement, namely humanity, impartiality, neutrality, independence, voluntary service, unity, and universality. The ICRC is also to recognize any newly established or reconstituted national society that fulfills the conditions for recognition. It is to work for the faithful application of international humanitarian law in armed conflicts and to endeavor at all times to ensure the protection of and assistance to military and civilian victims of conflicts. Also, the ICRC is to ensure the operation of the Central Tracing Agency and to contribute—in anticipation of armed conflicts—to the training of medical personnel and the preparation of medical equipment, in cooperation with the national societies, military and civilian services, and other competent authorities. Finally, it is to work for the understanding and dissemination of knowledge of international humanitarian law applicable in armed conflicts.

The role of the ICRC is not limited to situations provided for in the Geneva Conventions, but includes any humanitarian initiative that comes within its role as a neutral and independent institution and intermediary.[12] In situations not covered by international humanitarian law, such as disturbances and tensions, the ICRC could offer its services to a government to monitor conditions of detention of "security detainees" (sometimes called "political prisoners"). ICRC's mandate for these visits is contained in the statutes of the movement and in many resolutions adopted by International Conferences of the Red Cross and Red Crescent.

Since World War II, the ICRC has negotiated with governments access to visit some 750,000 security prisoners in more than one hundred countries and territories. ICRC makes confidential reports to governments describing conditions of detention and provides concrete proposals for improving the treatment of prisoners.[13] To ensure effective protection of prisoners and an objective assessment of the detention facilities, the ICRC delegates commonly ask to see all political prisoners; to talk freely and without witness to the prisoners of their choice; to return to detention facilities regularly; to receive a list of the prisoners; and to assist detainees and their families. The visits are often the first step for more comprehensive ICRC action. This was the case in Iran under the Shah, in El Salvador in 1979, and more recently in the former Yugoslavia and Soviet Union. Governments have no obligations to accept ICRC's services in internal strife. Incentives for accepting ICRC's visits could be domestic or international. Except in cases where delegates are direct witnesses, ICRC generally pursues quiet diplomacy. Going public on violations is exceptional and remains a last resort.

The ICRC is also an operational humanitarian organization that is active in the field on behalf of victims. It cannot be sidetracked by collecting information for the prosecution of humanitarian law violations or fact-finding.[14] Parties in conflict often have requested the ICRC to take such action. But these activities hamper ICRC's operational acceptance. This is the role of the International Fact-Finding Commission or of the States Party, individually or collectively, in cooperation with the United Nations or regional organizations.

The International Fact-Finding Commission

The International Fact Finding Commission, provided for in Article 90 of Protocol I, was established in 1991. Any High Contracting Party to the Protocol may declare at any time that it recognizes, in relation to any other High Contracting Party accepting the same obligation, the competence of the Commission to inquire into allegations of serious violations of the Geneva Conventions and the Protocol. Only thirty-one states so far have accepted the competence of this Commission,[15] and they have agreed to two prerequisites for the Commission's action. The facts must constitute a grave breach as defined in the Geneva Conventions and the Protocol or other serious violation, and the state bringing the allegations and the one against which the allegations are made must both have submitted the declaration.

The Commission is not only competent to inquire, but also to facilitate through its good offices the restoration of an attitude of respect for the Geneva Conventions and the Protocol among the parties to an armed conflict. The Commission also may conduct inquiries into serious violations, provided all the parties agree, even on an ad hoc basis. The fifteen members of the Commission independently serve for five years. The Commission has geographical and professional diversity. The findings and recommendations are confidential and submitted only to the parties. The Commission could play a complementary role to the ICRC's. The Commission's fact-finding could relieve the burden of humanitarian organizations, whose comparative advantage is to help and protect victims, not to judge facts or violators.

The United Nations

The United Nations as an institution has evolved substantially in its approach to humanitarian law. The world body initially ignored humanitarian law, reasoning that laws of war were not appropriate in view of the prohibition of war in the UN Charter.[16] The UN then sought to update its views by recognizing human rights in armed conflicts. Today, the world organization regularly declares its relevance and applicability, and strives to implement and enforce international humanitarian law. Since the session of the United Nations General Assembly after the 1968 International Conference on Human Rights in Teheran, the United Nations has recognized officially the value of international humanitarian law,[17] and has cooperated with the ICRC in promoting, disseminating, and implementing it.

United Nations resolutions (including those from the Sub-Commission on Human Rights, Commission on Human Rights, General Assembly, and Security Council) constitute evidence of *opinio juris* for determining the applicability of international humanitarian law and principles. The adoption of Security Council Resolution 688 in April 1991 opened the way to armed humanitarian intervention with Operation Provide Comfort in northern Iraq. This was viewed by many governments as a fragile precedent, particularly in light of abstentions by China and India, and negative votes by Cuba, Yemen, and Zimbabwe. Less than three years after the resolution, which was supposed to have limited replicability, the issue remains. Specifically, the tragedies of Somalia and Bosnia have suggested a growing determination by the international community to bring aid to victims, even against armed resistance, and to ensure the prosecution of war criminals.

The new roles are welcome efforts by the United Nations to address the issue of contributing to the implementation of international humanitarian law. Article 89 (Cooperation) of Protocol I in 1977 already mentioned the possible role of the UN for serious violations. The United Nations General Assembly regularly mentions international humanitarian law in its resolutions. In 1992, for example, several resolutions sought to promote universal accession: Resolution 47/36 (Status of the Protocols Additional to the Geneva Conventions of 1949 and Relating to the Protection of Victims of Armed Conflicts); Resolution 47/56 (Convention on Prohibitions or Restrictions on the Use of Certain Conventional Weapons Which May Be Deemed Excessively Injurious or to Have Indiscriminate Effects); Resolution 47/112 (Implementation of the Convention on the Rights of the Child); and Resolution 47/108 (Status of the Convention on the Prevention and Punishment of the Crime of Genocide). Still others sought to foster dissemination, training, and education of humanitarian law (for example, Resolutions 47/32, 47/36, 47/71, 47/128); advocate expert consultations by ICRC (Resolution 47/37); reaffirm the pertinence of international humanitarian law in the Middle East (Resolutions 47/63, 47/69, 47/70); condemn violations of the law in the former Yugoslavia (Resolutions 47/121, 47/80, 46/242, 47/147); and request belligerents in Afghanistan, Myanmar, the former Yugoslavia, the Sudan, and Iraq to cooperate with the ICRC (Resolutions 47/141, 47/142, 47/144, 47/145, 47/147).

On an operational level, the General Assembly also made clear linkages between effectiveness and the respect for international humanitarian law. Resolution 47/120 encouraged the Secretary-General "to continue to strengthen the capacity of the Organization in order to ensure coordinated planning and execution of humanitarian assistance programmes" and "to address the question of coordination, when necessary, between humanitarian assistance programmes and peace-keeping or related operations, preserving the non-political, neutral and impartial character of humanitarian action." Resolution 47/168 (Strengthening of the Coordination of Humanitarian Emergency Assistance of the United Nations) deserves special mention, "stressing the need for adequate protection of personnel involved in humanitarian operations, in accordance with relevant norms and principles of international law."

The Commission on Human Rights, and the Sub-Commission, both of which meet annually in Geneva at different times, are often relays to and from the General Assembly. They also increasingly make use of international humanitarian law in their deliberations, a concrete illustration of the bonds between the law and policy. The Sub-Commission was the first to mention the applicability of Protocol II in the conflict in El Salvador. This resolution facilitated ICRC negotiations with the parties to the conflict, breaking ground for the inclusion of most provisions of the 1977 Additional Protocol in the Salvadoran military instructions.

The Human Rights Commission had its first emergency session ever on a question relating to international humanitarian law in August 1992, and adopted a resolution condemning the atrocities committed in the former Yugoslavia, in particular within Bosnia-Herzegovina. The Commission appointed Tadeusz Mazowiecki, former prime minister of Poland, as Special Rapporteur.

Dozens of governmental delegations and a score of NGOs took the floor. The statements of the UNHCR and ICRC attracted particular attention. The concepts of war crimes and crimes against humanity came up frequently in debates. Many speakers described the policy of ethnic cleansing as a crime against humanity. The resolution condemned the practice "in the strongest terms" and demanded that the ICRC be granted access to all detention facilities. It called on all the parties to cease human rights violations immediately, and it recalled that they were bound to comply with their obligations under the Geneva Conventions. The Commission affirmed "the absolute necessity of ensuring access for humanitarian assistance to those in need," and specified that persons who committed or ordered the commission of grave breaches of the Geneva Conventions and their Additional Protocols would be individually responsible for the breaches. The Commission also affirmed that states were to be held accountable for human rights violations that their agents commit upon the territory of another state.[18]

Resolution 1992/S-1/1 of August 1992 made it possible to appoint a Special Rapporteur to investigate the human rights situation. His task was to seek relevant information about the human rights situation, not only from governments and individuals but also from intergovernmental and nongovernmental organizations. In 1992 the Special Rapporteur carried out three visits to the territory of the former Yugoslavia and submitted three reports to the Commission on Human Rights. These reports were also made available to the Security Council.[19]

International humanitarian law is also mentioned with increasing frequency in Security Council resolutions, which suggests the seriousness of governments to implement better the provisions of international humanitarian law. During the Gulf War, it raised disturbing questions such as: Can the Security Council adopt resolutions modifying provisions on the repatriation of prisoners of war or ignoring provisions of the 1949 Conventions on the prosecution of violations of international humanitarian law?

A detailed analysis of the Security Council's handling of humanitarian law in recent conflicts would be highly valuable in order to determine the relevance of humanitarian law in the selection of conflicts, violations, violators, and of different consequences for those not abiding by the resolutions adopted by the Council. In relationship to the conflict in the former Yugoslavia, international humanitarian law is of special interest in appreciating the significance of the following:

• Resolution 764 of July 1992 reaffirmed that all parties are bound to comply with the obligations under international humanitarian law. In particular, the Geneva Conventions were highlighted in that persons who commit or order the commission of grave breaches of the Conventions are individually responsible in respect of such breaches.

• Resolution 771 of August 1992 demanded that all parties immediately cease and desist from all breaches of international humanitarian law.

• Resolution 780 of October 1992 requested the UN Secretary-General to establish, as a matter of urgency, an impartial Commission of Experts to examine and analyze the information submitted according to previous resolutions. Together with other information that the Commission of Experts could obtain, the purpose was to provide the Secretary-General conclusions on the evidence of grave breaches of the Geneva Conventions and other international humanitarian law violations committed in the territory of the former Yugoslavia.

The International Law Commission has been deliberating for years about the Draft Code of Crimes Against Peace and Security of Mankind and the possible creation of an International Criminal Court. Recent Security Council action has been a significant step forward to face the consequences and urgency of ongoing conflicts. The unanimous adoption, in February 1993, of Resolution 808 should be hailed as a watershed in the history of international humanitarian law. Voting on a proposal by France, the Security Council decided that "an international tribunal shall be established for the prosecution of persons responsible for serious violations of international humanitarian law committed in the territory of the former Yugoslavia since 1991" and requested that the Secretary-General prepare a report within sixty days, detailing the specific structure and rules of procedure of a tribunal to prosecute war crimes perpetrated in the former Yugoslavia. The tribunal will be the first by the United Nations since Nuremberg and Tokyo, of which the principles now are being reaffirmed and will be enforced. This time, however, principle will apply not only against the vanquished.

The provisions of the 1949 Geneva Conventions—reaffirmed in 1977—would no doubt be sufficient to punish violations that have taken place in numerous conflicts since 1949. Actual prosecutions have been rare and unilateral. However, governments party to the Conventions, virtually all UN members, should be continuously reminded of their responsibilities to prosecute violators of humanitarian law.

Regional Organizations

Regional organizations play an increasing role in the promotion, dissemination, and implementation of international humanitarian law. The Arab League, the Conference on Security and Cooperation in Europe, the Council of Europe, the European Parliament, the Organization of American States, the Organization of the Islamic Conference, and the Organization of African Unity have all adopted resolutions on international humanitarian law.

As the continent where civil war is most prevalent, it would be illustrative of more general trends to examine Africa in detail. The OAU, in cooperation with ICRC, was instrumental in releasing prisoners of war in Chad, a precedent that shows the links between humanitarian action and regional security, and prepared the way for UN involvement in Somalia. In the postcolonial period, African governments were strongly against outside involvement in internal conflicts. It is worth quoting the report presented by the Secretary-General of the OAU to the Council of Ministers in Dakar in June 1992:

> The conspicuous lack of clarity regarding norms in international law which regulate the conduct of third parties is even more acute with respect to internal conflicts, whether with respect to the prevention or resolution of the latter. When, for instance, can the Secretary-General or the Bureau of the Assembly of Heads of State and Government "intervene" in a situation of escalating tensions in a Member State, to prevent the development of a full-scale conflict? In other words, what is the "entry-point?" The basis for "intervention" may be clearer when there is a total breakdown of law and order, as in the case of Liberia, and where, with the attendant human suffering, a spill-over effect is experienced within the neighboring countries. In such a situation, "intervention" may be justified on humanitarian grounds as well as on the need to restore law and order. However, pre-emptive involvement should also be permitted even in situations where tensions evolve to such a pitch that it becomes apparent that a conflict is in the making. This would transform into real terms the OAU's expressed commitment to conflict prevention.
>
> It is arguable therefore that within the context of general international law as well as humanitarian law, Africa should take the lead in developing the notion that sovereignty can legally be transcended, by the "intervention" of "outside forces," by their will to facilitate prevention and/or resolution,

particularly on humanitarian grounds. In other words, given that every African is his brother's keeper, and that our borders are at best artificial, we in Africa need to use our own cultural and social relationships to interpret the principle of noninterference in such a way that we are enabled to apply it to our advantage in conflict prevention and resolution. In developing the law, in this context, account should also be taken of the need to create and maintain an enabling environment for economic development and progress.[20]

Nongovernmental Organizations

The 1949 Geneva Conventions have provisions protecting "impartial humanitarian organizations such as the ICRC," both for civil wars and international armed conflicts. However, the activities of such organizations are subject to the consent of the parties to the conflict. Some nongovernmental organizations have emphasized gaining access to victims without waiting for an official authorization or consent to cross borders; some claimed that impartiality was not their objective and wanted to be able to denounce violations, even unilaterally. They were subjected to attacks by parties to conflicts. In some cases, their representatives were arrested and tried as spies or taken as hostages. In most cases, pressure from external governments brought these persons back to safety.

The security of NGO field staff in the field—as well as for UN and ICRC personnel—is now less an issue of humanitarian intervention or of publicly denouncing violations of humanitarian law, but rather an issue of law enforcement in situations where arson, murder, rape, torture, hostage taking, and pillaging are commonplace. NGOs could play an invaluable role in promoting the implementation of humanitarian law both in the field and within the international community. They should deploy more field workers in conflict situations (even with the security risks implied by today's conflicts) and play a more active role in lobbying the United Nations, including the Security Council and regional organizations, as well as informing public opinion.

Factors for Implementation

After discussing the institutional mechanisms, this section concludes with a discussion of seven other common legal and extralegal factors influencing the implementation of international humanitarian law. Reciprocity is not a legal condition for the application of humanitarian law. As was indicated at the outset, the four 1949 Geneva Conventions explicitly prohibit reprisals against protected persons, and Additional Protocol I prohibits reprisals against civilians, cultural objects and places of worship, objects indispensable to the survival of the civilian population, the natural environment and works, and installations containing dangerous forces. Similarly, Article 60 of the 1969 Vienna Convention in the Law of Treaties excludes reciprocity as a condition for application of humanitarian law. Reciprocity is an important aspect of the reality of armed conflict, a powerful factor in the application or nonapplication of humanitarian law. External humanitarians should appeal to belligerents and stress their mutual interests in abiding by limitations to warfare.

Public opinion is a second factor because it can deter or escalate violence. In World War II, it was used by both sides on the western front to step up retaliation bombings against civilian populations. In Algeria, French public opinion denounced and limited the use of torture by French paratroopers against Algerian prisoners. In Vietnam, domestic and international public criticism constrained U.S. bombing.

Efficacy is a third factor. Humanitarian principles and military necessity converge in the respect and protection of civilian populations and prisoners who surrender. Bombing populations into submission proved to be a tragic and counterproductive strategy both to the Third Reich against Britain and to the United Kingdom against Germany, and also to the United States in Vietnam and to the Soviet Union in Afghanistan. Killing prisoners is the best way to ensure that survivors will fight to their last cartridge rather than surrender to an inhumane adversary. Military instructions on the essentials of humanitarian law are part of maintaining discipline. French troops who believed that every blow was permitted against the enemy in Algeria soon proved to be a deadly threat to the civilian government in Paris. Violence should be used only against those using violence. In order to avoid alienating civilians, respect should be shown for persons and property. In order to obtain the surrender of combatants without unnecessary further combat, they should be guaranteed correct treatment and the prospect of release. In order to maintain discipline, enforcing humanitarian law is more effective than tolerating excesses against the enemy because the latter quickly leads to anarchy.

A fourth factor is economy. It is more costly for a party to a conflict to carry out indiscriminate attacks than to concentrate on military objectives; and there is a greater certainty that the target will be destroyed and the survival of the population that one claims to defend or liberate will not be unduly jeopardized. Article 3 of the 1907 Hague Convention IV was carried over in Article 91 of Protocol I: "A Party to the conflict which violates the provisions of the Conventions or of this Protocol shall, if the case demands, be liable to pay compensation. It shall be responsible for all acts committed by persons forming part of its armed forces." Article 51 reaffirms the customary principle of proportionality and prohibits attacks causing "excessive incidental civilian damage in relation to the concrete and direct military advantage anticipated."

Return to peace is a fifth factor because respect for humanitarian rules is important in preventing the degradation of moral and social values. Respect for humanitarian law keeps lines open for dialogue. Often the first signal for peace is the release of prisoners. Implementing humanitarian law eventually stabilizes conditions once the hostilities end, not only between former adversaries but also within their respective communities.

Preservation of civilization is a sixth factor. Wars provoke massacres, famine, disease, and mass exoduses with global consequences. Respect for humanitarian law—which in traditional civilizations was marked by the prohibition of burning crops, poisoning wells, killing cattle, and destroying temples or churches—is now an essential way to guarantee the survival of entire civilizations. The right to survival as the basis of humanitarian law is contained in the prohibition of attacks against wounded (First 1949 Convention), the sick and shipwrecked (Second 1949 Convention), and prisoners (Third 1949 Convention), as well as the civilian population (Fourth 1949 Convention and Part IV of both Additional Protocols of 1977).

Public conscience deserves special attention as the seventh factor. It is very much part of humanitarian law. The Martens Clause was introduced in the Preambles of the Hague Conventions in 1899 and 1907,[21] in the four 1949 Geneva Conventions (Articles 63, 62, 142, and 158, respectively, of the First, Second, Third and Fourth Conventions), and again in both Additional Protocols of 1977. It is perhaps clearest in Article 1 of Protocol I: "In cases not covered by this Protocol or by any other international agreements, civilians and combatants remain under the protection and authority of the principles of international law derived from established custom, from the humanity and from the dictates of public conscience."

Maintaining standards of humanity is a common task to every human being. If nothing is done or said against those who shoot down civilians in a remote country, ethnic cleansing could become admissible anywhere. President Woodrow Wilson considered using public opinion as part of a mechanism of sanctions based on collective security that aimed at repressing acts contrary to international order. Public opinion is not necessarily impartial. Public opinion can focus on humanitarian "fashions" and forget lengthy emergencies: Who cares about *la violencia* in Colombia that started in 1948? Who speaks now about the civilian victims of indiscriminate shelling or of mines in Afghanistan? Who is concerned about Central Asia or southern Africa? And who can guarantee the accuracy of facts, when truth is often the first casualty in war?[22] The Gulf War indicated how public opinion also could be manipulated,[23] just as it was during World War II when the public provoked an escalation of bombing of civilians in Germany and Great Britain.[24] Nevertheless, public opinion condemned and stopped torture by French paratroopers in Algeria,[25] disappearances in Chile and Argentina,[26] and killings of prisoners in El Salvador. Perhaps soon it will be adequate to halt ethnic cleansing in Bosnia and in other places.

Public opinion bestows legitimacy to governments, resistance movements, and individual fighters. Legitimacy also can be stripped away in case of repeated grave breaches of humanitarian law. The suspension of aid to the contras in Nicaragua and the suspension of the South African and Yugoslav delegations at the United Nations General Assembly for apartheid and ethnic cleansing are pertinent examples. As Albert Camus wrote about

Algeria: "Let's be careful to fight for (what we believe to be) a truth without destroying it by the very means used to defend it."[27] Everyone belongs to public conscience and contributes to making or unmaking this global civil society.[28]

Improving the Effectiveness of Humanitarian Law and Action

This chapter began with the premise that the basic framework of international humanitarian law is sufficient in the 1949 Geneva Conventions and 1977 Additional Protocols. What is necessary is to improve the operational effectiveness or implementation of these conventions. Several possibilities are described in this concluding section.

More and Safer Humanitarian Personnel

Emergency relief is only one way to cope with the needs of victims of today's conflicts. Protecting victims against acts of violence is a necessary complement to relief. In many cases, assistance would not be needed if appropriate protection were provided. Protection of human rights means prevention, and should be understood as the guarantee of the interests of all parties, as well as the safeguard for fundamental human values such as the freedom from summary execution, torture, and ill treatment. According to customary and treaty law, these are unassailable international standards. Protection requires immediate presence, with access to civilian victims in their villages and prisoners in their jails or makeshift detention camps.

More than any new structure in New York or Geneva, humanitarian action needs more field workers, more dedicated men and women ready to serve the victims in Bosnia, Colombia, Peru, Somalia, and the Sudan. The respect and proper use of protective emblems (red cross, red crescent, United Nations flag) is an important part of the protection of wounded and sick, as well as of ICRC delegates and UN workers in the field. Rather than military escorts, ICRC and Red Cross and Red Crescent National Societies choose first to rely on the protective emblem, and on constant contact with all parties to conflicts to inform them of their moves and to check with them that safe passage will be guaranteed. A second level of protection is granted by such passive measures as shelters. A third exceptional step, which was necessary in situations such as Lebanon and Somalia, was to hire local security personnel.

Safety of personnel is also a key problem for the United Nations in conditions of strife. In *An Agenda for Peace*, UN Secretary-General Boutros Boutros-Ghali proposed in June 1992:

> Given the pressing need to afford adequate protection to United Nations personnel engaged in life-endangering circumstances, I recommend that the Security Council, unless it elects immediately to withdraw the United Nations presence in order to preserve the credibility of the Organization, gravely consider what action should be taken towards those who put United Nations

personnel in danger. Before deployment takes place, the Council should keep open the option of considering in advance collective measures, possibly including those under Chapter VII when a threat to international peace and security is also involved, to come into effect should the purpose of the United Nations operation systematically be frustrated and hostilities occur.[29]

By late September 1992, the conditions had not improved:

The security and protection of staff and safe and effective delivery of relief materials are major concerns with regard to humanitarian efforts in conflict situations. Indeed, the situations in Somalia and the former Yugoslavia have demonstrated that it may not be a question of the capacity to deliver, but rather of the security conditions pertaining to distribution of relief supplies, which determine whether humanitarian assistance can be provided. Volatile security situations have led to the suspensions of operations. In other cases, relief operations have continued, but at a considerable hazard for those involved. United Nations and other humanitarian relief workers are often exposed to great dangers and many are risking their lives on a daily basis.[30]

Among the factors determining the parameters for UN personnel are the decisionmaking process within the UN secretariat, regional organizations, the main governments involved, and the private humanitarian organizations; the timing (beginning and duration) of the operation; and the objectives of the operation (humanitarian, settlement of the conflict, reestablishment of law and order, cessation of threats to the regional security).

The United Nations is increasingly integrating humanitarian and peace-keeping operations. In El Salvador (ONUSAL) and Mozambique (ONUMOZ and its UN humanitarian component), there have been elements of both. In Somalia humanitarian activities protected by soldiers were the entire operation beginning in December 1992. In Bosnia, armed elements of UNPROFOR have been crucial and could become an even stronger element in future operations.

Therefore, the presence of an impartial humanitarian body like the ICRC, independent of the United Nations, still will be very much needed. This may be more important in view of the increasingly political involvement by the UN in peacekeeping and humanitarian activities. Independence does not exclude cooperation that does not jeopardize ICRC's impartiality and neutrality in the eyes of all parties to a conflict. Cooperation should take place at various levels, between the Secretary-General of the UN and the President of the ICRC, in the field, and at UN headquarters. In situations of acute crisis, it may be desirable to place a few ICRC staff on the UN Secretary-General's small humanitarian staff.

Broadening the Humanitarian Network

As has been indicated elsewhere in this volume, humanitarian action needs to be conceived and implemented in the broader context of economic and social development. Moreover, it will operate increasingly side by side with peacekeeping, preventive diplomacy, peacemaking, law enforcement, and the prosecution of war criminals. Humanitarian organizations should limit themselves to emergency relief and protection. They will be overstretched soon if governments and other organizations do not produce results in the areas of development, rehabilitation, peacekeeping, and law enforcement.

Humanitarian organizations nevertheless should cooperate, even informally, with other organizations active in development or rehabilitation. They need to examine, on an ad hoc and case-by-case basis, what kinds of service could be delivered best by which agent to what kind of persons in need. In other words, a better international division of labor would benefit both donors and recipients.

There are many interrelationships among humanitarian activities, ranging from development, rehabilitation, and law enforcement to peacemaking. The role of humanitarian law in maintaining peace is clear. Breaches of humanitarian law have started conflicts. Serious violations of humanitarian law have sparked internal and international wars. Massacres of civilian populations in the Middle East, Latin America, Southeast Asia, and Europe all inflamed hatred and passion rather than imposing fear and submission. Breaches of humanitarian law have permitted conflicts to spread. Refugees are a good example. As victims of persecution in their homeland, they often transmit the violence to which they were subjected to neighboring or more distant countries. Another example is the rise of violence in war-affected countries, often years after the end of the war.

Humanitarian law also is linked to restoring peace. The possibility of dialogue is facilitated by avoiding degradation and excessive violence among adversaries, internationally and among one's own population internally. Unsolved humanitarian problems (refugees, prisoners, disappeared, missing in action) often become serious political issues. They hamper the resumption of normal relations among countries and belligerents, often years or decades after the actual cessation of combat. Vietnam's refusal to abide by the Third Geneva Convention and the unsolved case of U.S. MIAs brought about a seventeen-year-old trade embargo against Vietnam. In spite of these links, ICRC's humanitarian efforts are purposely kept separate from political efforts by regional or universal organizations to restore or enforce peace. However, limiting action to strictly humanitarian activities can have a direct and positive impact upon the eventual successful implementation of political negotiations.

Before political negotiations begin, humanitarian gestures help to institute a minimum of confidence and trust necessary for meaningful dialogue between or among adversaries. Such gestures include cease-fires—often tacit—between enemy positions; evacuation of the dead and wounded; truces to let civilians out or supply them with food and medicines; and contacts to exchange news of the latest captures or even prisoners. The co-chairmen of the Steering Committee of the International Conference on the Former Yugoslavia, Cyrus Vance and David Owen, placed human rights and humanitarian issues at the core of their peacemaking. At the commencement of the peace talks on Bosnia-Herzegovina on January 2, 1993, they made the following appeal to the parties to the conflict: "Your immediate release of all detainees is essential. It would not only be an indication of your peaceful intentions, but could also help to stop the drums of war, which are beating so loudly around us as we meet here today."[31]

A humanitarian truce may lead to a complete halt to the fighting. In Santo Domingo in 1965, for instance, the efforts of the ICRC delegate and the president of the local Red Cross were combined with those of UN and OAS representatives. They succeeded in halting fighting for twenty-four hours in order to collect the wounded, and during this time, negotiations were held that put an end to the armed clashes.

Adversaries usually wish to negotiate humanitarian clauses first. For example, the provisional government of the Republic of Algeria sought to begin negotiations with a "Special Agreement" with the French government, under Common Article 3 to the 1949 Geneva Conventions. After a refusal from Paris, it initiated the procedure for accession to the four 1949 Geneva Conventions. In 1984 in La Palma, El Salvador, the first item in the negotiations between the government and the FMLN guerrillas was "to humanize the war" ("humanizar la guerra"). The first contacts between Soviet representatives and mujahidins in Afghanistan dealt with the plight of prisoners of war. The first talks between various warring factions in the former Yugoslavia were held in Geneva in 1991 under the auspices of the ICRC to agree on such humanitarian issues as prisoner exchange and relief to civilians.

The treatment of prisoners and civilian populations plays an important role in the return to peace. Repatriation of refugees also is an essential component for the restoration of peace, which is difficult if villages have been razed and roads and fields strewn with mines. The question is highly relevant today for hundreds of thousands of Afghans, Angolans, Cambodians, and Mozambicans.

In noninternational or civil conflicts, amnesty corresponds to an essential feature of prisoner-of-war status, namely impunity for participation in the hostilities. It is also a powerful means of relieving antagonism, a measure of national reconciliation following a crisis, and a political solution to a conflict. It encourages partisans of armed struggle to turn or return to democratic forms of political competition. Article 6 of Protocol II of 1977 invites governments "to grant the broadest possible amnesty to persons who have participated in the armed conflict." The object of this provision is to encourage gestures of reconciliation that contribute to reestablishing normal relations in a divided nation.

More Preventive Action, Preparedness Training, and Education
Awareness of humanitarian rules and principles, and of their compelling character, can restrain violence. In the Gulf War, ICRC preventive humanitarian diplomacy took place from August 1991 to January 1992, with missions both to Baghdad and Washington, as well as to all capitals in direct contact with Iraq. It confirmed, after the adoption on November 29, 1990, by the Security Council, Resolution 678 that authorized member states to use "all necessary means" to liberate Kuwait by force as of January 15, 1991. The ICRC reminded all High Contracting Parties of the humanitarian principles involved. The ICRC dispatched representatives from headquarters to Baghdad, Washington, London, Paris, Tehran, Riyadh, Damascus, Amman, and Cairo.[32]

Dissemination, by both training and education, of international humanitarian law is a crucial obligation of the States Party to the Geneva Conventions. This is part of a preventive approach for implementing international humanitarian law, a duty reaffirmed and detailed in Additional Protocol I (Articles 83, 87, and 82). Targets for training and educational efforts include armed forces personnel, universities (not only law schools), civil servants, and diplomats. More effort should be spent on promoting the training of armed forces and police about the provisions of international humanitarian law. A special emphasis should be put on countries facing conflict, or that are conflict prone, and those that may provide or host UN peacekeeping forces, as has been suggested by the UN Secretary-General.[33]

Drafting, translating, printing, and distributing training material for armed forces and police should be a priority, especially because more and more of them are being called upon to participate in UN operations that have humanitarian dimensions. International humanitarian law and Red Cross and Red Crescent principles and mandates should be included in all training for UN peacekeeping forces and accompanying administrative personnel.[34] Instructions to force commanders stipulate that UN operations are to be conducted with full respect for the principles and spirit of international instruments applicable to the conduct of military personnel. In cooperation with the Department of Peace-keeping Operations and other offices within the UN secretariat, the legal counsel of the United Nations is taking a first important step by organizing training courses for legal advisers with peacekeeping missions.[35]

In addition to special efforts in operational areas like the Persian Gulf or the former Yugoslavia, where combatants were the priority target of dissemination efforts, ICRC has made with the International Institute on Humanitarian Law important contributions over the years in regularly organizing training of military personnel in San Remo, Italy. Recently, there is a new emphasis on regional seminars: Laws of War for Military Officers in Europe (Athens, Bucharest, Budapest, and Sofia in 1991); Conference on International Humanitarian Law for Armed Forces of States Members of

OAU (Nairobi in December 1991); and East Asia Military Seminar on the Law of War (Singapore in March 1992).

The production and distribution of publications, videotapes, cassette tapes, and educational CD-ROM on international humanitarian law and skills for humanitarian activities is required not only in the traditional written languages of the ICRC (English, French, and Spanish), but also in all official languages of the United Nations, as well as in the indigenous languages for areas in conflict. During the Gulf War, ICRC printed and distributed bilingual (Arabic/English) booklets on the laws of war and first aid for troops in the Persian Gulf, and posted an ICRC regional delegate to the armed forces in Amman, Jordan. In South Africa in 1991, about one hundred thousand copies of a comic strip were produced with the aim to put across the Red Cross principles to young people involved in communal violence. ICRC translated into Russian in 1992 the Geneva Conventions, which had been considered a confidential document by Soviet authorities. In 1993 a Summary of the Conventions, a Handbook for Armed Forces, and a leaflet on ICRC and the Red Cross/Red Crescent Movement were translated into fifteen languages of the former Soviet Union. ICRC's CD-ROM on international humanitarian law will be ready in English in June 1993. This should facilitate inexpensive access to large amounts of humanitarian documentation and data.

Seminars for diplomats on international humanitarian law are another training effort. They have been organized annually in New York (in collaboration with New York University Law School since 1983), Washington (with the American Red Cross and American University School of Law since 1983), and Geneva (with the Graduate Institute of International Studies since May 1992). These seminars are opportunities for informal dialogue between ICRC staff and multilateral diplomats. "Networking" is often the best way to explain ICRC's peculiar approach. ICRC neither crashes borders as some NGOs proudly proclaim, nor waits until a request comes from a government as is the rule for most UN organizations. It does not advocate the right to intervene on humanitarian grounds, but affirms the right of victims to receive assistance and protection, according to the relevant provisions of international humanitarian law. The ICRC maintains contact with all belligerents to guarantee the effectiveness and the security of its action on behalf of victims.[36]

Selection and training of expatriate field personnel for posting in conflicts requires more attention than in the past. The professionalism of expatriates and of local personnel largely determines the effectiveness of a humanitarian operation. A first step has been made in field medicine in cooperation with the World Health Organization (WHO) and the Geneva University School of Medicine to organize seminars for medical and sanitary personnel in emergency situations. This follows the ICRC's production in 1988 of a movie entitled *War Surgery: An Introduction* and the publication of field manuals. Training courses and materials need to be expanded and now are being considered in different locations, including in North America. They are available to personnel from intergovernmental and nongovernmental organizations, as well as to government officials.

As for local personnel, ICRC regional delegations are assisting national societies of the Red Cross and the Red Crescent to provide training in first aid, dissemination, and tracing activities to make them better able to cope during emergencies, unrest, and conflicts. One of these programs is the Community Organizers Program, in South Africa, where ICRC supports efforts to broaden the grassroots membership of the South African Red Cross in training local Red Cross volunteers in black townships.

International and local media are increasingly an ally of humanitarian efforts on matters of enhancing consciousness and agency visibility. As an expert group recently noted: "Humanitarian action will increasingly depend on the mobilization of public support throughout the world. Public education as to the causes and consequences of humanitarian emergencies is a matter of priority concern. New strategies for effective public information are needed to meet the new challenges of the post–Cold War era."[37] The media should be more active, not waiting until a BBC team comes to Ethiopia to "discover" a famine situation, for example, and aim to prevent violations of international humanitarian law against civilians, prisoners, and field workers of humanitarian organizations.

There is a need for a media campaign on humanitarian principles and action, with a special emphasis on continents, countries, and areas threatened by man-made disasters, and with the message tailored to local cultures and in local languages. The first step is identifying individuals in the media able to present the message effectively and credibly. The second step is to provide media representatives with substantive and up-to-date information on humanitarian issues and activities, and to support them with translations, transmission of images, and reproduction of printed or audiovisual materials.

For example, ICRC dissemination delegates in the former Yugoslavia strive to enlist the support and cooperation of the country's many local radio stations and newspapers. As ethnic warfare is no longer the business of professional soldiers and the course of hostilities is not always decided by the military, civilians and combatants must be reached through TV spots, eyewitness accounts, and reports on ICRC activities in the villages. Since local media very often are characterized by intolerance and extremism, the humanitarian message must counter these attitudes and build the image of a neutral, impartial organization whose activities benefit all victims.[38]

A third possible step could be to establish independent channels (newsletters, posters, broadcasting stations), either in cooperation with local organizations (the first candidate being the local National Society of the Red Cross/Red Crescent) or the ICRC itself (through small, mobile FM transmitters). This requires, especially in very poor countries, the distribution of cheap radio receivers to villages to increase the reception and acceptability of the message. Few combatants or civilians in today's conflicts read newspapers; most of them listen to the radio. Effective humanitarian messages could help prevent violations by spreading fundamental principles and information on humanitarian operations.

Collective Security Through Solidarity
Humanitarian action should become part of a new concept for national and international security. States should no longer attempt to argue that security is not imperiled by an uprising in a remote island or a confrontation in the Central Asian mountains. Even if there are no riches or direct geopolitical intent in those conflict areas, refugees will be seeking havens in all parts of the world.[39]

A new national security concept, based on collective security, is needed. Solidarity among countries and continents to guarantee international stability should help shift the emphasis away from military security toward more active, preventive approaches, including extended dialogues at national, regional, and universal levels to address situations before they become crises; the strengthening of multilateral institutions, including the United Nations and regional organizations, their peacekeeping and peacemaking capacity, and their preventive diplomacy efforts; a primary concern with economic issues and combating threats without enemies (environmental, population, and health issues); and global negotiations on mass destruction and conventional arms reductions, as well as convening a new conference on disarmament.

What is needed is a humanitarian mobilization for survival, not only of individual countries but also of humankind.[40] Humanitarians should formulate an action program:

1. Consider the best ways to implement common values to humankind, including respect for different values and peaceful settlement of disputes. Part of this strategy includes a more global approach toward controlling violence on the personal and collective levels and drawing concrete lessons from earlier humanitarian or peacekeeping operations.

2. Reaffirm humanitarian rules (ratify and implement existing instruments) and principles (promote ethical education).

3. Create a network of local and expatriate organizations and individuals willing and able to support humanitarian efforts. Resources can be made available to cope with civilian suffering.

4. Negotiate quietly first. Behind closed doors, people are more prone to listen and accept even difficult messages. Go public as the last resort.

5. Encourage independent broadcasting. Public opinion can be a powerful influence on any party to a conflict and should be used to guide energies toward humanitarian action—if necessary by exposing violations to enforce implementation—and not toward more hate. Governments should be

encouraged to use their individual and collective responsibility as States Party to the fullest extent of the law, including for the prosecution of war criminals. Information should be made available and intelligence shared with intergovernmental organizations (both the United Nations and regional organizations) so that they can switch their emphases toward prevention. NGOs have a key role in publicizing situations, issues, and violations, as well as in mobilizing public opinion so that governments and other belligerents will abide by their humanitarian obligations.

6. Have a global view of humanity. Bosnia and Somalia could have a direct impact on Europe and the United States. Chaotic and poor corners of the world could become places where drug producing and trafficking, weapons trade, and terrorism thrive. Humanitarian action is needed to keep open the dialogue among parties. Violations of humanitarian law provoke flows of refugees seeking food and shelter abroad, and failure by the international community to confront violations of humanitarian law in one part of the world is an abdication of our humanity and an invitation to further violations.

7. Work against all odds. There are no instant solutions to conflicts or to perilous emergencies. Assessment of needs, negotiation with all parties, patience, and perseverance are required to sustain victims of war. Today's outburst of violence could be met and checked best with a combination of firmness, respect, and compassion.

Notes

The opinions given here do not necessarily reflect the position of the International Committee of the Red Cross (ICRC).

1. On existing humanitarian law, see Geoffrey Best, *Humanity in Warfare: The Modern History of the International Law of Armed Conflicts* (London: Weidenfels and Nicholson, 1980); Hugo Grotius, *De jure belli ac pacis: The Law of War and Peace* (Indianapolis: Bobbs-Merril Co., 1963); Max Huber, *The Good Samaritan: Reflections on the Gospel and Work of the Red Cross* (London: Gollancz, 1945); *International Dimensions of Humanitarian Law* (Dordrecht: Martinus Nijhoff, 1988); Jean Pictet, *Humanitarian Law and the Protection of War Victims* (Leiden: Sijthoff, 1957); and Dietrich Schindler, "The Different Types of Armed Conflicts According to the Geneva Conventions and Protocols," *RCADI* 163, no. 2 (1979): 117–163.

2. See Jean S. Pictet (ed.), *The Conventions of 12 August 1949. Commentary*, 4 vols. (Geneva: ICRC, 1952–1960).

3. See Michael Bothe, Karl Josef Partsch, and Waldemar A. Solf, *New Rules for Victims of Armed Conflicts. Commentary on the Two Protocols Additional to the Geneva Conventions of 1949* (The Hague: Martinus Nijhoff, 1982); and Yves Sandoz, Christophe Swinarski, and Bruno Zimmermann (eds.), *Commentary on the Additional Protocols of 8 June 1977 to the Geneva Conventions of August 12, 1949* (Geneva: ICRC, 1986).

4. For the link between human rights and international humanitarian law, see Asbjørn Eide, "The Laws of War and Human Rights—Differences and

Convergences," in Christophe Swinarski (ed.), *Studies and Essays on International Humanitarian Law and Red Cross Principles in Honor of Jean Pictet* (Geneva: ICRC, 1984): 675–697; Hector Gros Espiell, "Derechos humanos, derecho internacional humanitario y derecho internacional de los refugiados," in Swinarski, *Studies*, 699–711; and A. H. Robertson, "Humanitarian Law and Human Rights," in Swinarski, *Studies*, 793–802.

5. For the link between disarmament and international humanitarian law, see Antoine Bouvier, "Protection of the Natural Environment in Time of Armed Conflict," *International Review of the Red Cross* (November/December 1991): 567–578; Knut Ipsen, "International Law Preventing Armed Conflicts and International Law of Armed Conflict—a Combined Functional Approach," in Swinarski, *Studies*, 349–358; Frits Kalshoven, *Constraints on the Waging of War* (Geneva: ICRC, 1987); Arthur H. Westing (ed.), *Environmental Hazards of War: Releasing Dangerous Forces in an Industrialized World* (London: Sage Publications, 1990).

6. Georges Abi-Saab, "The Specificities of Humanitarian Law," in Swinarski, *Studies*, 265–280; Robert Axelrod, *The Evolution of Cooperation* (New York: Basic Books, 1984); Emmanuel Bello, *African Customary Humanitarian Law* (Geneva: ICRC, 1980); and Geoffrey Best, *Humanity in Warfare: The Modern History of the International Law of Armed Conflicts* (London: Weidenfels and Nicolson, 1980).

7. For the implementation of international humanitarian law, see Georges Abi-Saab, *The Implementation of Humanitarian Law in the New Humanitarian Law of Armed Conflict* (Napoli: Giuffrè, 1979): 310–346; *Respect for International Humanitarian Law: ICRC Review of Five Years of Activity (1987–1991)* (Geneva: ICRC, December 10, 1991); G.I.A.D. Draper, "The Implementation and Enforcement of the Geneva Conventions of 1949 and of the Two Additional Protocols," *Recueil des Cours* 3 (1979): 1–54; David P. Forsythe, "Human Rights and the International Committee of the Red Cross," *Human Rights Quarterly* 12, no. 2 (May 1990): 265–289; Frits Kalshoven and Yves Sandoz (eds.), *Implementation of International Humanitarian Law* (Dordrecht: Martinus Nijhoff, 1989); George A. B. Peirce, "Humanitarian Protection for the Victims of War. The System of Protecting Powers and the Role of the ICRC," *Military Law Review* 90 (1980): 89–162; and Michel Veuthey, "The Global Reach of International Humanitarian Law," in R. C. Hingorani (ed.), *Humanitarian Law* (New Delhi: Oxford & IBH Publishing Co., 1987): 39–54.

8. See Luigi Condorelli and Laurence Boisson de Chazournes, "Quelques remarques à propos de l'obligation des Etats de 'respecter et faire respecter' le droit international humanitaire 'en toutes circonstances,'" in Swinarski, *Studies*, 17–35; and Michel Veuthey, "Pour une politique humanitaire," in Swinarski, *Studies*, 989–1009.

9. See Igor P. Blishchenko, "Responsibility in Breaches of Humanitarian Law," *International Dimensions*, 285.

10. On the various material scopes of application of humanitarian law, see Dietrich Schindler, "The Different Types of Armed Conflicts According to the Geneva Conventions and Protocols," *Recueil des Cours* 2 (1979): 117–164.

11. See Rosemary Abi-Saab, *Droit humanitaire et conflits internes* (Paris: Pedone, 1986); and Michel Veuthey, "Implementation and Enforcement of Humanitarian Law and Human Rights Law in Non-international Armed Conflicts: The Role of the International Committee of the Red Cross," *American University Law Review* 33, no. 1 (Fall 1983): 83–97.

12. See Yves Sandoz, "Le droit d'initiative du CICR," *Jahrbuch für Internationales Recht* (Göttingen) 22 (1979): 352–373.

13. Jacques Moreillon, *Le Comité international de la Croix-Rouge et la protection des détenus politiques* (Lausanne: L'Age d'Homme, 1973); and Roland Siegrist, *The Protection of Political Detainees: The International Committee of the Red Cross in Greece, 1967–1971* (Montreux: Editions Corbaz, 1985).

14. Until the eve of the Diplomatic Conference on the Reaffirmation and Development of International Humanitarian Law Applicable in Armed Conflicts (Geneva, 1974–1977) that established the International Fact-Finding Commission, the ICRC was often approached by parties to conflicts to forward protests by one party to the other on alleged violations. That was the case in the October War in 1973 between Egypt and Israel; this role did not enhance the ICRC's operational acceptance, but impeded it.

15. Algeria, Australia, Austria, Belarus, Belgium, Bolivia, Canada, Chile, Croatia, Denmark, Finland, Germany, Hungary, Iceland, Italy, Liechtenstein, Malta, Netherlands, New Zealand, Norway, Qatar, Russia, Seychelles, Slovenia, Spain, Sweden, Switzerland, Togo, Ukraine, United Arab Emirates, Uruguay.

16. See the *Yearbook of the International Law Commission* (New York: United Nations, 1949): para. 18.

17. See Resolution 2444 (XXIII) of December 1968 (Respect for Human Rights in Armed Conflicts).

18. Adrien-Claude Zoller, "Commission on Human Rights. Emergency Session on the Situation in the Former Yugoslavia," *Human Rights Monitor, International Service for Human Rights*, no. 17–18 (September 1992): 42–45.

19. See documents A/47/418-S/24516, A/47/635-S/24766, and A/47/666-S/24809.

20. "Report of the Secretary-General on Conflicts in Africa: Proposals for a Mechanism for Conflict Prevention and Resolution," Addis Ababa, Organization of African Unity, document CM/1710 (LVI), presented to the Fifty-sixth Ordinary Session of the Council of Ministers in Dakar (Senegal), June 22–27, 1992, 12.

21. Paragraph 9 of the 1899 Convention and paragraph 8 of the 1907 Convention. See Shigeki Miyazaki, "The Martens Clause and International Humanitarian Law," in Swinarski, *Studies*, 433–444.

22. See Phillip Knightley, *The First Casualty from Crimea to Vietnam: The War Correspondent as Hero, Propagandist, and Myth Maker* (New York: Harcourt, Brace Jovanovich, 1975).

23. See John R. MacArthur, *Second Front: Censorship and Propaganda in the Gulf War* (New York: Hill and Wang, 1992); Hedrick Smith (ed.), *The Media and the Gulf War: The Press and Democracy in Wartime* (New York: Seven Locks Press, 1992); and Philip M. Taylor, *War and the Media* (Manchester: Manchester University Press, 1992).

24. See Frits Kalshoven, *Belligerent Reprisals* (Leyden: Sijthoff, 1971).

25. See John E. Talbott, *The War Without A Name: France in Algeria, 1954–1962* (New York: Knopf, 1980).

26. See Iain Guest, *Behind the Disappearances: Argentina's Dirty War Against Human Rights and the United Nations* (Philadelphia: University of Pennsylvania Press, 1990).

27. "Se battre pour une vérité en veillant à ne pas la tuer des armes mêmes dont on la défend." Albert Camus, *Actuelles III. Chroniques algériennes 1939–1958* (Paris: Gallimard, 1958): 24.

28. See Richard Falk, "New Dimensions in International Relations and the Infancy of Global Civil Society," *ICIS Forum* 22, no. 2 (April 1992): 85–91.

29. Boutros Boutros-Ghali, *An Agenda for Peace* (New York: United Nations, 1992): para. 68.

30. Boutros Boutros-Ghali, "Report on the Work of the Organization from the

Forty-sixth to the Forty-seventh Session of the General Assembly," document A/47/1, para. 158.

31. See Annex I of "International Conference on the former Yugoslavia. The Co-Chairmen of the Steering Committee and Human Rights Issues in the Former Yugoslavia. Report of the Secretary-General on the Activities of the International Conference on the Former Yugoslavia," document S/25221, 1993, paras. 1 and 5.

32. See Angelo Gnaedinger, "Travels, Negotiations and Innumerable Meetings: Persistent Humanitarian Diplomacy," in *The Gulf 1990–1991. From Crisis to Conflict. The ICRC at Work* (Geneva: ICRC, 1991): 10–11.

33. Boutros Boutros-Ghali, *Agenda,* para. 52.

34. See Yves Sandoz, "The Application of Humanitarian Law by the Armed Forces of the United Nations Organization," *International Review of the Red Cross* (September/October 1978): 274–284; and Dietrich Schlinder, "United Nations Forces and International Humanitarian Law," in Swinarski, *Studies,* 521–530.

35. See Carl-August Fleischhauer, UN Under-Secretary-General for Legal Affairs, statement delivered at the Tenth Annual ICRC Seminar for Diplomats on International Humanitarian Law, New York University, January 19, 1993.

36. See Yves Sandoz, "'Droit' ou 'devoir d'ingérence' and the Right to Assistance: The Issues Involved," *International Review of the Red Cross* (1992): 215–227; Maurice Torrelli, "From Humanitarian Assistance to Intervention on Humanitarian Grounds," ibid., 228–248; Jarat Chopra and Thomas G. Weiss, "Sovereignty Is No Longer Sacrosanct: Codifying Humanitarian Intervention," *Ethics and International Affairs* 6 (1992): 95–117; and International Institute of Humanitarian Law, "The Evolution of the Right to Assistance," selection of reports submitted and interventions made at the 17th Round Table on Current Problems of Humanitarian Law, San Remo, Italy, September 2–4, 1992.

37. Refugee Policy Group, *The Bellagio Statement on Humanitarian Action in the Post Cold War Era* (Washington, D.C.: Refugee Policy Group, 1992): 10–11.

38. Gilbert Holleufer, "The Media and Advance Protection," *ICRC Bulletin,* no. 203 (December 1992): 2.

39. See "Note on International Protection," presented by the Director of International Protection of the UNHCR to the UNHCR Executive Committee in October 1992, document A/AC.96/799, and the comments by member governments in the "Report of the Sub-Committee of the Whole on International Protection," document A/AC.96/802.

40. Jean-Christophe Ruffin, *L'Empire et les nouveaux Barbares* (Paris: J. C. Lattes, 1991).

■ 8 ■

Humanitarian Assistance in the Post–Cold War Era

FREDERICK C. CUNY

The end of the Cold War—and of U.S. Cold War administrations—created a unique opportunity to profoundly change the international humanitarian system. There will be new challenges, many resulting from the collapse of the Soviet Union, and a reordering of the international power structure. It is unlikely that the vacuum left by Russia's withdrawal from superpower competition will remain empty. Contenders to fill the void could include China, Japan, India, or a combination of these. But for the time being, the absence of superpower rivalry will provide opportunities to resolve many of the conflicts on the periphery of the East-West confrontation. Opportunities will arise for making fundamental changes in the international humanitarian system. Major flaws in the United Nations system can be corrected; new organizations can be created to reach groups of victims that were once unreachable; and the major powers can focus on trying to stem the growing tide of human rights abuses, separatist wars, and ethnic conflicts.

This window of opportunity is not likely to remain open for long. Indeed, the forces that opened the window also added new stresses to the international environment. The dissolution of the Soviet Union left a dozen unstable countries in its wake and weakened the controls that kept ethnonationalism and racial and cultural prejudices in check. The current relief system, which is already under major strain, could face a 50 percent increase in caseload by the end of the 1990s.

Recent Political Changes and Developments

Four international developments will shape humanitarian assistance in the next decade and beyond:

1. The reordering of Western power resulting from the end of the Cold War;
2. The resurgence of Islamic power;

151

3. The reemergence of ethnonationalism; and
4. The shift toward market-based democracies.

Each of these presents new opportunities and poses new constraints on international relief and development agencies, and are discussed below.

The End of the Cold War

The end of the Cold War is the dominant event of the 1990s and, indeed, of the latter half of the twentieth century. From a geopolitical standpoint, the most significant factor to emerge is Western collective preeminence as the dominant world power. In military terms, the West is the coalition forged by the United States to confront Saddam Hussein in the Gulf War. That war demonstrated the superiority of Western military technology and ended the United States' self-imposed, post-Vietnam restraint from an interventionist foreign policy.

Another event caused by the Gulf War opened a new chapter in relief operations: the humanitarian intervention to protect the Kurds in northern Iraq. In terms of military operations, it was only a footnote to the end of the war, but Operation Provide Comfort had major implications for post–Cold War humanitarian crises. It demonstrated what could be done by using Western troops to create safe havens to permit the Kurdish repatriation, and by summoning the will to impose restraints on the Iraqi government to stop the killing.

As Operation Provide Comfort ended, there were summonses for similar military-civilian interventions in the former Yugoslavia, the Caucasus, and Somalia. It is clear that if the Western powers choose to intervene, they have the capability to do so—and to do it effectively. However, interventions of this sort contradict the post-Vietnam military doctrines adopted by the United States, as elaborated first by former Secretary of Defense Caspar Weinberger and reiterated by the Chairman of the Joint Chiefs of Staff, General Colin Powell. This doctrine calls for nonintervention unless the government of the United States is committed to total victory, a resolution of Congress expresses popular support for the action, and there are clear and attainable objectives. Before Operation Provide Comfort, few legislators would have called for military intervention in a humanitarian crisis. But Operation Provide Comfort was successful—without the loss of one coalition soldier— and it demonstrated that joint military and civilian operations could give relief agencies a chance to accomplish their humanitarian work safely.

The Cold War ended because of the economic collapse and implosion of the Soviet Union. The breakup of the Soviet empire has led to the realignment of vast geographic areas. The eastern European states of the former Warsaw Pact have essentially jumped from East to West, and their economies have moved ever closer to those of the European Community. The newly independent central Asian republics have not yet found their way.

They are actively being courted by Turkey, which is acting as a surrogate for the West, Iran, which is hoping to extend its influence and power northward, India and Pakistan, which are looking for new markets, and Russia, which wants to maintain favorable trade relations with its former satellites.

Russia was transformed from power to pauper. Its massive military-industrial complex lies idle, its currency is scorned by its own citizens, and its vaunted social welfare system, which offered at least some protection against personal poverty for most citizens, is on the brink of collapse. The decline of Russia has major consequences for the international humanitarian system. As the Russian food and economic system is reoriented, it is likely to require massive food aid from the West. Ethnic divisions and rivalries—long suppressed by Moscow—have reemerged in the former Soviet republics and throughout the Russian federation. Dozens of conflicts have displaced hundreds of thousands of people. Ethnic Russians who moved to the central Asian republics during the past century find that they are largely unwelcome in their adopted lands; hundreds of thousands of people have left central Asia, with more likely to leave in the immediate future.

The movement of large numbers of people inside Russia has put severe strains on the social support system, contributed to the disruption of agriculture, and slowed the integration of markets between Russia and the other former Soviet republics. Russia's massive aid requirements will compete with those of the Third World. Russia, once an aid giver, is today a major aid receiver.

Former Soviet client states, especially in the Third World, have moved from centralized to market economies, and this move stimulated disenchantment with centralized government. Socialist government structures were abandoned in favor of market-supported democracies. In essence, many revolutionary movements were stripped of an ideology and a doctrine upon which to base their social revolutions; they simply ran out of steam. Democracy movements around the world gained momentum, and as the global economy expands, their chances for survival increase. In Latin America, the number of dictatorships dropped from fourteen to four in a decade. As the superpower rivalry fades, Western donors have increased the pressures on authoritarian regimes of all stripes to liberalize and share power.

These developments have two implications. First, there is less tolerance of dictators. What was justified as strategic pragmatism in the Cold War is now viewed with disdain. Human rights abuses are less tolerated, and gross misconduct of a government against its citizens is likely to be roundly condemned. Second, there has been a corresponding increase in the West's willingness to aid these victims and, in some cases, intervene. Intervention may take the form of sanctions, but the West is showing a greater willingness to support operations inside a country, or to support measures to gain access for humanitarian operations—measures that constitute an intrusion into the internal affairs of the offending country. After the breakup of the Soviet Union,

Russia no longer cares what happens to the former client states of the Soviet Union, and even if it did, there is little it could do about it.

Resurgence of Islamic Power

The collapse of the Soviet Union also has accelerated the rise of Islamic influence as a major force in the post–Cold War era. As long as the southern republics of the Soviet Union were bound together as a nation, the Muslims were a minority, albeit a large one. With the dissolution of the union, six new—and potentially powerful—Islamic nations have emerged: Kazakhstan, Tajikistan, Uzbekistan, Turkmenistan, Kyrgystan, and Azerbaijan. Five of these republics sit on major oil reserves, and all have important strategic minerals. More Islamic states are likely to emerge from the ruins of the former Soviet Union, and Islamic politics are apt to be an increasingly important factor in Russian internal affairs.

An increase in the number of Muslim states affected by Islamic fundamentalist movements is of major concern to the West. Much fundamentalist rhetoric is based on anti-Western sentiment and is a rejection of Western values. Even as its influence on world politics increases, the Islamic world is divided by the pro- and antifundamentalist sentiments that are swirling throughout the Muslim community. The West is largely unable to influence these events, and trying to do so would be counterproductive. But Western relief agencies for the most part will have to pick up the pieces and deal with the consequences of the internecine strife between Muslim and non-Muslim societies. No one should underestimate the significance of this human fallout. In 1950 Muslim refugees represented only 12 percent of the world's refugee population. In 1970 they made up 50 percent. In 1990 almost 75 percent of the world's refugees were Muslim. Furthermore, if one looks at the next decade's potential trouble spots, the total number of Muslim refugees could represent well over 90 percent of the world's refugee and displaced populations.

Juxtaposed against Islamic instability has been an increase in the power of many Islamic states—some by themselves and many in groups. Their power goes far beyond their military means. Except for a few Middle Eastern states, few Islamic countries have the ability to project power outside their own borders. They have gained influence because of their oil resources. Before 1991 Islamic states controlled 60 percent of the world's oil production. With the breakup of the Soviet Union and the emergence of the Islamic republics of central Asia, that portion has increased to 74 percent.

The concentration of wealth within an area of intense ideological competition and religious fervor has major implications for the international community. The Islamic world does not have the military power to challenge the West and must rely on outsiders to fuel its many arms races, but the economic power it commands will be a force to be reckoned with in the post–Cold War environment.

Reemergence of Ethnonationalism

As superpower rivalry fades, the forces that helped hold multiethnic nations together have begun to weaken. This is the case not only in the former Soviet Union, but also in many Third World nations. The superpowers once believed it was in their interest to support one faction's national hegemony over rival ethnic groups, but today there is less adherence to the inviolability of national borders and less tolerance of regimes that use repression to hold ethnic groups together.

Hundreds of ethnic minorities have realized that they may have a unique opportunity to seek self-identity. As recently as 1990, few international leaders would have supported the idea of the breakup of Yugoslavia; today six new countries have arisen. In 1990 there was one Soviet Union; today there are fifteen independent states. In Africa Eritrea has started divorce proceedings from Ethiopia and may soon be followed by other regions. In northern Iraq the Kurdish areas are moving stealthily toward something greater than regional autonomy.

Violence increasingly accompanies the proliferation of separatist and nationalist movements. For example, ethnic clashes trouble the former Soviet republic of Georgia in its northern provinces, along its border with Russia. Armenia and Azerbaijan are fighting over the disputed Nagorno-Karabakh enclave, and Russia, Turkey, and possibly Iran may be drawn into the fray.

The establishment of each new ethnostate often has consequences beyond its borders. There are often large numbers of people of the same ethnic, cultural, or linguistic group living in neighboring countries. For example, Turkey, Syria, and Iran all fear that if Iraqi Kurdistan becomes independent, their own large Kurdish minorities will try to join the new state, and Tajik and Turkmen minorities in Afghanistan and Iran hope that they might be united with newly independent Tajikistan and Turkmenistan.

Countries on every continent contain national groups that have aspirations challenging the idea of a single state. In South Africa the Zulus pose the biggest test to the postapartheid government and may yet rend that country apart in fratricidal warfare. Even Europe has not remained untouched by these problems: Czechoslovakia has split in two, and in Spain the Basques continue their struggle for independence. In North America Canada is continuously challenged by both indigenous Americans and French Québecois.

One by-product of the emergence of ethnonationalism has been the corresponding rise in racial and cultural intolerance. Much of this intolerance has been focused on foreign migrant workers and refugees. National governments, anxious to stop the violence, have begun closing the doors to asylum seekers and guest workers. This means that Third World countries will have to bear the burden of refugee problems, since resettlement possibilities are shrinking.

This has two likely outcomes. First, more people will be held in refugee camps for longer periods, thereby increasing the cost of care and maintenance. Second, and more important in terms of human rights, host governments are more likely to abuse refugees than in the past, largely on the theory that refugees who find it uncomfortable may go home. There will be greater pressures to deal with the problem in the country of origin, for example, by creating havens or secure areas where displaced persons can get help in relative safety. There is also likely to be more emphasis on repatriation, and relief agencies should expect pressures from host governments to encourage refugees to go home quickly.

Under these circumstances, relief agencies will find themselves working more frequently in conflict zones. The difficulties of operating under these conditions without the protection of an organization such as the United Nations will be one of the greatest challenges to international relief agencies. Ideally, the United Nations will finally create an agency to deal with the victims of conflict in their home areas, or will extend the mandate of the United Nations High Commissioner for Refugees to include displaced persons and those trapped in conflict zones. It may be possible to push through some of the long-stalled structural reforms in the humanitarian assistance system that are needed to help victims of conflict.

A Shift Toward Market-Based Democracies

The perceived victory of the West and of market-based democratic governments over centralized, government-controlled economies has led to rapid abandonment of socialist systems in many Third World countries. Most "democratic" socialist republics were never much more than dictatorships espousing a Marxist line to get support from the Eastern bloc. But the realization that centralized planning was creating havoc in their struggling economies convinced many leaders that the postcolonial flirtation with Marxism had to end. As governments loosened the controls on enterprise, democracy movements flourished, but the new capitalists quickly found their operations limited by corrupt centralized governments and realized that the old order had to go. On every continent democracy movements have successfully challenged a variety of authoritarian governments both on the left and the right.

Time may be running out for many remaining dictators. No longer can they play East against West to obtain weapons and influence. In some situations, there may be a relatively smooth transition, as in the Philippines in 1986, but in cases where the strongmen will not step down voluntarily, there is bound to be trouble.

The shift away from centrally directed to market-based economies and the proliferation of democratic governments will open new opportunities for relief and development agencies. For example, the establishment of new democracies will permit long-standing refugee problems to be resolved.

Repatriation and reintegration of refugees and displaced persons is likely to be one of the major roles of the humanitarian system in the coming decade.

Operational Implications

What are the operational implications of these changes? The international relief system is facing a major increase in the numbers of areas in need, governmental entities, and people in the relief caseload. Before 1991 emergencies in the Soviet Union were, with a few exceptions, the exclusive domain of the Russians; now more than half of the newly emerging states are likely to be seeking international relief within five years. Many of the new states are unstable and beset with the same problems that faced African and Asian countries when they emerged three decades ago from years of colonial domination.

Foremost among their problems is ethnonationalism. In Kazakhstan alone there are over a hundred ethnic groups, many demanding autonomy and several demanding independence. Some other geographic areas are also especially ripe for trouble. For example, the Fergana Valley—which lies between Uzbekistan, Tajikistan, and Kyrgystan—contains more than fifty ethnic groups, all vying for the same economic resources. A conflict originating in that area, one of the most densely populated zones of the former Soviet Union, could generate hundreds of thousands of new refugees and displaced persons.

The international community is woefully unprepared to deal with crises in the former Soviet Union, much of which lies in the higher latitudes, where winters are fierce. The relief system is largely oriented toward providing assistance in tropical areas. If relief operations are required in colder regions, the cost per capita would be much higher than in tropical areas. The people of the former Soviet Union are used to a much higher standard of living and require a more robust diet to sustain them in winter. Operations in cold climates will require additional investment in some of the basic relief materials; shelter costs will be higher since tents are not suitable for winter weather; sleeping bags would have to replace blankets.

Another feature of a post–Cold War era is the challenge of assisting an increasingly Islamic caseload. The international relief system is not culturally prepared to deal with Islamic refugees and displaced persons, or to operate in an environment of jihad (holy war). More than 90 percent of the world's relief agencies are based in the West. The body of international law and doctrine that protects refugees and displaced persons largely originates from Judeo-Christian heritage and legal principles. The concept of nations interacting under rules of international law and principles of humanitarian service does not always translate well in the Muslim world. In the 1980s agencies assisting Afghan refugees found themselves severely constrained by the Islamic tradition of purdah (the seclusion of women). Even in the less restrictive Muslim societies, relief agencies often have found it difficult to approach women and children. Since they make up the largest group of victims and have proven to be the most vulnerable to disease and human rights abuses in conflicts, restricted access to them is a major obstacle.

An unstated, but more serious problem, is the attitude of fatalism inherent in some Islamic societies. In some cases, political leaders have used fatalism to disavow their responsibility to ensure that war victims in their areas receive adequate food, water, and medical attention. Nowhere is this more evident than in Somalia, where clan leaders denied responsibility for the famine deaths that resulted from their preventing relief agencies from reaching victims. Not only did they deny their own people relief supplies, but their indifference toward security for relief agency personnel created an atmosphere in which nongovernmental organizations had to travel under armed escort to protect themselves from bandits.

In such an environment, demands that governments or people in charge adhere to international principles of behavior and guarantee humanitarian access often have been futile. Relief agencies have turned to new approaches to ensure that food gets to at least some sufferers. In the worst cases, they pay bribes to get supplies through; in the best, they resort to selling food to merchants and relying on market forces to deliver food to areas that the agencies cannot reach. The idea of selling food in famines, especially to many of the same people who are creating the problem, is hard for many humanitarian agencies to accept, but operations increasingly will require market-based interventions. The best way to overcome fatalism or the lack of concern by clan or faction leaders for their own people will be to make it profitable for someone to deliver food and other relief supplies.

Some agencies have tried to adapt Western principles and conventions to Islamic law. In one instance, the International Committee of the Red Cross (ICRC) asked a group of noted Islamic scholars in Jiddah, Cairo, and Istanbul to identify common themes between Islamic law and the Geneva Convention. The scholars refused, saying that the conventions should originate from Islamic law, not the reverse. The anecdote illustrates the difficulties that the international system is likely to encounter.

The Struggle for Leadership Among Islamic Nations
The rise in prominence of the Islamic states has sparked a competition for leadership and influence, especially over the newly emerging Islamic republics in the former Soviet Union. In the 1950s the leadership of the Islamic world was unquestionably in Cairo. Egypt was the leading military power, and Gamal Abdel Nasser was the Islamic world's most dynamic leader. In the 1970s influence, if not power, moved away from Egypt and the military states surrounding Israel. With the 1970s oil embargo and the rise in oil prices, a significant portion of the world's wealth shifted to the Persian Gulf states, principally Saudi Arabia and Iran, and the focus of power in the Islamic world shifted with it.

Saudi Arabia, the protector of the holy shrines of Islam, was able to use its oil wealth to extend its influence far beyond the region. By offering aid to developing Islamic countries in return for strict compliance with Islamic law, the kingdom was able to influence political developments in such areas as the Sudan, Yemen, and, more recently, the Islamic republics of the former Soviet Union. Because of their dependence on Persian Gulf oil, the Western powers have been reluctant to try to moderate Saudi Arabia's influence, even where the regimes that the Saudis support routinely engage in human rights abuses in the name of Islamic purity.

Turkey is emerging as a leader, especially in the countries that have developed from the breakup of the Soviet Union, because most Muslims in five of the six new Islamic states are of Turkish origin.[1] Both the United States and Russia have encouraged Turkey to pursue this course in hopes that the republics emulate the Turkish model of secular government. This has brought Turkey into direct competition with Iran, which also hopes to expand its influence in the region and promote its Islamic revolution as a model.

This struggle for leadership in the Muslim world has many implications for how humanitarian agencies will operate. Where the Turkish model is adopted, relief agencies should have the same flexibility that they have in non-Islamic areas. If a more fundamentalist model of government or law is adopted, agencies can expect the difficulties they faced in Afghanistan and Pakistan. In the rest of the Muslim world, access to disaster victims will rely upon how the society comes to grips with the modern world, on what inroads fundamentalism makes in the society, and on which Islamic donors the country attracts.

The Lessening of Concern About National Sovereignty

During the Cold War, every dictator had a superpower sponsor. As long as the dictator voted in the right column on international issues, especially at the UN Security Council, his sponsor was likely to back him if another superpower threatened to intervene in his country's internal affairs. In this atmosphere, the most repressive regimes in the world were able to carry out massive human rights violations virtually unchallenged. With China and Russia backing the Khmer Rouge, the West ignored the situation in Cambodia as the government murdered up to a quarter of its citizens.

In the 1980s the approach changed. Rather than intervening to extend humanitarian protection, the United States and the Soviet Union began to support rebel factions and conduct proxy wars in order to drain the other superpower economically and militarily. This simply increased the level of violence and produced millions of displaced persons and refugees.

The Soviets are no longer around to back every petty dictator who calls himself a socialist and for the time being the Chinese have little chance to extend their influence and protect friendly regimes much beyond their borders.

Few nations are willing to protect a repressive regime. Many major powers are more willing to ignore the national sovereignty of a nation controlled by authoritarian leaders who violate international standards of decency. There is more willingness to support intervention for humanitarian purposes. Intervention will be limited mostly to supporting relief operations in areas not controlled by the host government, but in some cases, military force may be used to create opportunities for humanitarian assistance, as in northern Iraq in 1991 and Somalia in 1992–1993. In the next decade, relief agencies may be able to gain greater access to war victims in areas outside government control and find donors to support crossborder operations. It is also likely that the international community will be more willing to impose sanctions on outlaw governments. In some cases, this could lead to increased access to displaced persons in government-controlled areas.

Intervention will not be uniformly applied. There will be more in sub-Saharan Africa, where there are no credible patrons to raise a protest, and those in the Islamic world will be fewer and more circumspect. There will be more assistance to displaced persons and an increased emphasis on trying to solve refugee crises in the country of origin (i.e., preventing people from leaving and becoming a burden on neighboring countries). This should stimulate major structural changes in the international humanitarian assistance system, especially that of the UN.

Paradoxically, while opportunities to intervene, and the willingness to do so, have increased, the fact that few conflicts involve the strategic interests of the West means there will be less interest in getting involved. In the past, even the most obscure conflicts often were elevated to undeserved prominence when they attracted the attention of one of the great powers.[2] In the future, a crisis will have to be extremely serious before international donors respond. Remote struggles in far-off corners of the world will have trouble attracting international support. NGOs are likely to be the only standard-bearers.

Inherent in this situation is a reduction in funds available for humanitarian assistance. Given the current world economic malaise, it will be more difficult for donor governments to rally support for massive relief operations in remote areas. This, however, may have a positive side effect. Many of the approaches used today are ineffective and have been used simply because they are part of the conventional wisdom. As funds become scarcer, caseloads increase, and costs per capita rise, relief agencies will be forced to adopt more pragmatic and result-oriented approaches. Massive, free feeding programs will decrease, and there should be a shift to more market-oriented approaches.

Increased Use of the Military in Relief Operations

As geopolitical rivalry decreases, the political agendas of aid donors will become more transparent and less threatening because of real or imagined ulterior motives. Donors will deploy military forces to support relief operations at unprecedented levels. The military has always supported peacetime humanitarian operations, providing planes, vehicles, and soldiers in earthquakes, floods, and other natural disasters. However, the use of the military to support humanitarian efforts in conflict areas has always been more circumspect. Developing countries worry about hidden motives, and relief agencies of all stripes have concerns about being painted as spies or surrogates of the military. In the aftermath of Vietnam, most relief agencies adopted policies that kept their involvement with the military at arm's length. For example, as recently as the Gulf War, few agencies were willing to work with displaced civilians in Kuwait or southern Iraq because the U.S. military was involved.

That restraint is beginning to be tempered. Analysis of Operation Provide Comfort has convinced many people in the relief community that military forces and resources can be integrated successfully into humanitarian operations. The deployment of allied forces in Somalia in December 1992 may signal greater involvement of international military forces in humanitarian emergencies.

Western military establishments now are debating whether the role of the military in humanitarian operations should be expanded. NATO has pushed to redefine its mission largely in terms of peacekeeping and humanitarian interventions. In 1992 the U.S. Department of Defense elaborated its post–Cold War strategy, which stated that a military priority is "ensuring our forces provide needed levels of forward presence to influence emerging security environments, as well as maintain our strategic deterrent."[3] One way that forward presence was to be maintained was participation in humanitarian operations in unstable areas.[4] In his last address to the UN General Assembly in September 1992, then-President George Bush described his administration's commitment to using the military in humanitarian operations. He pledged to introduce special training for peacekeeping operations into the curricula of the U.S. military academies, develop humanitarian response doctrines, and increase support for humanitarian operations with a wider variety of assets. However, there are sharp differences of opinion about the issue in the Western foreign policy and military establishment. Before Bush's address, General Powell, chairman of the Joint Chiefs of Staff, gave an interview to the *New York Times* in which he responded to criticisms within the U.S. government of his reluctance to commit U.S. forces for humanitarian operations in Bosnia.[5]

The military's preference for self-preservation will probably determine its role in humanitarian operations. In an era of reduced superpower tension, allied military establishments have difficulty finding a role that permits their presence outside their national boundaries. The military will have to commit forces to humanitarian operations or lose much of its strategic deployment capability.

Will there be more Iraq- or Somalia-style humanitarian interventions?

The answer is yes, but not as many as one might think. It is important that policymakers understand the situations that helped create these incidents. In Iraq the allied powers were facing a conventional military force that moved in massive, easy-to-monitor formations, whose behavior was easy to predict. Having just been savaged in the Gulf War, the Iraqis knew what the allied powers could do and were understandably reluctant to challenge them again. There was international support for the intervention; Saddam Hussein was still a pariah, and no one cared whether his national sovereignty was violated. In Somalia there was no government to object to the intervention, and the armed forces on the ground were lightly armed and poorly organized.

These operations illustrate what can be done when all the right factors converge, but to imply that all those factors will recur in the next humanitarian emergency is not realistic. Despite problems, there are likely to be more cases where national leaders will feel compelled to commit the military to support humanitarian operations and, if necessary, use force to allow relief agencies to perform their work.[6]

Implications for Humanitarian Institutions

Despite the many changes and opportunities that have come about with the end of the Cold War, there is unlikely to be substantial change in the way the international humanitarian system functions. Donors will continue to rely primarily on NGOs to reach the victims of conflict; the institutional arrangements between donors and NGOs are likely to be strengthened and the NGO capabilities expanded.

International NGOs will continue to bear the brunt of operations. While many new local NGOs will spring up and some of the existing ones may expand and become more professional, most will find it difficult to work in conflicts because their own governments can pressure them to comply with government policies. While there have been some notable exceptions— several Red Cross societies and various church groups in Central America, for example—generally international NGOs, supported by donors, can stand up better to repressive governments.

Not all NGOs welcome donors' willingness to put them on the front lines. NGOs in the former Yugoslavia and Somalia resent their sponsoring governments' willingness to place them in harm's way without providing adequate security, either by peacekeeping forces or direct intervention. They also resented the UN's inability to play a major role as an intermediary between them and the factions in Somalia.

Despite their reluctance, NGOs still have the key strengths of flexibility and on-the-ground experience that make them invaluable. They are less bureaucratic than UN organizations and can quickly gear up to respond to new requirements, which makes them ideal to implement relief programs. Even with the increased number of NGOs, there are still many technical gaps in the relief system. While a few organizations such as Oxfam, CONCERN, Save the Children/UK, and CARE are highly competent, many NGOs are unprofessional, and they deliver assistance of uneven quality. Most agencies still focus on providing medical and nutritional assistance. Few, with the notable exception of the International Rescue Committee and OXFAM, work on such critical areas as water and sanitation.

Third World governments and sometimes insurgent groups are very suspicious of NGOs. In some countries, host governments have become bolder in harassing NGO staff. Many NGOs are well aware that they are exposed and vulnerable. Yet it is a testament to their commitment that they continue to work, despite these pressures.

As more governments become democratic, donors will be more willing to work through government institutions. Close cooperation between donors and governments is likely to develop in cases where rebel movements threaten newly democratic governments. There are many advantages to working with governments. Investments in training, for example, can pay off well since government workers are more likely to remain on the job, unlike NGOs, which have high staff turnover. The primary disadvantage is that governments, whether democratic or not, are always a party to a conflict and therefore are not disinterested in dealing with internally displaced persons and refugees.

Just as donors will be more willing to work with democratic governments, they will be less interested in cooperating with repressive governments. In the past, donors such as the United States often wasted millions of dollars to prop up ineffective and corrupt ministries dealing with internally displaced persons simply because donors wanted to put on a good face for their clients. Many of the functions normally carried out by governments now will be transferred to larger NGOs. For example, immunization programs, which are normally carried out by ministries of public health, are more likely to be assigned to UNICEF or the larger medical NGOs.

The end of the Cold War could bring more changes to the United Nations than to almost any other organization. However, the UN is unprepared for change. The organization suffers from major structural problems. No UN organization is specifically assigned to provide assistance to persons affected by war in areas outside the host government's control. In addition, no agency has a mandate to help people who have crossed international boundaries as a result of famine or severe economic crises (refugees are afforded international protection only when they are fleeing from war). Furthermore, no UN agency is prepared to deal with the expulsion of resident guest workers, such as those who were forced to flee Kuwait and Iraq immediately before the Gulf War.

Because agencies are not assigned responsibility for these groups, operations to help them are always handled in an ad hoc manner, sometimes effectively, as in the case of Operation Lifeline Sudan, but usually ineffectively, as in Somalia. Assembling an ad hoc operation by drawing resources from many different UN agencies takes time and is always hampered by bureaucratic obstacles within the participating agencies.

Unfortunately, the UN is probably unable to fix these problems itself. The major member states have not shown much sophistication in addressing the problem. They have consistently tried to deal with reform by making executive changes at the top. Instead, they have created only new layers of bureaucracy and confusion. The establishment of the Department of Humanitarian Affairs (DHA), which was supposed to improve coordination, has done just the opposite. The problems of the UN are fundamental. They include the way staff is hired, trained, and promoted; how the organization is structured; the mandates and responsibilities of each agency; the way decisions are made; and the way funds are raised, allocated, and spent. Until its foundations are repaired and strengthened, the UN house will continue to teeter; changes on the upper floors will not help.

The end of the Cold War has provided a window of opportunity for making substantial changes in the UN system. This opportunity must be exploited. The UN has tremendous potential. It can provide an umbrella under which NGOs can operate in conflict zones, and coordination at the local level could be greatly enhanced with better UN leadership. The disadvantages of UN participation must be addressed. These include excessive bureaucracy, expensive operations, and staff of mixed quality. In addition, the UN must work through local governments, which effectively limits its coordination role.

Coordination of Humanitarian Response
Within the last few years, there has been much discussion about the need to coordinate humanitarian response in the international system. As a result of growing donor frustration and the inability of the United Nations to respond effectively to the various crises surrounding the Gulf War, the UN was encouraged to improve the coordination of its agencies. In late 1991 DHA was established, with broad responsibilities for coordinating the various specialized UN agencies.

The establishment of an interagency coordinating mechanism is certainly laudable. However, without major structural reforms within each UN organization, true coordination will remain elusive. The emphasis on coordination, rather than structural reform, means that in every operation the United Nations will throw together ad hoc structures to deal with problems. Opportunities for training teams that could work together and improve with experience will be lost. In the recent reforms, the donors failed to grasp the essence of the problem. They pushed for better coordination when what they really need is more effective delivery of services. The best coordination in the world will not overcome structural deficiencies.

Early Warning

Many observers believe that with the end of the Cold War the United Nations finally will be able to establish an information collection and analysis system that can provide early warning of developing humanitarian crises. Since the West and East are no longer locking horns in the Third World, the argument goes, their combined intelligence assets can be pooled to alert the UN and other humanitarian agencies to situations that are beginning to threaten the peace. Presumably the major powers could use their influence to prevent conflicts from getting out of hand.

Accurate early warning is technically within reach. The problem, however, is not early warning; it is early response. The international system is still not willing to utilize resources until problems are critical. The mechanisms to raise money work only after the problem is on the front pages of the world's newspapers. Thus, we are unlikely to see any real results from the establishment or improvement of early warning systems.

New Actors

In the post–Cold War decade, a number of new players are likely to appear on the international humanitarian scene, while many of the old actors will adopt new roles.

The governments of the newly independent states of the former Soviet Union will probably be an important group for the next few years because few credible NGOs exist in the former Soviet Union. Therefore, aid will need to be channeled through government or parastatal organizations. For example, the Azeri refugees created by the fighting in Nagorno-Karabakh are cared for almost exclusively by Azeri government organizations. They are housed in camps and hostels owned by the government or parastatal industries; they receive stipends from the government's refugee assistance organization and food from government-run stores; and they receive government coupons for their personal needs. The only assistance received from NGOs is a small stipend given to widows with dependent children. In all the former Soviet republics, the tradition of government primacy in social welfare is likely to continue for some time. In humanitarian crises, international agencies will need to work largely with those governments for some time. Church organizations, except for those in Armenia, are not strong and will take time to develop.

For the near future, the Russian government will need a tremendous amount of assistance to meet the needs of displaced persons and refugees within its borders. At the same time, improvements in agriculture as a result of privatization and the switch from a socialist to a market economy could make Russia a food exporter before the end of the 1990s. Furthermore, it will continue to be a major source of assistance to the other former Soviet republics, because it wants to maintain good relations for trade and there are still substantial Russian minorities in the new states. To increase the effectiveness of their aid and provide a wide range of technical assistance, the Russians will seek partners among international organizations.

Whether or not Russia becomes a major actor on the international humanitarian scene is still in question. The Russians have neither the experience nor a real interest in working outside their immediate sphere of influence. However, they do have assets. Russian transport planes and cargo ships are showing up in increasing numbers in relief operations. Half of the NGO-contracted aircraft ferrying relief supplies to the Kurds in northern Iraq were Russian planes operating under European charter companies. In Africa, Russian Antonovs served side-by-side with Western transports in Somalia and southern Sudan.

National Red Cross and Red Crescent societies are likely to play a more important role in disasters. There have been many moves to improve the quality of emergency services through the International Federation of Red Cross and Red Crescent Societies in Geneva, with particular emphasis on building more professional societies in Africa. In the former Soviet Union, the Red Cross and Red Crescent societies are undergoing major transformations. In many countries, they are becoming more independent and are beginning to expand their services beyond the supplemental welfare support that they traditionally provided through the Soviet social protection system. Technical assistance is being provided by Western Red Cross personnel, and in the various ethnic conflicts in the Caucasus and central Asia, the Red Cross and Red Crescent societies are likely to play a major role.

The proliferation of NGOs is likely to continue, especially at the national level within developing countries. A movement has taken place within the international NGO community to encourage "twinning," or linking international NGOs with local ones. Results have been mixed, largely due to cultural and linguistic differences, but the practice is likely to expand.

Turkey and Saudi Arabia will become the most active new bilateral donors as they compete for influence in the former Soviet Union. Saudi Arabia will seek preeminence in other parts of the Islamic world as well. Both will be influential in the sense that they can offer a wide array of technical or financial assistance, but they are not likely to develop the clout of the United States, the European Community, or Japan.

Among the potential new actors, the biggest question mark is whether a new UN agency for the internally displaced will be established. Most of the discussion has focused so far on creating a new agency or expanding the role of the UNHCR. The best route would be to identify the groups affected by war and civil conflict that are not adequately served or protected by the international system—those who are dislocated by conflict, as well as those who remain in the conflict zones—and prepare a new mandate for a High Commissioner for War Victims. This would permit the international system to get access to people from the moment they are affected by strife. Early access could have a major impact on mitigating the level of conflict and should help reduce migration and refugee flows. The artificial and restrictive definitions of refugees now can be replaced by a more protective and expansive approach, without frontiers. The question is whether the UN can make it happen. It may be necessary for donors to establish an organization, similar to the International Committee of the Red Cross, outside the UN system.

Old Actors, New Roles
There are some efforts within the UN system to make members work more effectively. Among the more interesting are the efforts in the Horn of Africa to establish a new working relationship among UNHCR, UNICEF, and the United Nations Development Programme. In the drought and famine zone that spans Ethiopia, Somalia, and Kenya, they have agreed to cooperate in a crossborder/crossmandate approach. Essentially, every person coming into the program area of an operational agency will be assisted by that agency. For example, people displaced by drought in Kenya coming into one of the towns where UNHCR has established refugee camps for Somalis could apply for food and rations equivalent to those given to the Somalis. All three agencies work together to establish basic minimum standards for those in need in their theaters of operation, and each agency provides assistance through its programs or centers. This approach has enabled the agencies to establish single logistics systems and has improved coordination in many areas.

The United Nations Disaster Relief Organization, which is now part of DHA, is being revitalized and plans to take on a larger role in conflicts. Two areas that are likely to expand are logistics and communications support.

A number of changes should substantially improve UNHCR performance. It has allied itself with NGOs to provide services under the UNHCR umbrella. Groups such as the International Rescue Committee, the Norwegian Refugee Council, and the Danish Refugee Council have been contracted to provide standby cadres of relief workers so that UNHCR can expand rapidly when emergencies arise. These agreements give the participating subcontractors a chance to recruit well in advance of crises, train teams to deploy, and stockpile equipment to support them in the field.

UNICEF extensively expanded its role in conflicts during the 1980s. Because of its flexible mandate and superb leadership at both the international and regional levels, UNICEF often was designated the lead UN agency in conflicts. Because of its reputation, UNICEF will continue to play a central role in many crises and will lose preeminence only if the United Nations finally creates an effective agency for the displaced. UNICEF got where it is professionally by focusing on a limited number of services and delivering them well: immunization, water and sanitation, and maternal-child health care. In the next decade, UNICEF may expand into one or two additional areas, but the organization is not likely to have the same impact in those because few other technical areas lend themselves as easily to standard approaches.

The World Food Programme (WFP) is another UN agency that is likely to undertake new roles. The wisdom of focusing exclusively on distribution of free food in emergencies is increasingly being called into question. In several emergencies in the early 1990s, WFP participated in programs that involved selling its food in local markets and using the proceeds to finance cash-for-work and other income-support projects. These were markedly successful. When carried out with targeted feeding programs, they provided a much faster way of easing a famine. As a result, some of the restrictions that prevented WFP from selling donated food are being relaxed, permitting the organization to initiate changes in its operations.

Two other institutions should be mentioned: the International Committee of the Red Cross (ICRC) and the International Organization for Migration (IOM). The ICRC has been justly praised for its recent work in Africa, especially in Somalia. Many observers see a new openness in the organization and a willingness to cooperate with other groups, especially NGOs. The ICRC has been forced to assume wider responsibilities in many countries because NGOs and the UN system were unable or unwilling to enter into the fray. In Somalia the ICRC was engaged in major food-relief operations on a scale that dwarfed those of other organizations. It also helped repatriate refugees and managed a major airlift that supported both NGOs and UN organizations. While its mandate includes providing assistance to civilians in conflicts, the ICRC has tended to focus on medical assistance and protection for displaced persons.

Despite its openness in recent operations, ICRC is likely to return to its normal activities and secrecy in most future operations. The nature of its work in protection, family reunification, prisoner visitation, and counseling combatants on the rules of war requires confidentiality to maintain the trust of all sides. Thus, the role of ICRC is not likely to expand significantly beyond its present mission.

IOM is well positioned to expand its efforts. As an intergovernmental organization, it can focus on a wide range of issues dealing with migration and spans the gap between refugees and internally displaced persons. IOM's constitution gives its president the latitude to address many of the problems ignored by the UN system. IOM organized the repatriation of third-country nationals from the Gulf region before and after the Gulf War and initiated the repatriation of the Kurds along the Turkish border while the UN was sorting out its role. IOM has been working quietly on the problems of internally displaced persons in many African countries. If the UN system does not change rapidly, IOM is likely to expand and fill the gap.

Notes

1. The Tajiks originated in Persia.

2. See Jeane J. Kirkpatrick, "The Problem with the United Nations," in *The Reagan Phenomenon—and Other Speeches on Foreign Policy* (Washington, D.C.: American Enterprise Institute, 1983): 92–98.

3. Richard Cheney, "Annual Report to Congress," January 22, 1991, p. v.

4. Eduard Koll, "Strategic Planning and the Role of Civil Affairs," presentation at the annual U.S. Army Civil Affairs Association Conference, New York, 1992.

5. Michael Gordon, "U.S. Military Chief on Bosnia: Stay Out," *New York Times*, September 29, 1992.

6. In situations where the U.S. military is asked to provide security, the United States will probably be able to insist that all forces be placed under U.S. command and the military commander be put in overall charge of both military and civil operations. This was the case in Operation Provide Comfort.

■ 9 ■

The Future Architecture
for International
Humanitarian Assistance

JAMES INGRAM

For humanitarian agencies helping disaster victims in the Third World, 1991 and 1992 were years of unprecedented activity and enormous strain. In 1991 the massive and unexpected movement of millions of Kurds, perched on the mountainous frontiers of Iraq, captured the most attention, but equally taxing was the civil war in Ethiopia and the chaotic movement of millions of people after it ended. The Somali dictatorship was overthrown but the result was continuing conflict, the breakdown of government, and the breakup of the country. Moreover, conflicts affecting millions continued in Afghanistan, Angola, Mozambique, and Liberia. Natural disasters, as always, burdened the same humanitarian agencies. The most devastating and eye-catching was a cyclone in Bangladesh that killed 140,000 people and turned about twelve million out of their homes. Drought again gripped northern Sudan, and millions faced food deprivation and possible death.

If anything, 1992 turned out to be even more taxing. The breakup of Yugoslavia and the ensuing civil war showed how difficult it is for the international community to intervene quickly and effectively to help all the victims of internal conflict. The same can be said for Somalia. In both cases, political factors constrained decisive intervention. The slow media focus on Somalia also allowed donors and the UN Secretary-General to avoid making the decisions to prevent a famine that was predicable six months before television screens were filled with horrific images of starvation and death.

United Nations humanitarian agencies have been key players for years in humanitarian emergencies. Indeed, donor governments and nongovernmental organizations have increasingly looked to the UN to coordinate the international response to major emergencies. Twenty years ago the UN General Assembly set in place a comprehensive framework to organize the UN humanitarian response.[1] However, it made little real difference to the generally haphazard way in which the UN disaster agencies went about their business. Over the years, donor governments and NGOs increasingly criticized the UN's performance in emergencies. The UN's perceived shortcomings in the Kurdish crisis and Bangladesh cyclone were the last straw.

Even earlier, several major outside studies had called for the reform of the UN's management of emergencies.[2] They focused on institutional changes at the margin, building on what were seen as the UN's successes in the African famine of the early 1980s and Operation Lifeline Sudan. The latter in particular was seen as a new precedent in getting access to victims of civil conflict. Indeed, some observers saw the process of persuading the warring parties to agree to UN access as itself helping to promote peace. With the passage of UN Security Council Resolution 688, which insisted on access by humanitarian organizations "in all parts of Iraq," a further dimension was added to the debate about the changes that should be made in the UN humanitarian response system. The result was progress toward the idea of a right of humanitarian intervention, that is, a right to forcibly deliver assistance to people being deprived of the necessities of life or otherwise abused by their governments.

On both scores—institutional arrangements and the advancement of international humanitarian law—the stage seemed to be set for real advance by the UN. The General Assembly debated the issue at length at its forty-sixth session at the end of 1991. After intense negotiations a comprehensive resolution was adopted.[3] However, I believe the new institutional arrangements, while they show progress over previous arrangements, remained deeply flawed. Despite some potentially significant modifications intended to improve coordination among UN agencies, donor governments, and NGOs, little changed. Indeed, the net effect could be to slow the UN response, with only an appearance of greater cohesion.

In making that judgment, I have in mind mainly humanitarian emergencies caused by armed conflict within states, and sudden major natural catastrophes such as the cyclones that devastated Bangladesh. Armed conflict has led over the last few years to an explosion in numbers of refugees and internally displaced persons. In 1991 the World Food Programme was feeding some fourteen million refugees and displaced persons in more than thirty countries.[4] Human suffering caused by civil wars in developing countries often is aggravated by a fragile food production and distribution system. Drought and war are an unbeatable combination for increasing suffering. But while the international aid community, including the United Nations, is relatively good at dealing with suffering caused by drought, we are much less good at helping *all* the victims of conflicts. In practice, we are selective, not only among the victims of specific conflicts, but also among conflicts.

Resolution 46/182 is disappointing in another sense: it does nothing to advance the application of humanitarian law. It provides no guidelines to define the circumstances under which international humanitarian interventions may be done, other than in response to a request from the government of the affected country.

I contend that further efforts to build around the United Nations an appropriate structure for dealing with humanitarian disasters arising from armed conflicts within states are likely to be disappointing. The UN's institutional structure for dealing with disasters is inherently cumbersome and ponderous in action. Without root and branch changes in the structure, for which governments have shown little support, only marginal improvements can be expected. Even if the United Nations could be made a reasonably efficient instrument for dealing with large-scale and rapidly evolving humanitarian disasters, we should ask: Is the United Nations the best instrument for relieving human suffering in armed conflict? My view is that it is not. First, I will deal with the limitations of the United Nations system and impediments to its improved functioning.

The Limitations of the United Nations Humanitarian Response System

How to create an effective United Nations disaster response mechanism has been a vexing issue since the UN established twenty years ago what was expected to be a comprehensive disaster response system. The General Assembly has reviewed its decision many times,[5] finally passing Resolution 46/182 in December 1991.

Nevertheless, every important element in twenty-year-old Resolution 2816 (XXVI) found a place in Resolution 46/182, but with some important differences of detail and emphasis. Resolution 2816 (XXVI) called upon the Secretary-General to appoint a disaster relief coordinator at the Undersecretary-General level to report directly to him. Resolution 46/182 called for a "high-level" official to be appointed as emergency relief coordinator, with "direct access" to the Secretary-General. As it happened, the actual appointee is also at the Undersecretary-General level. However, the new resolution does place great weight on the leadership role of the Secretary-General, which is rightly said to be "critical." In the earlier resolution this was implied. Putting the responsibility squarely on the Secretary-General is critical because even within the UN system he is only first among equals. Some of the heads of specialized agencies and programs do not readily accept leadership from UN officials whom they do not regard as peers.

Resolution 2816 (XXVI) gave the disaster relief coordinator clear-cut power. He was authorized on behalf of the Secretary-General "to mobilize, direct and coordinate the relief activities of the various organizations of the UN system." In Resolution 46/182 the powers of the new senior official are rather fuzzy. He is to "process" requests for assistance, "systematically pool and analyze early warning information," "organize" joint interagency needs assessment missions, "serve as a central focal point" with governments and intergovernmental and nongovernmental organizations, provide "consolidated information" to interested governments, "actively promote" the smooth transition from relief to rehabilitation, and prepare an annual report for the Secretary-General. The most substantive tasks are "coordinating and facilitating" (but not directing) the United Nations emergency response, "managing" a central emergency revolving fund, and, as noted above, "actively facilitating" access by humanitarian organizations to people in need.

In short, governments have been dissatisfied for twenty years with the coordination system they have established, but are unable to agree on anything significantly different. Resolution 46/182 introduces some potentially useful changes. For example, the humanitarian coordinator[6] is to establish a central register of specialized personnel to summon on short notice, and the UN is to have access to governments' emergency relief capacities, emergency food reserves, and personnel. But the problems of efficient UN disaster management are deeper than these measures can reach. They go back to the way in which the UN system has been constructed and how it functions.

Coordination and the United Nations
It may be useful to say something about coordination in general, what it means in this context, and why it is necessary. When discussing deficiencies in the UN response to disasters, donor government representatives use the word as an ill-defined catchall. Their comments often sound unfair from the point of view of the heads of UN organizations who are acting responsibly, and who are not averse to dovetailing the work of their organizations with others'. For their part, heads of some UN agencies belittle the importance of coordination so as to avoid the imposition of restraints on their freedom of action.

Nevertheless, coordination is needed to secure an effective response. Coordination is one of the principal, top-level managerial tasks in all complex, large organizations. Successful management requires a strategic plan understood by and acceptable to the various units needed for division of labor or other reasons. Successful management also requires a scheme of implementation delimiting organizational roles, systems to promote cooperation between units, and a means of gathering and feeding back information in order to monitor progress and make adjustments in the plan. The greater the number of autonomous units, the more complex the task.

Major humanitarian emergencies are inherently complex. Even if their management was in the hands of a single autonomous agency, efficient operations would require good coordination. With so many UN agencies involved, good coordination is even more important. Management must have the power of direction. At least in Western management culture, committees cannot coordinate. Military operations, which require a great deal of coordination, epitomize management by a commanding general who is held personally responsible for the outcome. Major, sudden humanitarian crises require a military-type response to be effective. In the much-praised Operation Provide Comfort, the military commander was in overall charge of both military and civil operations. The UN system is inherently incapable of mounting a similar intervention. For this reason, it is nonsense for governments to accuse it of failing to do what it is unable to do.

Four factors explain the UN's limitations:

1. The United Nations Structure. The United Nations is not a single organization, but a loosely organized system of independent, specialized agencies set up by separate treaties and autonomous programs, usually established by General Assembly resolutions, with a very large measure of de facto independence.

At least six entities have seen themselves as playing a key role in the first response to disasters: UNDP, UNDRO (now subsumed within the Department of Humanitarian Affairs by virtue of the adoption of General Assembly Resolution 46/182), UNHCR, UNICEF, WFP, FAO, and WHO. However, Resolution 2816 (XXVI) also placed weight on the relationship between an emergency, rehabilitation, development, and management of the emergency phase (as emphasized in previous chapters). Therefore, development agencies also have a claim to be involved in the United Nations response. While theoretically sound, this is a case of the best being the enemy of the good. When development agencies become involved in an emergency, development is not promoted, but emergency intervention is impeded. The more actors involved, the more difficult and drawn out the coordination task becomes.

Of the six key actors in humanitarian disasters, two (FAO and WHO) are specialized agencies over which the Secretary-General has no legal authority. His authority tends to be circumscribed even toward the other four, which are all quasi-independent boards composed of government representatives to whom their executive heads report. As with FAO and WHO, the government representatives on those bodies share with their secretariats an interest in the continuing independence or autonomy of their agencies. Since few, if any, states pursue mutually consistent policies toward United Nations organizations, Secretaries-General have rarely sought or felt able to exercise their authority, moral or legal, or even to test the limits of that authority. Given this reality, the other agencies saw UNDRO, even though directly responsible to the Secretary-General, as essentially impotent. Consequently, its timid efforts at coordination were easily ignored or sidetracked. On the other hand, its ineffectual interventions were seen by the operational agencies as time-wasting complications.[7]

In a system lacking central authority, even to arbitrate interagency disputes, a fundamental obstacle to getting an effective UN response is conflict and gaps among mandates of the six agencies. For instance, UNHCR and UNICEF deal with an overlapping category of beneficiaries. Refugees include women and children, so at the early stages of a conflict, the roles of these two organizations may not be clear. UNICEF, WHO, and UNHCR have expertise in health and sanitation; in regard to nutrition FAO also has staked a claim. WFP's competence in mobilizing and delivering food has conflicted at times with UNHCR's efforts, although this problem now has been worked out by the two agencies. UNICEF's desire to provide supplementary foods to vulnerable groups sometimes has been at odds with a rational division of labor with WFP. Despite WFP's recognized logistical capability, it has no recognized mandate for systemwide logistical management; UNDRO and UNICEF, for example, have made their own arrangements in some circumstances. WFP and FAO contest the responsibility for assessing food aid needs.

Even with a disaster relief coordinator, coordination has been consistently and persistently muddled. While UNDRO always asserted its competence for sudden, high-profile emergencies, an outside coordinator was usually appointed by the Secretary-General for situations like Ethiopia and Afghanistan because the main donors did not believe UNDRO was up to the job. And, since the UNDP resident representative in each country was also the Secretary-General's resident coordinator—at UNDP insistence—he or she also was asked by the Secretary-General to play a coordination role. Lack of experience in or aptitude for emergency work and eagerness by the resident coordinator to advance the interests of UNDP occasionally complicated the task of operational agencies like WFP.

Much interagency conflict results because agencies are funded voluntarily and they compete for the same resources. Each is eager to demonstrate action when an emergency arises, which has frequently led to the issuance of separate appeals by each agency. Donors urge use of consolidated appeals as the general rule for major emergencies.

An integrated appeal became an end in itself. An appeal must be based upon a sound assessment of needs. This is difficult in an emergency, especially in the least developed countries. The necessary involvement of several agencies and the increasing desire of donors to intrude means that a hastily produced document is given unwarranted authority. It is difficult to alter such an appeal later. The reductio ad absurdum is embodied in Resolution 46/182, which asks the Secretary-General to produce an initial consolidated appeal, in consultation with the affected state, within *one* week.

A further consideration inhibiting effective UN field coordination is the United Nations doctrine, deriving from the concept of national sovereignty, that coordination is the responsibility of the government of the affected country. Since quite often the government is unable to discharge the task, a lot of effort has to go into establishing institutional structures that give the appearance of government coordination and in negotiation with the government on many aspects of implementation.

2. *Personalities.* Two points are relevant. First, unless the Secretary-General has a strongly charismatic personality and a good sense of the

practical problems of emergency management, he or she is not really able to give coherent leadership to the many agencies claiming a role in the UN emergency response system. Given the high profile of the UN's humanitarian work and declining interest in its development work, more UN agencies are asserting their competence in humanitarian emergencies. Neither the current Secretary-General nor his predecessor have these qualities. In any event it can be argued that no matter how gifted a single person may be, one person cannot effectively oversee the whole UN system, or even the UN proper and the programs linked to it. Inevitably and properly, the Secretary-General has to give the most attention to diplomatic issues. It was considerations such as these that led governments in 1991 to favor the creation of Deputy Secretary-General positions under the Secretary-General to oversee the principal spheres of UN activity. This approach was not supported by the incoming Secretary-General.[8]

Second, merit and suitability are less significant than political connections in determining who is appointed to senior United Nations posts. Given that the United Nations is the international organization most closely associated with foreign ministries, most appointees tend to be diplomats, and posts are frequently filled in response to political pressures from national governments. Major and minor powers are assiduous in pushing their perceived interests in this respect.

Diplomatic skills are essential attributes for top-level UN appointees, but diplomats are renowned neither for their management skills nor for their sense of what is feasible in response to concrete situations such as natural or man-made disasters. Governments privately attributed much of their dissatisfaction with UNDRO to the fact that neither of its successive chiefs had professional experience of disaster management, even though both were senior professional diplomats.

3. Donor Policies. Donor pressure for consolidated appeals gives the appearance of better coordination. While satisfying the internal bureaucratic requirements of donors, this pressure has not led to improved coordination on the ground in affected countries. A more fundamental problem is the donors' practice of allocating most of their emergency resources bilaterally, usually through nongovernmental organizations. Even the Nordic countries allocate only 31 percent of their emergency assistance through multilateral organizations.[9] One reason is internal politics in donor countries. The lobbying power of NGOs is formidable during emergencies that attract media attention. Governments respond by channeling resources through them. While key NGOs may or may not be more efficient than UN agencies, the practical effect is that in almost all disasters a large number of NGOs is involved on the ground. NGOs often have conflicting aims and agendas, and often insist on working in particular regions of affected countries. The task of harmonizing the total effort, which falls to the UN, is far from easy. Very often the representatives of donor embassies insist on being involved. While their efforts can sometimes be helpful, more often than not they add to the coordination burden.

Food and its transport, in terms of volume and value, is usually the largest part of the cost of emergency humanitarian responses. The task of coordinating the supply and distribution of food would be much easier, more timely, and less costly if provided on a genuinely multilateral basis through WFP. Even consignment through WFP would be a significant improvement. Depending on the circumstances of each country, distribution in both cases would continue to use NGO capabilities to the maximum extent feasible. If the WFP had a free hand to procure the most appropriate commodities, rather than having to depend on food chosen by donors, it would be easier to reach the suffering with fewer delays, and complaints about sending the wrong types of food for local habits would diminish.

While donor governments are interested in magnifying the domestic political impact of their humanitarian interventions, and therefore favor prominent local NGOs as recipients of their largesse, donor bureaucracies are interested in accountability and simplicity of presentation. Thus they have a powerful appetite for feedback about how their resources were used. Experience at WFP is that donors are slow in providing information to the UN about what they are doing with food aid, bilaterally or through NGOs. Without such timely information, coordination is hamstrung. Much of the justified criticism of scanty or excessive food aid and its untimely delivery in emergencies is due to donors' insistence on independent decisionmaking and foot-dragging in giving data on their actions to the coordinator. The situation in Somalia in October 1992 illustrated dramatically how dangerous the effects of individual donor decisionmaking can be. Not only was the port of Mogadishu clogged with unscheduled ships (a routine occurrence in any major famine no matter how much lead time has been given to donors), but some donors were shipping commodities (dates, wheat flour, rice, sugar) that were highly prized on the black market and whose high value led to intervention and theft by armed looters.[10]

The provision of the kind of data sought by donor aid ministries leads to centralized coordination at UN headquarters by many generalists. But an effective intervention requires leadership at the country level by a person experienced in disaster management, who also has the ability to persuade the parties involved to work together under his or her broad direction. The coordinator needs considerable autonomy and cannot discharge the task efficiently if subject to a burdensome reporting requirement to headquarters, which inevitably leads to undue intervention. More often than not the consequence is simply to slow down decisionmaking or, in the worst cases, paralyze it.

4. United Nations Management Culture. An effective emergency response requires the capacity for quick decisionmaking, flexibility, and improvisation, as well as a capacity for expeditious organization and planning. None of these qualities is particularly characteristic of national civil services. Yet, not only have United Nations relief agencies been set up and staffed along civil service lines, but their multinational and multicultural composition make them much more rulebound and inflexible than most civil services. The full elaboration of this point would require a chapter in itself, but it is an important reason why UN agencies usually are not seen as especially effective in emergencies. Most senior UN staff, with or without field service, are experienced in development work, which has compounded the difficulty of locating the skills required for the successful management of emergencies.

UN officials in the field are sometimes criticized for being deskbound and generally ineffectual in disasters. Their performance, and what is seen as their often premature withdrawal from dangerous posts, is contrasted unfavorably with NGO performance. This criticism is misplaced. The professional staffers of UN agencies have accepted employment in an international civil service. They are not hands-on volunteers such as the employees of NGOs recruited for disaster work. In practice, many career UN officials are ready to accept extremes of discomfort and danger that are not expected of diplomats from national foreign services.

The Impact of Resolution 46/182
As already noted, Resolution 46/182 has attempted to overcome these impediments, but apart from structural changes, few improvements can be achieved through legislation. It is arguable that the General Assembly should have insisted on the application of a selection process for the humanitarian coordinator along the lines advocated in the Urquhart/Childers report.[11] Given the predominantly political role of the UN, however, the present mode of choice may be inescapable.

As regards management culture, the existence of the problem is implicitly recognized in the resolution. Paragraph 30 calls for special procedures for spending, procurement, and recruitment. To a large extent the main UN relief organizations had already done or were doing this. My experience is that it is very difficult to achieve a good balance between speedy action and an acceptable audit trail. The funds involved are considerable, but in the last resort much weight is necessarily placed on the personal probity of staffers, their good judgment, and their willingness to take responsibility and calculated risks. These characteristics are rare in all civil services. For large-scale emergencies many temporary staffers have to be taken on. A great deal of supervisory responsibility, arguably an unfair burden, is borne by a handful of permanent UN staff in each affected country. Nothing in the resolution puts pressure on donors to put concerted international interventions ahead of their own individual national interests, or even to simplify and harmonize the differing accountability requirements that they place on UN agencies.

The resolution does (albeit timidly) try to come to grips with the critical problem of overlapping mandates. It created a $50 million voluntary fund "as a cash-flow mechanism to ensure the rapid and coordinated response of the organizations of the system." The fund will be used to make advances to the UN agencies responding to disasters. It is to be replenished from "voluntary contributions received in response to consolidated appeals." The idea is to give the humanitarian coordinator power over the purse—something that was not given to the earlier post established under Resolution 2816 (XXVI). The Secretary-General also is enjoined to ensure that arrangements between the humanitarian coordinator and "all relevant organizations are set in place, establishing responsibilities for prompt and coordinated action in the event of emergency." In short, the Secretary-General is asked to sort out who is to do what.

Elsewhere in the resolution the coordinator is enjoined always to show regard for "existing mandates" (paragraphs 19, 21, 34). Even in relation to the central fund, the humanitarian coordinator is asked to manage the central fund "in consultation with the operational organizations concerned." Overlapping mandates or gaps in mandates handicap a rational division of tasks, and consultation in the UN system is usually a protracted bargaining process and a powerful inhibitor of clear decisionmaking. So much will continue to depend on the personalities and political skills of the Secretary-General and humanitarian coordinator in determining whether real progress is made on this key issue.

A worrisome aspect of the resolution is that it seems to rule out the appointment of high-level, in-country disaster coordinators. The resolution provides that the new humanitarian coordinator should combine the functions carried out by existing representatives. At the same time, the resolution states that the UN resident coordinator should normally coordinate the humanitarian assistance of the United Nations system at the country level. The humanitarian coordinator is to provide leadership to the resident coordinator on humanitarian assistance. However, resident coordinators are UNDP staff members with UNDP salaries. They will inevitably find it difficult to subordinate UNDP interests to those of the humanitarian coordinator. Moreover, very rarely are they experienced or skilled in disaster management, which is not surprising since they are appointed to administer economic and social development.

Faced with several disasters simultaneously, the humanitarian coordinator may find it hard to carry out the leadership tasks. While the system of using UNDP resident representatives has not worked well, changing it would require donors to move away from their strong attachment to the idea that all UN field coordination should be carried out by the UNDP resident representative. For the effective management of sudden humanitarian emergencies, there is no substitute for the appointment of a single, high-level, appropriately qualified person based in the field, with the authority to direct in-country operations if necessary.

The Somalia crisis of 1992 showed the continuing inability of the United Nations to deal decisively with this problem. At the beginning of the year, the UNDP resident representative was resident coordinator for Somalia. He was based in Nairobi and responsible for the overall UN effort. He was replaced by a UNICEF official appointed as coordinator for humanitarian assistance in Somalia. Subsequently, a special representative of the Secretary-General responsible for "overall leadership" also was appointed. On October 19, 1992, the Secretary-General appointed an outsider, Philip Johnson, executive head of CARE USA, as operational manager of the program, while retaining the two existing appointments. The operational manager was to bring about "optimal coherence between the programs and activities of nongovernmental organizations, United Nations agencies and other institutions concerned and to strengthen United Nations support of the many humanitarian aid organizations in Somalia." About this time the special representative resigned, and on November 3 a successor was appointed.

The centralized, overly elaborate approach to coordination, designed essentially to meet the administrative requirements of donors, was formalized—indeed somewhat intensified—by the resolution. In this regard, attention already has been drawn to the weight given to consolidated appeals, the early involvement of development organizations in emergencies, and the emphasis on the preparation of consolidated information. The humanitarian coordinator is to work closely with the ICRC and other major organizations, indeed with all relevant NGOs. The process is, however, institutionalized through the establishment of an Inter-Agency Standing Committee with a standing invitation to the ICRC, the League of Red Cross and Red Crescent Societies, and the International Organization for Migration. Relevant NGOs are to be invited to participate on an ad hoc basis. Such a committee could lead quite easily to a slower international response. Much time is spent in reconciling the differing perceptions of the several headquarters, based on the imperfect flow of up-to-date information about rapidly changing situations received from their separate field representatives.

Our experience at WFP was that centralized coordination imposes a heavy additional workload at WFP country and headquarters offices. A great deal of time of key operational officials, who are a very scarce resource, is spent in attending coordination meetings. The appearance of improved coordination at the center does not necessarily lead to more effective and timely interventions in the field.

Possible Alternative Modes of Organization

With so many players inside and outside the UN system, and with donor government representatives insisting on keeping a close eye on the process of coordination and intervention, it is hard to envisage workable alternatives to the approach described in Resolution 46/182. For slowly developing droughts and long-running but stable refugee situations, it is cumbersome but workable. I have no doubt that in such situations a capable humanitarian coordinator, supported by a good staff with hands-on experience, could slowly bring about a better United Nations and international response. Indeed, in these types of disasters, the system has not been working badly and has been improving. The danger is that the structure will prove to be top-heavy, aggravating the deficiencies that make the system of UN agencies an imperfect instrument for dealing with emergencies.

A simpler organizational approach to slowly maturing famines that are serious enough to warrant concerted international intervention is possible. It would require explicit recognition of WFP's appraisal and management role, and a related adjustment of the functions of other concerned UN agencies. It would also require donors to exercise greater self-denial regarding when and how they respond bilaterally and through NGOs to such famines. Resolution 46/182 is seriously flawed in failing to sort out disaster categories, and the most appropriate means of dealing with each of them.

The new structure is unsuitable for dealing with sudden conflicts that lead to movement of internally displaced persons. In the early stages of such a crisis, as UNHCR has pointed out, a quick response requires "clear authority and direct lines of command," as well as "decentralization and rapid decision making."[12] "When confronted with a disaster emergency, managers must be able to move away from the consensus and control-based activities," the document states. To do that requires that one person be in charge who is able to "direct," as was envisaged in Resolution 2816 (XXVI) but dropped from Resolution 46/182.

To some extent, this requirement has been met in the past by designating a lead agency for a particular disaster. UNHCR eventually accepted this responsibility in the Kurdish situation in Iraq. But this method requires other agencies with complementary skills to subordinate their work to that of UNHCR. As UNHCR has acknowledged, cooperation with WFP in that crisis was exemplary.[13] Broadly speaking, the problem of conflicting mandates and the autonomy of agencies—which is tolerated by governments and encouraged by secretariats—prevents the lead agency approach from being a sufficient answer.[14] Moreover, the UN management culture prevents any UN agency from using the single-mindedness of a military-style operation, even if it had at its disposal the necessary resources of skilled personnel and money.

In any event, the lead agency idea is not consistent with the overall thrust or detailed prescription of Resolution 46/182, and therefore is probably no longer a realistic option. An alternative arrangement by which the Secretary-General appointed skilled, high-level delegates of the humanitarian coordinator to take charge of UN disaster operations at the outset could work. This would require that the preparatory work of sorting out in-country roles of the agencies had been done, and that everyone involved understood that all relevant agency in-country staff were subordinate to the delegate's staff and answerable to them. The agency in-country staff would need full backup from its headquarters. This could work only in a more unified UN system, within which the Secretary-General could direct agencies to do what was required.

A more realistic option might be to create a new UN agency dedicated to managing operations at the onset of sudden disasters. The existing agencies would carry out operations at a later stage, after the situation has settled down, much in the way that ICRC sometimes looks to WFP to take over feeding responsibilities after the initial crisis has been surmounted.

Governments have sought to remedy the deficiencies of UN agencies by creating new ones. Keeping the original agency in existence has led to the proliferation of largely autonomous agencies with overlapping mandates. It is to the credit of governments that Resolution 46/182 did not do this and that UNDRO has been subsumed within the Department of Humanitarian Affairs. Moreover, while governments remain eager to restrain spending by UN agencies, and remain skeptical of the ability of the UN to surmount its management and organizational problems, there has been great reluctance to consider solutions that could lead to the creation of new agencies.

Governments are prisoners of a system that they have unwittingly created, a system in which many agencies dealing wholly or partly with aspects of disaster identification, relief, and rehabilitation are entangled. This system is not and probably cannot be centrally managed while the UN institutions remain individually answerable to different intergovernmental bodies of sovereign states. But there is no reason why a coordinated international humanitarian response should be built around the United Nations. There are many important international agencies dealing with critical issues that are not part of the UN system. It might in fact be more fruitful to look to organizations outside the UN system on which to base a restructured humanitarian order. Before doing so, however, let us examine the relationship between international humanitarian law and a more desirable humanitarian architecture.

Sovereignty and Humanitarian Interventions

Existing humanitarian law on the protection of civilians and the duty of states to accept "exclusively humanitarian and impartial" relief operations on behalf of civilian populations is well defined.[15] This law is embodied in the 1949 Geneva Conventions and more especially in the 1977 Additional Protocols. While many states are signatories, few of the principal powers, including the United States, have ratified these protocols. While a significant number of developing countries have done so, many have not lived up to their assumed obligations. Most developing countries continue to put greater weight on national sovereignty.

The formation of stable, enduring sovereign states has been beset by conflicts, often extending over hundreds of years. The process of state formation is complete in few Third World and some European countries. Immediately after independence, government leaders of developing countries were successful in using the shared anticolonial struggle to foster a sense of national consciousness, but its roots were often not deeply planted. The internal disorder we see today in much of Africa, for example, is the result. Religious and ethnic divisions have assumed more importance in internal politics. Government leaders' priorities are to preserve the state and to maintain their own personal power. Broadly speaking, outside humanitarian assistance is tolerated, even welcomed, provided outsiders do not complicate the state preservation task.

The United Nations Charter is based upon the principle "of the sovereign equality of all its members" (Article 2[1]). Given the enormous economic and political inequality of states and uncertainty about the permanence of many, it is not surprising that developing countries continue to insist upon the primacy of their sovereign rights and regard the Charter provisions concerning human rights as essentially subsidiary. Even if there is, as some contend,[16] an inherent contradiction in the Charter between sovereignty and human rights, few are prepared to assert a right of humanitarian intervention as inherent in the Charter.

General Assembly Resolution 46/182 and Sovereignty

General Assembly Resolution 46/182 steered clear of the issue. Although ambiguous in places, it does not go beyond Resolution 2816 (XXVI). That resolution concerned "prompt, effective and efficient response to a Government's need for assistance." To that end a disaster relief coordinator was appointed inter alia to coordinate relief activities in response to "a request for disaster assistance from a stricken State" and to "assist the Government of the stricken country to assess its relief and other needs." Disasters encompassed natural and man-made situations.

The guiding principles of the new resolution state that "the sovereignty, territorial integrity and national unity of States must be fully respected in accordance with the Charter of the United Nations," and that humanitarian assistance is to be provided with the "consent of the affected country," thereby avoiding use of the word "request." Instead, assistance is to be provided "in principle on the basis of an appeal by the affected country." At the same time, affected states have the primary role in initiating and implementing humanitarian assistance within their territories. Where the situation is beyond their capacity, "international cooperation is of great importance" and "should be provided in accordance with international law and national laws." "States in proximity to emergencies are urged to participate closely with the affected countries," in other words, not to act contrary to their wishes.

The role of intergovernmental and nongovernmental organizations "in supplementing national efforts" is recognized, though they must work "impartially" and with "strictly humanitarian" motives. The one new element is that affected states are "called upon" to facilitate the work of such organizations where access to victims is essential. In this regard, a high-level official appointed by and answerable to the Secretary-General, the humanitarian coordinator, has responsibility to actively facilitate access by operational organizations to emergency areas, by negotiation if needed, "by obtaining the consent of all parties concerned."

When presenting this resolution to the General Assembly, the chairman of the group of countries that negotiated it avoided any reference to the resolution as advancing humanitarian law.[17] In debate, the major donor countries did not seriously contest the emphasis placed by developing countries on the continued overriding importance of respect for national sovereignty. This outcome is not necessarily regrettable. I am not convinced that the best way of advancing humanitarian law is to give the United Nations the central role in leading and coordinating the efforts of the international community in all conflicts, which has become conventional wisdom. The UN has a vital role, but it should not be all-encompassing.

The United Nations and Internal Conflict

In thinking about this issue I start from the proposition that the right to life is the most basic human right. In conflicts the first humanitarian goal is to relieve life-threatening suffering. Actions with additional goals are unlikely to achieve that objective.

Saving lives and relieving life-threatening suffering in civil conflicts means that underlying causes are not addressed. Feeding civilians can prolong the conflict. Socioeconomic factors that are at the root of conflict and that are not addressed also may cause the conflict to be prolonged. The problems with this line of argument are many. First, doing something about fundamental causes or bringing about cease-fires, let alone peaceful settlements, takes a great deal of time. Meanwhile, lives are lost. If I were in a conflict and faced death by starvation, I would prefer to stay alive, even if the circumstances of its provision meant that the conflict were prolonged and my life remained at risk. Second, given universally shared values about saving civilian lives, especially those of women and children, getting access to all victims ought to be a realistic goal, though it can be hard to achieve. Dealing with causes and the long-term effects of interventions involves making judgments that one side or the other may see as politically motivated and hence unacceptable. While the end is laudable, the means for achieving it leads to loss of life in the interim. Further, the long-term consequences of all outside interventions are problematic. To assume we know correct answers to conflicts in other societies is Western hubris. Just as politics is the art of the possible, so must our humanitarian action address what is possible; saving more civilian lives in internal conflicts is an achievable goal.

Relieving suffering requires access to all affected people. This may be best achieved by gaining the consent of both parties to the conflict rather than through coercion. In the most spectacular intervention to date against the wishes of an affected state, namely Iraq, the various Security Council resolutions and the accompanying supervisory machinery to oversee the operation of sanctions have handicapped United Nations humanitarian operations that could have benefited all suffering Iraqis. The political goals of the Security Council in relation to Iraq were of overriding importance.

Getting the parties to a dispute to agree to a free flow of food is difficult precisely because this will confer politico-military advantages or disadvantages on one side or the other. The indispensable condition for gaining the consent of belligerents is for the negotiator to be seen "working impartially and with strictly humanitarian motives" (Resolution 46/182). This is not a political goal but its achievement requires that political conditions be right, as they were in Sudan in 1989. The government in office at that time was willing to compromise in seeking an end to conflict with its opponents in southern Sudan. When replaced by the hard-line fundamentalist El Bashir government, a different policy was followed. Ever since then, Operation Lifeline Sudan (OLS) has been very uncertain, falling short of the achievements of its first year.

In another sense, the political conditions have not been right since 1989. In 1989 there was tremendous NGO and media interest in southern Sudan, and much pressure was put on the United States and other governments to do something to prevent a recurrence of the loss of life of 1988. These governments in turn pressured the United Nations. More recently, there has not been the same interest, even though the situation remains bad. It was not so much the authority of the Secretary-General per se that strengthened his negotiator's skillful hand,[18] as it was the fact that the UN was seen as a surrogate for the United States and its allies.

WFP's negotiations in 1990 with the Eritrean People's Liberation Front (EPLF) and the Ethiopian government on the reopening of the port of Massawa and the delivery of food to besieged Asmara were also successful. However, they, too, owed much to propitious political circumstances and U.S. government pressure on both parties. Through their economic dominance and power as aid dispensers both bilaterally and through the World Bank and International Monetary Fund (IMF), industrialized countries led by the United States strongly influenced the policies of Third World governments. Their power has increased with the collapse of the Soviet Union. When Western governments have little strategically or economically at stake, as is the case now in much of Africa, NGOs—especially when working with the media—can exert decisive influence on Western governments in getting them to push for UN humanitarian action. In turn, those governments can have leverage in influencing the parties in internal conflicts to submit to negotiations concerning access.

Equally, in negotiations in 1991 with the Sudanese government for the relief of Nasir following the expulsion from Ethiopia of Sudanese People's Liberation Army (SPLA) supporters who had taken refuge there, success was helped by serendipitous timing. The Sudanese government was divided over whether to make an all-out onslaught on the SPLA, or to refrain so as not to jeopardize IMF financial assistance. I headed a team that flew in without clearance, and our presence and argumentation seem to have been a factor in temporarily tipping the balance of decisionmaking away from a new military offensive. The result was that the Sudanese agreed to allow assistance to the returning refugees by air and by river transport that had been denied for several years.

In asserting the need for the access negotiator to focus on increasing the numbers of people to be helped, I am not excluding the possibility that there can be a positive political spinoff, such as movement toward conflict resolution or peacemaking. However, the negotiator is unlikely to succeed in getting access if any goal other than the relief of civilian suffering is pursued. Having the trust of the parties is the prerequisite for success. In all negotiations I have observed, I was struck by the profound lack of trust by the opposing parties and their desire to use the negotiations to advance their own political goals. At least one goal invariably has been to demonstrate to the outside world that they share Western humanitarian values and that it is the other party that is blocking access. Further, in relation to the reopening of Massawa and access to Asmara, the main obstacle to successful negotiations was the desire of the EPLF to use negotiations to advance recognition of its sovereignty, even as the Ethiopian government had precisely the opposite objective.

If political factors play a part in successful negotiations over access, isn't the United Nations the appropriate agency to carry out the negotiations? I think not. The United Nations is too political. Even if acting impartially, the parties will tend to see the UN as having goals that go beyond saving lives and that threaten their interests. The United Nations is above all an organization of states, and even its humanitarian agencies are not apolitical. The main ones (UNHCR, UNICEF, WFP) are almost entirely funded by voluntary contributions from the major industrialized countries. They set their agendas, define their priorities, and influence the distribution of resources to needy countries. As an example, in most conflicts there is a need for food. Indeed, it is usually the main component by volume and value. An ever-present complication is the insistence by major donors on controlling the destination of their food. This can happen even after title is transferred to WFP and the food is physically in its possession. Thus, WFP loaned food to the International Committee of the Red Cross to support its operations inside Iraq. The food was of U.S. origin. However, WFP action was sanctioned reluctantly and only after a considerable delay and much negotiation. The concern of U.S. officials was that the ICRC had been using the food for purposes that, though humanitarian, appeared to breach specific public remarks by President Bush.

In none of these negotiations do I think that the role of the United Nations was a decisive factor, although the explicit backing of the Secretary-General was very helpful. The parties were fully aware of and susceptible to United States pressure exerted directly or through international organizations. Also of crucial importance was Grant's reputation (and I believe my own) for evenhandedness.

The head of a major NGO trusted by the parties and known to be apolitical may have done as well, provided the political circumstances were also right. Some NGOs insist on publicly identifying the underlying causes of human suffering while offering succor. In the eyes of the parties, taking a position means taking sides in a political conflict. Such efforts to negotiate access are likely to be viewed suspiciously or even rejected by the affected states. NGOs have every right to be selective in deciding whom they will help and under what circumstances. Nor do I deny their right to advocate the cause of those whom they see as the victims. To the extent that NGO actions are viewed as serving political ends, however, their claim to be humanitarian is regarded skeptically by Third World governments. While governments can and do make distinctions, the more that organizations show a preference for one side over the other, the more they help to confirm already strong suspicions about the motives of NGOs generally. The possibilities of reaching victims may thereby be weakened.

However, none of these objections applies to the ICRC, which, by its mandate, is forbidden from taking a political position in relation to conflicts within and between states. Certainly the head of the ICRC could have done as well as Grant and Ingram.[19]

Conditions for United Nations Intervention
From a humanitarian perspective, UN intervention would appear to be clearly justified by government collapse, as in Somalia. Nevertheless, intervention there was shamefully slow.

Following the overthrow of Siad Barre in January 1991, government effectively ceased in that country, and the former British Somaliland declared its independence. By early in 1992 anarchy reigned. Armed conflict among several factions, who failed to establish conditions within their areas that would allow the orderly distribution of food, cried out for a concerted international effort to impose enough order to allow the victims of conflict to be succored. But nothing happened. The main donors had ceased to have any real interest in Somalia after the end of the Cold War. East African states were unwilling, and to some extent unable, to do what West African countries had done in Liberia following the overthrow of President Tubman. Even by mid-1992, when the media had at last focused on the appalling famine, decisive UN action to restore order was not taken. A consensus that would enable such an operation to be mounted by the Secretary-General was slow to emerge.

The Secretary-General takes the view that he will intervene only with the specific authority of the Security Council. This is appropriate for three reasons. First, it is doubtful that under the UN Charter the Secretary-General has authority to initiate humanitarian interventions contrary to the views of the affected state. Second, given the very strong attachment of states, especially developing countries, to national sovereignty, a long-term stable international order is best built on consensus, which is best articulated through the Security Council. Security Council decisionmaking about Iraq, Libya, Somalia, and the former Yugoslavia showed that getting and keeping consensus is not easy, and that religious and ethnic divisions remain potent factors in international relations. Third, the main thrust of the United Nations should continue to be on peacekeeping and conflict resolution, issues very much within the purview of the Council. Unless the parties are to be coerced, the process of getting access to conflict victims requires an impartial negotiator. The UN's peacemaking and peacekeeping roles will not always sit well with the role of impartial access negotiator.

Role of the ICRC

There are likely to be internal conflicts where a party other than the United Nations might be a more appropriate access negotiator. It is possible to go further and argue that from the start another agency dedicated solely to the humanitarian value of the sanctity of human life should normally carry out this task. If that agent was unsuccessful, the United Nations could appropriately consider what actions, including coercion, should be taken.

The ICRC is the obvious choice. Indeed, in a great many situations it already does so, and with considerable success. The bravery and competence of ICRC staff are beyond reproach and have aroused great admiration. The growth of conflicts has imposed strains on the organization. All its delegates are Swiss nationals, and the recruitment of staff with the right skills and attitudes is becoming more challenging, given the relatively small population on which to draw. The ICRC has sought to overcome this limitation by integrating more staffers seconded by national societies in its field operations, although none is an ICRC delegate. As of July 1, 1992, over 250 national society personnel were on mission with ICRC.

The ICRC is not an international organization but remains a private, independent Swiss institution subject to Swiss law.[20] Its governing bodies are composed of Swiss nationals. Given Switzerland's neutrality policy and nonmembership in the United Nations, its Swiss character has brought many advantages. Nevertheless, my own experience has persuaded me that the multicultural, multinational composition of United Nations organizations does promote a greater sensitivity to the values and concerns of other nations and cultures. In WFP's dealings with governments in conflicts, we have sometimes found suspicion of the ICRC as an arrogant European organization lacking appreciation of the aspirations and concerns of developing countries. An internationalized ICRC would almost certainly enjoy more confidence with developing countries and therefore be more effective in negotiating access to all victims of internal conflict, provided of course that the political conditions were propitious for such interventions.

Internationalization of the ICRC in a way that avoids the defects of UN organizations is feasible. The international agricultural research organizations grouped within the Consultative Group for International Agricultural Research (CGIAR) could be a model. One small change in line with that model would be for membership of the supreme governing body of twenty-five members, the Committee, to be borrowed from the International Red Cross and Red Crescent Movement. These would be people known for their international experience and devotion to humanitarian values. The president could continue to be elected by the Committee, but the pool of nationalities from which delegates are chosen would need to be widened.

In short, I am recommending a dual system. Access would normally be negotiated by an internationally recognized and constituted NGO with no other function than the relief of life-threatening suffering. A remodeled ICRC could fulfill this role. In the event that access could not be achieved by the new ICRC, the way would be open for Security Council authorization for intervention by the United Nations, forcibly or otherwise. In situations akin to that in Iraq in 1991, action could be initiated by the Security Council without prior ICRC negotiations. The underlying rationale is that the suffering of more people will be alleviated more quickly if the political functions of conflict resolution and forcible intervention are separated as much as possible from the function of increasing access to the victims of conflicts. The United Nations is necessarily a highly political body, the work of whose humanitarian agencies is influenced by the political goals of national governments.

To say this is not to denigrate the United Nations, or the dedication and selflessness of many officials working in its various humanitarian agencies, or their very considerable humanitarian achievements. My plea, however, is that the UN should focus on resolving disputes between or among states and, where appropriate, within states in accordance with its Charter, and as interpreted through orderly decisionmaking by the Security Council. A durable international order that gives greater weight to shared humanitarian values is best advanced through precedent rooted in progressive expansion of the area of consensus among states. Meanwhile, human suffering arising from internal conflict is in most situations likely to be dealt with best by an internationalized ICRC.

A remodeled ICRC could also provide the nucleus for quicker and more effective international action in disasters arising from internal conflicts.

United Nations agencies, including UNHCR, would assume responsibilities in line with their mandates and capabilities only after the ICRC had brought the relief picture under control. At that point UN instrumentals and NGOs would act as agents for the ICRC, under its overall direction.

The ICRC would retain responsibility for negotiations with the warring parties for access to victims, in accordance with its responsibilities under the Geneva Convention and Additional Protocols, and the ICRC would assume responsibility for coordinating the entire international relief effort. To be successful, the ICRC would require increased financial backing from donor governments. These governments would need to refrain from interference, make their financial support to UN agencies and NGOs conditional on their acceptance of ICRC's central role, and ensure that their representatives in the governing bodies of United Nations agencies act consistently to support the recommended division of responsibilities. This approach should be welcome by developing countries in that it accords with their conception of the sovereignty of states.

Other Alternatives

In broadening its operational responsibilities along these lines, the ICRC would be substantially expanding its already significant involvement in relief operations. To some extent the ICRC has become more heavily involved in such activities for lack of a better alternative, but this kind of activity could impair its role as custodian of international humanitarian law and its related functions of protecting war victims and the like. Moreover, the ICRC might be reluctant to initiate the restructuring needed to enable it to discharge the dual roles.

It may well be, therefore, a more appropriate course for governments to create a new organization outside the United Nations to deal with relief operations for the victims of internal conflict, including the access negotiation function. In order to avoid the problems associated with United Nations agencies, such an organization should be constituted along the lines of my proposal for a remodeled ICRC, an organization fully backed by governments but not, strictly speaking, an intergovernmental organization.

There has been some movement towards the assumption by UNHCR of these functions. Setting aside UNHCR's current limitations and the reasons why UN agencies are inherently unfit to run the highly organized, complex, military-type operations required in conflicts, there is a more basic reason for avoiding this step. UNHCR's protective functions in regard to refugees are and should remain its essential raison d'être. Those functions are well established in international law. Refugee problems are clearly issues of state relations. Protection and succor of the victims of internal conflict, if pursued vigorously, is bound at times to create serious problems with states, which could easily detract from UNHCR's credibility and effectiveness.

Conclusion

The United Nations should place its primary emphasis on the prevention and settlement of conflicts among states and, as feasible and appropriate, within states. I fear that when these highly political functions are mixed with humanitarian relief operations, the international community will be less effective in both areas. Minimizing national sovereignty as the governing principle of international organization is a poor foundation for building a durable world order. A new dominance based on the military power of the United States and a few allies will not bring a lasting order. Moreover, the conflicting goals of national governments and the inevitable desire of ambitious civil servants to assert a competence based on the broadest possible interpretation of organizational mandates have created a loose and incoherent UN system unable to reach the level of performance in humanitarian disasters now demanded by public opinion.

Governments are transfixed by their investment in existing UN agencies. Since UN agencies are virtually impossible to abolish and donor governments are legally or practically obliged to provide funds, governments feel that the only realistic option open to them is to reform them. But as I have shown, more than twenty years of efforts have yielded precious little improvement in efficiency or effectiveness. We are haltingly building a pluralistic multilateral world order, many of the elements of which are not contained within the United Nations system. Reducing the humanitarian costs of conflicts might be better achieved by accepting the logic of the ICRC's custodianship of humanitarian law, its political neutrality, and its operational effectiveness, and building on these strengths or, alternatively, creating a new body outside the United Nations.

Notes

1. General Assembly Resolution 2816 (XXVI) of December 14, 1971 (Assistance in Case of Natural Disaster and Other Disaster Situations).

2. See Kristen Edwards, Gunnar Rosen, and Robert Rossborough, "Responding to Emergencies: The Role of the UN in Emergencies and Ad Hoc Operations," report no. 14, *The Nordic UN Project*, September 1990.

3. General Assembly Resolution 46/182 of December 17, 1991 (Strengthening of the Co-ordination of Humanitarian Emergency Assistance of the United Nations).

4. World Food Programme, *Annual Report of the Executive Director: 1991*, Doc CFA: 33/P/4, March 13, 1992, 5.

5. Between December 14, 1971, and December 21, 1990, no less than seventeen resolutions and decisions were adopted, namely, 2816 (XXVI), 3243 (XXIX), 3340 (XXX), 3532 (XXX), 33/429, 34/55, 35/107, 36/225, 37/144, 38/202, 39/207, 41/201, 42/433, 43/131, 43/204, 45/100, and 45/221.

6. Resolution 46/182 does not assign a title to the official to be appointed to carry out the prescribed functions. They are in fact exercised by the Undersecretary-General for Humanitarian Affairs. Hereinafter he is referred to as

the humanitarian coordinator, as distinct from the disaster relief coordinator appointed under Resolution 2816 (XXVI).

7. To strengthen its hand, UNDRO developed an advisory body among government delegations accredited to the Geneva office of the United Nations, whose members often became UNDRO advocates in donor capitals. Rivalry between the United States and some Western European governments was certainly a factor affecting the perception that UNDRO, unlike New York–based agencies, was more attuned to the interests of Europe.

8. The resolution adopted by the General Assembly on March 2, 1992, Revitalization of the United Nations Secretariat (document A/46/L.67), was much less specific about organizational structure.

9. *The Nordic UN Project*, 41.

10. *The Canberra Times,* October 2, 1992.

11. B. Urquhart and E. Childers, *A World in Need of Leadership: Tomorrow's United Nations* (Uppsala, Sweden: Dag Hammarskjöld Foundation, 1990).

12. General Assembly document A/AC.96/788, December 11, 1991.

13. Ibid.

14. If ever there was a clear case for making a UN agency the lead agency, it was to put UNHCR in this role for the repatriation of Afghan refugees in 1989. UNHCR sought the role and WFP gave its full support although other agencies resisted. The Secretary-General appointed a high-level coordinator, Prince Sadruddin Aga Khan, based in Geneva.

15. Article 70 of Protocol I and Article 18 of Protocol II. Texts as published in Adam Roberts and Richard Guelff, *Documents on the Laws of War* (Oxford: Clarendon Press, 1982).

16. Thomas G. Weiss and Jarat Chopra, "Sovereignty Is No Longer Sacrosanct: Codifying Humanitarian Intervention," *Ethics and International Affairs* 6 (1992): 108.

17. Statement by Jan Eliasson, permanent representative of Sweden to the United Nations and chairman of the ad hoc Group for Informal Consultations on agenda item 143, December 19, 1991. Eliasson was later appointed by the Secretary-General to the post of humanitarian coordinator.

18. James Grant, executive director of UNICEF. The author, together with UN Undersecretary-General A. Farah, participated with Grant in the negotiations with the Sudanese government that resulted in its acceptance of the OLS concept.

19. A distinguished and respected person appointed by the president of the ICRC might be an alternative, just as the UN Secretary-General has frequently appointed outsiders to represent him in peace efforts, for example, Cyrus Vance in relation to the former Yugoslavia.

20. The International Committee of the Red Cross, "What It Is, What It Does," ICRC Publications, Geneva, undated.

About the Authors

MARY B. ANDERSON is president of the Collaborative for Development Action, Inc., and a consultant, case writer, and trainer on women's roles in economic and social development. A development economist, her clients include USAID, the World Bank, the Population Council, UNFPA, and UNIFEM. She has written about education and gender issues, as well as development in times of disaster. She is the coauthor of *Rising from the Ashes: Development Strategies in Times of Disaster.*

FREDERICK C. CUNY is a registered planner and founder and chairman of INTERTECT, a professional disaster management consulting firm based in Dallas, Texas. Since 1969, he has participated in numerous relief operations that concentrated on refugee camp planning, administration, emergency management, and reconstruction, most recently in Somalia and Bosnia. He is an editor of *Disasters, The International Journal of Disaster Studies and Practice* and has written widely on disaster planning and management.

EDWARD GIRARDET is an independent journalist and producer who covers wars, refugees, and drought situations for European and U.S. television. He has reported for the *"MacNeil-Lehrer News Hour," U.S. News and World Report,* and the *Christian Science Monitor.* A citizen of both the United States and Switzerland, he served as group leader of a Yale Law School–sponsored human rights trip to southern Africa. He is also editor of *Crosslines*, a monthly global report on development, relief, and the environment.

JAMES C. INGRAM directs the Australian Institute for International Affairs, following a decade as executive director of the UN World Food Programme. Earlier he served as director-general of the Australian Development Assistance Bureau and ambassador to Canada, several Caribbean states, and the Philippines. He is currently writing on Australian policy toward the UN at the Australian National University, Canberra.

EPHRAIM ISAAC directs the Institute of Semitic Languages, Inc., in Princeton, New Jersey. An Ethiopian national active in peace efforts, he is cofounder of the National Literacy Campaign Organization and coordinator of the Ad Hoc Peace Committee in Ethiopia. A Fellow of Harvard University, he has taught and published widely in the areas of African languages, ancient religions and black civilizations, Ethiopian history, and the concept and history of slavery.

JAMES O. C. JONAH is Undersecretary-General for Political Affairs at the United Nations in New York. A career international civil servant who has traveled widely on UN troubleshooting missions, he was formerly Assistant Secretary-General for Research and the Collection of Information, for Field Operational and External Support Activities, and for Human Resources Development. A national of Sierra Leone, he coordinated activities relating to the Second Decade for Action to Combat Racism and Racial Discrimination.

JOHN MACKINLAY is senior research associate at Brown University's Thomas J. Watson Jr. Institute for International Studies, where he directs the research project Second Generation Multinational Forces. During an active career in the British army, he held international staff appointments in Europe and Washington, D.C., and was a peacekeeper in the Sinai. He has written on UN and other peacekeeping operations, as well as on using military resources in humanitarian emergencies, including *The Peacekeepers*.

LARRY MINEAR has been actively involved in humanitarian and development issues since 1972, both as an official of Church World Service and Lutheran World Relief and as a consultant to UN organizations and the U.S. government. In 1990 he headed an international team that carried out a case study of Operation Lifeline Sudan. He currently codirects the Humanitarianism and War project and is based at the Refugee Policy Group and Brown University's Thomas J. Watson Jr. Institute for International Studies.

GAYLE E. SMITH serves as a consultant for many organizations involved in international humanitarian assistance, including Oxfam Canada, USAID, the U.S. Department of Agriculture, and Dutch InterChurch Aid. She is the former Africa Development Program Coordinator for the Development Group for Alternative Policies and has published widely on hunger, war, postconflict reconstruction, and other issues in the Horn of Africa.

MICHEL VEUTHEY heads the International Organizations Division of the International Committee of the Red Cross in Geneva. He has represented the ICRC at the United Nations General Assembly in New York and at many conferences on humanitarian issues. A Swiss national with training as an international lawyer, he has published widely on various aspects of international humanitarian law.

THOMAS G. WEISS is associate director of the Thomas J. Watson Jr. Institute for International Studies, associate dean of the faculty at Brown University, and codirector of the Humanitarianism and War project. Previously, he held a number of UN posts (at UNCTAD, the UN Commission for Namibia, UNITAR, and ILO) and served as executive director of the International Peace Academy. He has written extensively on development, peacekeeping, humanitarian relief, and international organizations. He is also executive director of the Academic Council on the United Nations System.

The Sponsoring Institutions
and the Project Publications

The Sponsoring Institutions

Brown University's Thomas J. Watson Jr. Institute for International Studies was established in 1986 to ensure that the University continuously develop its international dimension for the benefit of students, faculty, and, ultimately, society. Based in Providence, Rhode Island, the Watson Institute provides a universitywide focus for teaching and research on international relations and foreign cultures and societies, and is the focal point for generating support for international studies. It furnishes financial support for faculty teaching and research, and sponsors lectures, conferences, and visiting fellows. Its thirteen affiliated centers and programs engage in a broad range of activities, from improving the teaching of international studies to contributing to policy-oriented research and public outreach. The Watson Institute provides material support for the university's libraries, promotes faculty development, and advises on international programs.

The Refugee Policy Group was established in 1982 as an independent center for policy research and analysis on international and domestic refugee issues. RPG serves as a catalyst for policy improvements by enhancing the quality of information and analysis available to decisionmakers concerned with refugee and related humanitarian issues. RPG promotes increased understanding of the broader contexts in which refugee problems occur so that issues can be addressed in a longer-range and more comprehensive manner. It promotes evenhanded, less ideologically based policies that give first priority to humanitarian considerations. RPG serves as a center for the exchange of information and for symposia and policy briefings. RPG's Resource Center, which contains more than twenty thousand documents, is open to policy analysts and scholars. RPG is headquartered in Washington, D.C. and has an office in Geneva, Switzerland.

Chronological List of Humanitarianism and War Project Publications, 1990–1993

- *Humanitarianism Across Borders: Sustaining Civilians in Times of War*, edited by Thomas G. Weiss and Larry Minear. Boulder: Lynne Rienner, 1993.
- *Humanitarian Action in Times of War: A Handbook for Practitioners*, by Larry Minear and Thomas G. Weiss. Boulder: Lynne Rienner, 1993.
- *United Nations Authority in Cambodia*, by Jarat Chopra and Larry Minear. Providence: Watson Institute, forthcoming 1993.
- *Collective Security in a Changing World*, edited by Thomas G. Weiss. Boulder: Lynne Rienner, 1993.
- "Making the Humanitarian System Work Better," by Larry Minear, in Kevin Cahill, ed., *A Framework for Survival: Health, Human Rights and Humanitarian Assistance in Conflicts and Disasters.* New York: Basic Books and Council on Foreign Relations, 1993.
- "Groping and Coping in the Gulf Crisis: Discerning the Shape of a New Humanitarian Order," by Larry Minear and Thomas G. Weiss. *World Policy Journal* 9, no. 4 (Fall/Winter 1992–1993): 755–788.
- "New Challenges for UN Military Operations: Implementing an Agenda for Peace," by Thomas G. Weiss. *Washington Quarterly* 16, no. 1 (Winter 1992): 51–66.
- "Regional Organizations and Regional Security," by Neil S. MacFarlane and Thomas G. Weiss. *Security Studies* 2, no. 3 (Fall/Winter 1992–1993): 6–37.
- *The Challenges of Famine Relief: Emergency Operations in the Sudan*, by Francis M. Deng and Larry Minear. Washington, D.C.: Brookings Institution, 1992.
- *United Nations Coordination of the International Humanitarian Response to the Gulf Crisis, 1990–1992*, Occasional Paper no. 13, by Larry Minear, U.B.P. Chelliah, Jeff Crisp, John Mackinlay, and Thomas G. Weiss. Providence: Watson Institute, 1992.
- "Sovereignty Is No Longer Sacrosanct: Codifying Humanitarian Intervention," by Jarat Chopra and Thomas G. Weiss. *Ethics and International Affairs* 6 (1992): 95–118.
- "Humanitarian Intervention in a New World Order," by Larry Minear. *Overseas Development Council Policy Focus* 1 (February 1992).
- "Do International Ethics Matter? Humanitarian Politics in the Sudan," by Larry Minear and Thomas G. Weiss. *Ethics and International Affairs* 5 (1991): 197–214.
- "Military Humanitarianism," by Thomas G. Weiss and Kurt M. Campbell. *Survival* 33, no. 5 (September/October 1992): 451–465.
- *Humanitarianism and War: Learning the Lessons from Recent Armed*

Conflicts, Occasional Paper no. 8, by Larry Minear, Thomas G. Weiss, and Kurt M. Campbell. Providence: Watson Institute, 1991.

- *Humanitarianism Under Siege: A Critical Review of Operation Lifeline Sudan,* by Larry Minear in collaboration with Tabyiegen A. Aboum, Eshetu Chole, Koste Manibe, Abdul Mohammed, Jennefer Sebstad, and Thomas G. Weiss. Trenton: Red Sea Press, 1991.
- *Soldiers, Peacekeepers and Disasters*, edited by Leon Gordenker and Thomas G. Weiss. London: Macmillan, 1991.
- *A Critical Review of Operation Lifeline Sudan: A Report to the Aid Agencies*, by Tabyiegen A. Aboum, Eshetu Chole, Koste Manibe, Larry Minear, Abdul Mohammed, Jennefer Sebstad, and Thomas G. Weiss. Washington, D.C.: Refugee Policy Group, 1990.

Forthcoming 1993–1994

- *Humanitarian Challenges in Central America: Lessons from Recent Armed Conflicts,* by Cristina Eguizabal, David Lewis, Larry Minear, Peter Sollis, and Thomas G. Weiss. Providence: Watson Institute, June 1993. This will also appear as *Desafios Humanitarias en Centroamérica: Lecciones Aprendidas en los Recientes Conflictos Armados*. San José: Arias Foundation, 1993.
- "Sovereignty Under Siege: From Humanitarian Intervention to Humanitarian Space," by Thomas G. Weiss and Jarat Chopra, in Gene Lyons and Michael Mastanduno, eds., *Beyond Westphalia? National Sovereignty and International Intervention.* Berkeley: University of California Press, 1993.
- *Humanitarianism and War: Reducing the Human Cost of Armed Conflict*, by Larry Minear and Thomas G. Weiss. Boulder: Lynne Rienner, 1994.

Index

Emerging Global Issues

THOMAS G. WEISS, SERIES EDITOR